The Americanization of the World; or, The Trend of the Twentieth Century

REMOTE STORAGE

THEODORE ROOSEVELT,
President of the United States of America.

By W. T. STEAD.

THE
AMERICANISATION
OF THE
WORLD

1^{s}/-

THE AMERICANISATION

OF THE WORLD

OR

The Trend of the Twentieth Century.

"We fervently believe that our only chance of national
prosperity lies in the timely remodelling of our system, so
as to put it as nearly as possible upon an equality with the
improved management of the Americans" — RICHARD
COBDEN, 1835

BY

W T. STEAD.

PUBLISHED AT

THE "REVIEW OF REVIEWS" OFFICE,

MOWBRAY HOUSE, NORFOLK STREET, LONDON, W.C

1902

LONDON :
PRINTED BY WILLIAM CLOWES AND SONS, LIMITED, STAMFORD STREET, S.E.,
AND 28 GREAT WINDMILL STREET, W.

PREFACE.

THE advent of the United States of America as the greatest of world-Powers is the greatest political, social, and commercial phenomenon of our times. For some years past we have all been more or less dimly conscious of its significance. It is only when we look at the manifold manifestations of the exuberant energy of the United States, and the world-wide influence which they are exerting upon the world in general and the British Empire in particular that we realise how comparatively insignificant are all the other events of our time.

The result of the rapid survey which I have embodied in this Annual will, I trust, enable my readers to see in its true perspective the salient fact which will dictate the trend of events in the Twentieth Century.

This survey is intensely interesting to all men, but it is of transcendant importance for my own countrymen. For we are confronted by the necessity of taking one of those momentous decisions which decide the destiny of our country. Unless I am altogether mistaken, we have an opportunity—probably the last which is to be offered us—of retaining our place as the first of world-Powers. If we neglect it, we shall descend slowly but irresistibly to the position of Holland and of Belgium. No one who contemplates with an impartial mind the array of facts now submitted to his attention, will deny that I have at least made out a very strong *prima facie* case in support of my contention that, unless we can succeed in merging the British Empire in the English-speaking United States of the World, the disintegration of our Empire, and our definite displacement from the position of commercial and financial primacy is only a matter of time, and probably a very short time. If, on the other hand, we substitute for the insular patriotism of our nation the broader patriotism of the race, and frankly throw in our lot with the Americans to realise the great ideal of Race Union, we shall enter upon a new era of power and prosperity the like of which the race has never realised since the world began. But "if before our duty we, with listless spirit, stand," the die will be cast, and we must reconcile ourselves as best we can to accept a secondary position in a world in which we have hitherto played a leading *rôle*.

If, on the contrary, we are resolute and courageous, we have it in our power to occupy a position of vantage, in which we need fear no foe and dread no rival. We shall continue on a wider scale to carry out the providential mission which has been entrusted to the English-speaking Race, whose United States will be able to secure the peace of the World.

It is, therefore, in no spirit of despair, but rather with joyful confidence and great hope that I commend this book to my fellow-countrymen.

December 1, 1901.   W. T. STEAD

THE AMERICANISATION OF THE WORLD;

OR,

THE TREND OF THE TWENTIETH CENTURY.

PART I.

THE UNITED STATES AND THE BRITISH EMPIRE.

CHAPTER I.—THE ENGLISH-SPEAKING WORLD

THE Americanisation of the world is a phrase which excites, quite needlessly, some resentment in Great Britain. It is even regarded as an affront to England to suggest that the world is being Americanised. Its true destiny of course is to be Anglicised. And many are quick to discern something of anti-patriotic bias in the writers who venture to call attention to the trend of the Twentieth Century.

To all such irate champions of England and the English it is sufficient to reply that, as the creation of the Americans is the greatest achievement of our race, there is no reason to resent the part the Americans are playing in re-fashioning the world in their image, which, after all, is substantially the image of ourselves. If we are afflicted with national vanity we can console ourselves by reflecting that the Americans are only giving to others what they inherited from ourselves. Whatever they do, all goes to the credit of the family. It is an unnatural parent who does not exult in the achievements of his sons, even although they should eclipse the triumphs of his sire, as much as the victories of Hannibal threw into the shade the exploits of Hamilcar.

Whatever may be the objections that are raised from one side or the other, I hope the reader, if he is a Briton, will at least be able to go so far with me as to rejoice in contemplating the achievements of the mighty nation that has sprung from our loins, and if he is an American, to tolerate the complacency with which John Bull sets down all his exploits to the credit of the family. Without that element of mutual sympathy, it is to be feared the survey of the process which I have dubbed the Americanisation of the World, is not likely to tend to edification, but rather to recriminations, cavillings, and bitterness of spirit.

Of one thing the Briton is assured. However he may be outstripped and overshadowed by the American, no one can deprive us of the traditional glories which encompass the cradle of the race. "The purple mist of centuries and of song" will never lift from these small islands on the northern seas. We may lose our primacy in the forging of iron and steel, but no "invasion" can deprive us of the indestructible renown possessed by the land which gave birth to Alfred and Cromwell, to Shakespeare and Milton, to Burns and Scott. And as men will ever think more highly of the City of the Violet Crown with its Groves of Academe, peopled with poets and sages, than of the geographically vast expanse of Asiatic empires, so it may well be that England may be a name worn ever nearer the great heart of mankind than that of the Continent-covering son of Anak, whose bulk overshadows the world.

At the same time—and I hasten to make this admission to pacify irate American readers resentful of the suggestion that John Bull stands to Brother Jonathan as Athens to Persia—it is possible that the American may stand to the Briton as Christianity stands to Judaism.

As it was through the Christian Church that the monotheism of the Jew conquered the world, so it may be through the Americans that the English ideals expressed in the English language may make the tour of the planet. The parallel is dangerously exact. For there is too much reason to fear that many Americans regard the English with the same unfilial ingratitude that many Christians regard the Jew. It is as useless to remind them that the men of the *Mayflower* were English, as it is to remind anti-Semites that Christ and His apostles were Jews. Yet it was through the Christian Church, too, often unmindful of its Jewish parentage, that the ethical ideals of the Jew permeated and civilised the world. The philosopher recognises

THE POSSESSIONS OF THE ENGLISH SPEAKING RACE

"Here is the people of one language"—See Gen. Genry

British Empire

United States

that the world-mission of the Jews was only fulfilled through the Nazarene whom they crucified; and so in years to come the philosophical historian may record that the mission of the English fulfilled itself through the American The Americanisation of the world is but the Anglicising of the world at one remove.

That the United States of America have now arrived at such a pitch of power and prosperity as to have a right to claim the leading place among the English-speaking nations cannot be disputed. The census returns at the beginning and the end of the Nineteenth Century are conclusive The figures stand thus —

	1801	1901
The United Kingdom	15,717,287	41,454,578
The United States	(1800) 5,305,925	(1900) 76,299,529

If it be objected that the population of the United Kingdom is only a fraction of the King's subjects, let us add to the population of the United Kingdom every white-skinned person in the British Empire, and let us at the same time deduct from the population of the United States all men of colour. The figures will stand thus —

	1801.	1901
The British Empire	16,000,000	55,000,000
The United States	4,300,000	66,000,000

If any one objects that we have not included the myriads of India among British citizens, the answer is easy We are comparing the English-speaking communities The right of leadership does not depend upon how many millions, more or less, of coloured people we have compelled to pay us taxes It depends upon the power, the skill, the wealth, the numbers of the white citizens of the self-governing State

It may be said that it is absurd to group together as English-speaking men millions who, like the Canadians of Quebec and the colonists in Mauritius, only speak French, or, like the Dutch of South Africa, only speak the Taal This, it may be objected, unfairly swells the British total But against this we must offset the millions of emigrants who have studded the United States with patches of the Old World, and who, until the next generation, cannot be described as English speakers. Roughly speaking, the figures given above may be said to represent the comparative numerical strength of the two sections of the English-speaking world. The Republican section has forged ahead of that which clings to the Monarchy Nor is there any prospect that their relative positions will be reversed. As John the Baptist said of Jesus of Nazareth, so Britain may say to the United States, " He must increase, but I must

decrease " The Baptist did not repine, neither should we

The Briton, instead of chafing against this inevitable supersession, should cheerfully acquiesce in the decree of Destiny, and stand in betimes with the conquering American The philosophy of common-sense teaches us that. seeing we can never again be the first standing alone, we should lose no time in uniting our fortunes with those who have passed us in the race. Has the time not come when we should make a resolute effort to realise the unity of the English-speaking race? What have we to gain by perpetuating the schism that we owe to the perversity of George the Third and the determination of his pig-headed advisers " to put the thing through " and chastise the insolence of these revolted colonists by " fighting to a finish "? As an integral part of the English-speaking federation, we should continue to enjoy not only undisturbed, but with enhanced prestige, our pride of place, while if we remain outside, nursing our Imperial insularity on monarchical lines, we are doomed to play second fiddle for the rest of our existence Why not finally recognise the truth and act upon it? What sacrifices are there which can be regarded as too great to achieve the realisation of the ideal of the unity of the English-speaking race?

Consider for a moment what at present is the distribution of the surface of this planet among the various races of mankind Instead of counting Britain and the United States as two separate and rival States, let us pool the resources of the Empire and the Republic and regard them with all their fleets, armies, and industrial resources as a political, or, if you like, an Imperial unit.

The English-speaking States, with a population of 121,000,000 self-governing white citizens, govern 353,000,000 of Asiatics and Africans Under their allied flags labour one-third of the human race.

The sea, which covers three-fourths of the surface of the planet, is their domain Excepting on the Euxine and the Caspian, no ship dare plough the salt seas in Eastern or Western hemisphere if they choose to forbid it. They are supreme custodians of the waterways of the world, capable by their fiat of blockading into submission any European State contemplating an appeal to the arbitrament of war

Of the dry land, they have occupied and are ruling all the richest territories in three continents. With the exception of Siberia they have seized all the best gold-mines of the world There is hardly a region where white men can breed and live and thrive that they have not appropriated They have picked out the eyes of every continent They reign in the land of the

Pharaohs, they have conquered the Empire of Aurungzebe, and have seized with imperious hand the dominions of Spain. They have despoiled the Portuguese, the French, and the Dutch, and have left to the German and the Italian nothing but the scraps and knuckle-bones of a colonial dominion.

The net result works out as follows :—

	Square miles.	Populations.	
		White.	Coloured.
The United States	3,754,000	66,000,000	20,000,000
The British Empire	11,894,000	55,000,000	333,000,000
TOTAL	15,648,000	121,000,000	353,000,000

The rest of the world cuts but a poor figure compared with the possessions of the English-speaking allies.

	Square miles.	Population.	
		White.	Coloured.
Russia	8,754,000	121,000,000	12,000,000
China	1,327,308	.. ..	400,000,000
Latin America	8,215,855	15,000,000	60,000,000
France	3,845,000	39,000,000	46,000,000
Germany	1,238,000	55,000,000	15,000,000
Rest of the world	13,293,000	134,000,000	129,000,000

The lion's share of the world is ours, not only in bulk, but in tit-bits also. The light land of the Sahara is not worth a centime an acre. The vast area of German South Africa would hardly provide a livelihood for the population of a middle-sized German village. With the exception of the Rhine, the Danube, the Amour, the Volga, and the Plate Amazon, nearly all the great navigable rivers of the world enter the sea under the Union Jack or the Stars and Stripes. The Valley of the Yang-tse Kiang is ear-marked as the sphere of our influence. The whole of the North American Continent, from the North Pole to the frontier of Mexico, is within the ring fence of the English-speaking race, and from the whole of Central and Southern America all trespassers have been emphatically warned off by the proclamation of the Monroe Doctrine.

Population should be weighed as well as counted. In a census return a Hottentot counts for as much as a Cecil Rhodes; a mean white on a southern swamp is the census equivalent for Mr. J. P. Morgan or Mr. Edison. A nation which has no illiterates can hardly be counted

off against the Russians, only three per cent. of whom can read or write. Excluding France and Germany and the highly civilised group of small states, Scandinavian, Dutch and Swiss, the English-speaking world comes out easily on top, no matter what test of civilisation is employed. We have more schools to the square mile, more colleges to the county, more universities to the State than any of the others. We print more books, read more newspapers, run more libraries. We have more churches per hundred thousand of the population, and attend them better. Our death-rate is diminishing even more rapidly than our birth-rate, our pauperism is decreasing, our criminal statistics are reassuring. Only in one respect do we fall below the average. We are the most drunken race in the whole world—the most drunken and in both our branches the most pharisaical. We are as piratical as the worst of our neighbours, but we alone make broad our phylacteries while we are plundering, and pray while we prey. In all the material tests of advancing civilisation, railways, steamships, telephones, telegraphs, electric trolleys, sanitary appliances, and the like, we beat the world.

If from a comparison between the English-speaking duality and the rest of the planet we pass to a comparison between the two English-speaking races, some curious results come out. The United States, which has shot ahead of us in population, has comparatively only a small area. The total superficial area of the United States is only 3,603,844 square miles on the mainland. The total area of Cuba, Porto Rico, and the Philippine Islands will not add more than 100,000 square miles to that total. But the British Empire has 3,456,383 square miles in Canada, 3,076,763 in Australia, and 1,808,258 in India. The vast expanses of Canada and Australia are but sparsely peopled ; there is elbow room in both for a greater population than that which the United States carries to-day. The following comparison of populations is interesting, excluding coloured persons :—

	1901		1900
England	31,231,684	United States (not including those below)	57,422,000
Wales	1,294,032	Virginia	1,854,184
Scotland	4,471,957	Illinois	4,821,550
Ireland	4,456,546	New York	7,118,012
Canada	5,185,990 (1900)	Pennsylvania	6,302,115
Australia	3,726,450	Missouri	3,106,665
New Zealand	773,440	Connecticut	908,355
South Africa and Miscellaneous	1,000,000 (estimated)	Nebraska	1,068,539

These figures do not pretend to be exact. No one really knows how many white citizens of the British Empire are scattered over the myriad-peopled regions where we maintain the Roman peace, how many are on the high seas, and how many are doing sentry-go all round the world. A million is probably not an unfair estimate. The comparison is interesting, and may be suggestive to some readers who have never quite realised that there are single states in the American Union with a population greater than that of the whole Dominion of Canada or of the kingdom of Scotland.

When the comparison is made between finance, railways and shipping, and there is no distinction made between coloured and white men, the British Empire, with its multitudinous host of dark-skinned races, is easily preponderant. The comparison works out somewhat as follows :—

	Area.	Revenue.	Railways.	Shipping.	Exports and Imports.
	Sq. Miles.	£	Miles.	Tons.	£
United Kingdom . .	121,000	120,000,000	21,659	9,104,000	815,000,000
Colonies and Dependencies	11,429,000	110,000,000	54,000	1,019,808	201,078,891
TOTAL, ...	11,550,000	£230,000,000	75,659	10,183,808	1,016,078,891
United States . . .	3,700,000	139,000,000	184,278	4,864,000	380,000,000
GRAND TOTAL . .	15,250,000	£369,000,000	259,937	15,047,808	1,396,078,891

Mr. Chauncey McGovern contributed to *Pearson's Magazine* last October a curious comparison between the English-speaking States and Russia, France, and Spain, from which I extract the following Table :—

The English-Speaking United States of the World.		Russia, France, and Spain.
Area	15,636,000 square miles.	12,320,000 square miles.
Population	473,500,000	217,218,000
Revenue	£379,800,000	£133,103,000
National Debts . . .	£1,560,705,000	£2,281,951,000
Railways	267,150 miles.	67,260 miles.
Exports	£825,251,600	£239,920,600
Merchant Ships . . .	19,236,000 tons.	3,037,000 tons.
Naval Guns	13,319	10,993

A more detailed comparison between the English-speaking States and France, Russia, and Germany, was made by Sir Richard Temple in September, 1899. I quote his figures as they stand without attempting to bring them up to date :—

English-Speaking.		Russia, Germany, and Spain.

Population.

White . .	125,000,000	White . .	221,000,000
Coloured .	350,000,000	Coloured .	64,000,000
	475,000,000		285,000,000

Area.

15¼ millions square miles. | 13¾ millions square miles.

Coast Line.

62,000 miles and 19 first-rate harbours. | 17,000 miles, 5 harbours.

Railways.

258,000 miles. | 79,500 miles.

Annual Trade.

£1,600,000,000 | £1,120,000,000

English-Speaking.	Russia, Germany, and France.

Shipping.

11,000,000 tons. | 3,750,000 tons.

Fisheries.

320,000 | 100,000

Coal Output.

405,000,000 tons. | 138,000,000 tons.

Iron Ore.

25,000,000 tons. | 20,000,000 tons.

Revenue.

£377,000,000 | £405,000,000

Armies.

1,000,000 | 7,000,000

Navies.

410 ships. | 381 ships.

This represents a greater factor of organised force than has ever before been at the disposal of a single race.

The question arises whether this gigantic

THE LATE PRESIDENT McKINLEY.

aggregate can be pooled We live in the day of combinations. Is there no Morgan who will undertake to bring about the greatest combination of all—a combination of the whole English-speaking race ?

The same motive which has led to the building up of the Trust in the industrial world, may bring about this great combination in the world of politics. This is not a sentimental craze. The question is prompted by the most solid of material considerations. Why should we not combine ? We should be stronger as against outside attack, and what is of far greater importance, there would be much less danger of the fierce industrial rivalry that is to come leading to international strain and war New York competes with Massachusetts and Pennsylvania with Illinois, but no matter how severe may be the competition, its stress never strains the federal tie States in a federal Union are as free to compete with each other as are towns in an English county, but being united in one organic whole the war of trade never endangers the public peace. Why should we not aim at the same goal in international affairs ? If the English-speaking world were unified even to the extent of having a central court for the settlement of all Anglo-American controversies, our respective manufacturers would be free to compete without any risk of their trade rivalry endangering good relations between the Empire and the Republic. And that would be again worth making no small sacrifice in order to secure.

The tendency of the last half century has been all in favour of the unification of peoples who speak the same language It is not likely to slacken in the new century. The Nineteenth Century unified Germany and Italy Will the Twentieth Century unify the English-speaking race ?

It is a momentous question. The remembrance of the *via dolorosa* of blood and tears by which the German race attained to unity may well deter the timid from suggesting that the English-speaking world should essay to reach the same goal. But the story of how the Germans realised their national unity is full of suggestion for us, both for encouragement and for warning. For the German race a hundred years since was very much like the English-speaking race to day. Austria then was what Great Britain is now.* She had the prestige

of antiquity, the Imperial aureole was round her brow, she reigned over many races of various tongues, and she was as proud as Lucifer Over against her were the Prussians —the Americans of their time. They were young and enterprising, the Hohenzollerns were but upstart parvenus beside the Hapsburgs, but they had the genius for organisation, the instinct for education, and a passionate patriotism Between these two lay the minor German States, who corresponded not inaptly to the various English-speaking Colonies which look to Britain as their natural head, very much as the South German States regarded Austria, who presided over the Bund, as the pivot of the German political system In the presence of national rivalries so intense, and political barriers so innumerable, the idea of German unity seemed an idler dream in 1801 than the idea of English-speaking unity seems in 1901.

We are all familiar with the consequence of allowing the German race to persist in its dual organisation As Bismarck wrote in 1856 " For a thousand years, ever since the reign of Charles V., German Dualism has regularly resettled its mutual relations once a century by a thorough going internal war, and in this century also that will prove to be the only feasible expedient for arranging matters satisfactorily *

Ten years later Bismarck, at Sadowa, settled matters to his satisfaction at least, but to this day one menace to the peace of central Europe

---

* When I was revising the proofs of this chapter, I was considerably surprised to find that the London correspondent of the *Novoye Vremya* in October last had already called attention to the analogy between Great Britain and Austria He pushed the parallel still further home He declared that the true parallel of the present situation must be sought not in the relations that

existed at the beginning of the nineteenth century between Prussia and Austria, but rather in those which existed at present between the German Empire and Austria, for in his opinion the United States have already established over Great Britain the same kind of protectorate as the German Empire has established over the Austrian member of the Triple Alliance He says —

"Everthing proves that Great Britain is now practically dependent upon the United States, and for all international intents and purposes may be considered to be under an American protectorate

"Just as Germany has used Austria for her own purposes, while guarding her from external and internal dangers, so does America take advantage of British needs and weakness, caring for England only in so far as self interest prompts it The United States has but just entered upon the policy of exploiting the protected kingdom . . .

"The British have lost all pride in their relation to the United States They admit that they cannot successfully resist the republic They no longer trust to their strength, but place their reliance on the racial, literary, and social ties which attract the Americans to England. In this surrender to the Americans there is a sentimental motive as well as a practical one Losing her maritime, commercial, and even financial primacy, England can bear with more resignation the passing of this primacy to a nation akin to her in language, civilisation, and even blood "

* " Our Chancellor " Busch, vol 1 p 322

arises from the fact that some eight million Germans were left outside the national fold.

Between the two sections of the English-speaking race there has been one war a century so far There is too much reason to fear that the average will be kept up, unless in some way or other the mischievous work of George III can be undone. It is, of course, manifestly impossible, even if it were desirable, for the Americans to come back within the pale of the British Empire But if that is impossible, there remains the other alternative Why should not we of the older stock propose to make amends for the folly of our ancestors by recognising that the hegemony of the race has passed from Westminster to Washington, and proposing to federate the Empire and the Republic on whatever terms may be arrived at after discussion as a possible basis for the reunion of our race?

The suggestion will be derided as a dream But to quote the familiar saying of Russell Lowell, "It is none the worse for that, most of the best things we now possess began by being dreams."

Mr. Balfour, six years ago, declared "that the idea of war with the United States of America carries with it something of the unnatural horror of civil war." Since then many things have happened to strengthen that sentiment. But even then he could use these eloquent words :—

"I feel, so far as I can speak for my countrymen, that our pride in the race to which we belong is a pride which includes every English-speaking community in the world We have a domestic patriotism, as Scotchmen or Englishmen or as Irishmen, or what you will, we have an Imperial patriotism as citizens of the British Empire, but surely, in addition to that, we have also an Anglo-Saxon patriotism which embraces within its ample folds the whole of that great race which has done so much in every branch of human effort, and in that branch of human effort which has produced free institutions and free communities."

And he added some words of wisdom with which I will close this chapter —

'We may be taxed with being idealists and dreamers in this matter I would rather be an idealist and a dreamer, and I look forward with confidence to the time when our ideals will have become real and our dreams will be embodied in actual political fact For, after all, circumstances will tend in that direction in which we look'

In a subsequent chapter, I attempt to describe some of these circumstances which already enable us to foresee the trend of the Twentieth Century —

> " Where is a Briton's Fatherland ?
> Will no one tell me of that land ?
> Tis where one meets with English folk,
> And hears the tongue that Shakespeare spoke,
> Where songs of Burns are in the air,
> A Briton's Fatherland is there

> Our glorious Anglo-Saxon race
> Shall ever fill earth's highest place,
> The sun shall never more go down
> On English temple, tower and town,
> And wander where a Briton will,
> His Fatherland shall hold him still. '

Chapter II.—The Basis for Reunion.

Let it be admitted, if only for the sake of our argument, that the establishment of English-speaking unity is a matter to be desired in the interest alike of the peace of the world and the liberties of mankind. The question next arises, how can this unity most easily and effectually be brought about? In attempting to answer this question, I disclaim in advance any accusation that I am imperilling the end in view by an inconsiderate precipitance in pressing for the adoption of measures that promise to lead in that direction. I only seek to discuss tendencies, to estimate forces, and to forecast the probable course of the natural evolution of the existing factors in the Empire and the Republic, and in the nations on their frontiers In presence of a problem so immense, fraught with consequences so momentous for the weal or woe of mankind, it would be presumption to attempt to proclaim solutions before the governing factors have been clearly discerned.

Nevertheless, it may not be impossible for even the cursory observer to see the trend of events, if he keeps his attention fixed upon the salient features of the situation. If the two English-speaking States are to come together, it is obvious that there must be some approximation towards a system which may be accepted by all the world-scattered communities of English-speaking men This being admitted, the question immediately arises as to whether the Empire will approximate to the Republic, or the Republic to the Empire Are we to Americanise our institutions, or may we expect to see the Americans anglicising their Constitution? Or may we anticipate that the future normal system of polity for the English-speaking world will be arrived at by such an exact balance between the English and American elements, that the product will be strictly Anglo-American, and not more American than it is Anglo?

It is not very difficult to answer these questions In the first place, what is the fundamental difference between the British and American Constitutions? That which differentiates them much more than the fact that the head of one is hereditary and of the other elective, is the fact that we have no written Constitution of any kind, whereas the American Constitution is the best known type of a written Constitution in

Bernard Partridge

Punch, Nov. 27, 1912

COLONEL JONATHAN J. BULL;

Or, What John B. may come to.

existence   The Constitution of the reunited English-speaking race must of necessity be written.   Not even the most uncompromising Britisher would venture to suggest that mankind will ever again attempt to repeat the experiment which has worked for so long with such miraculous success in Great Britain   If we seek for confirmation of this, we have only to turn to the recent history of our greatest colonies.   When the Dominion of Canada was constituted, the federation was embodied in a written Constitution.   Last year the same thing occurred in the creation of the Commonwealth of Australia   If Mr. Gladstone had succeeded in carrying his Home Rule Bill, that measure would have been the written Constitution or fundamental Charter of the new Government of Ireland   The adoption of some sort of written Constitution is therefore inevitable, and by its adoption the fundamental feature of the Re-united States would become American, not British.

After the difference of written and un-written Constitutions, the Empire and the Republic differ most visibly in the way in which they appoint their heads   The Americans elect their President for four years.   The British crown for life the eldest son of the deceased sovereign.

The comparative advantages of a Constitutional Monarchy and of a democratic Republic need not be discussed here.   The Americans themselves might be the first to object to the disappearance of the Monarchy.   The Crown might remain as a picturesque historical symbol, as a distinctively British institution as local as, although much more ornamental than, the London fog.   But not even the most perfervid Royalist in his wildest dreams can conceive the possibility of the Americans ever consenting to become the loyal subjects of a descendant of George III   Even if they developed a taste for monarchy, they would make it the first condition of their sovereign that he should be a thorough American.   No foreign-born citizen, no matter what service he may have rendered the State, no matter how long he may have been naturalised, can occupy the presidential chair, even for the space of four years.   If the Head of the State were to occupy the American throne for life, and leave it to his sons and his sons' sons after him, the condition of genuine native born Americanism would be insisted upon more passionately than ever   The conversion of the Americans to the principle of monarchy, instead of facilitating the race union, would create a new and very serious obstacle in the shape of rival dynasties   Of that, however, there is fortunately no danger.   If, therefore, race union is to be accomplished,

the future head of the Reunited States will be elective and republican, even if the monarchy continues to be cherished in these islands as a distinctly local institution.   Here also the mould of the future destinies of our race will be American and not British

After the monarchy, the American differs from the British Constitution chiefly in the repudiation by the former of the principle of hereditary legislation and of an Established Church, and the acceptance, with all its logical consequences, of the principle of government of the people by salaried representatives chosen by constituencies in strict proportion to their numbers, as ascertained at each decennial census.   These are the notes which, to the casual observer, differentiate the two Constitutions   Which of them will be the key-note of the Constitution of the Reunited Race ?

In discussing this question let us assume that the Americans themselves will be passive in this matter, and that the decision to be taken will rest solely with the subjects of the King   If a plebiscite were to be taken to-morrow, and every white male adult in the Empire were to be asked to vote for or against hereditary legislation, an Established Church, and our present illogical system of unpaid Parliamentary representation, what would be the result ?   It is more than probable that even now the majority of British subjects would be in favour of the American view

In England, no doubt, the majority would be in favour of the ancient time-honoured institutions   But Wales and Ireland would cast heavy majorities on the other side, and it is extremely doubtful whether Scotland would not go the same way.   The most significant factor, however, remains to be noticed.   We boast that we have encircled the world with self-governing colonies, but without a single exception every one of these colonies, while rejoicing in the shelter of the Union Jack, and enthusiastically loyal to the person of the Sovereign, has organised its own Constitution on American as opposed to British lines   Not a colony has transplanted across the seas either a hereditary chamber, an Established Church or the English system of unpaid unequal representation   The descendants of George the Third retained the allegiance of the colonies by allowing them one and all to frame their constitutions on the principles of George Washington.   The English segment of Great Britain may be true to the distinctive British institutions, but Greater Britain repudiates them with absolute unanimity.

Mr Whitelaw Reid was the American special representative at the Jubilee of 1897.   He saw London in the very heyday of British loyalty and enthusiasm.   Among the thousands who thronged our capital, none were more demon-

GEORGE WASHINGTON.

stratively loyal, more impassioned in their expressions of devotion to the Old Country and its institutions than the Colonial Premiers   But Mr Whitelaw Reid, who studied them closely, was startled to discover that one and all of these highly placed Ministers of the Crown were, to quote his own phrase "downright Yankees" I asked him to explain that dark and Delphic saying   He replied "What I mean is that these men are not in the least like British Ministers or any of your English politicians Their point of view is American   Their political ideas are the same as ours   They are loyal to the Queen, no doubt, but that is a thing apart. In their work-a-day politics they are as Republican as ourselves.   They start from the same principles, they reason in the same way, and they arrive at the same conclusions.   Not one of them would tolerate a House of Lords in their own colony, or an Established Church. Even on Free Trade their ideas are more American than British   In talking to them I am never conscious of that break of gauge which I constantly feel in talking to a British statesman "

We may take it, then, as tolerably manifest that the distinctively British institutions of a hereditary legislature and an Established Church will not figure among the institutions of the Reunited Race, even though they may be left for a time to linger in England   It is even possible that the growth of a popular desire in England itself to rid ourselves of these institutions may lead indirectly to union with the great English-speaking community which is freed from their evil influence?   All this means one thing and one thing only. It is we who are going to be Americanised, the advance will have to be made on our side, it is idle to hope, and it is not at all to be desired, that the Americans will attempt to meet us half way by saddling themselves with institutions of which many of us are longing earnestly to get rid.

Even if there were no other reason for this, sufficient cause would be found in the fact that while every American is an enthusiastic believer in his own Constitution, it is difficult to find an Englishman who does not admit that his own Constitution is in a very bad way.

I do not confine this remark to the Irish, the Welsh, and the English and Scotch Liberals. They are naturally in revolt against the permanent veto upon all Liberal legislation vested in the permanent majority which their political opponents enjoy in the Upper House.   I find the bitterest complaints against the breakdown of the constitutional machine in the Conservative *Quarterly*, and in the speeches of thorough-going Ministerialists   The Parliamentary machine

has broken down before our eyes   That fact there is none to dispute   Authorities differ as to the cause of the breakdown, and they differ still more widely as to the remedy to be employed   But not even the most self-satisfied advocate for things as they are speaks of the spectacle at Westminster except in accents of shame and despair

Contrast this with the tone in which every American habitually speaks, and what is more, actually thinks, of his Constitution.   Mr. Bryce, in the very first page of his admirable work on the American Commonwealth, calls attention to the immense, almost religious, respect which the Americans pay to their institutions.   It is not merely, says Mr Bryce, that they are supposed to form an experiment of unequalled importance on a scale unprecedentedly vast.   It is because they are something more than an experiment : "they are believed to disclose and display the type of institutions toward which, as by a law of fate, the rest of civilised mankind are forced to move, some with swifter, others with slower, but all with unresting feet."

When you have two parties in counsel, one of whom is heartily ashamed of his system, while the other is absolutely convinced that his system is so perfect that its ultimate universal adoption is only a matter of time, it needs no prophet to foresee which system will be adopted as the result of their consultations.   Nor can we be surprised at the American's reverence for his Constitution when we read the terms in which it has been spoken of by eminent Englishmen. Was it not Mr. Gladstone who declared—

" The American Constitution is, so far as I can see, the most wonderful work ever struck off at a given time by the brain and purpose of man   It has had a century of trial, under the pressure of exigencies caused by an expansion unexampled in point of rapidity and range, and its exemption from formal change, though not entire, has certainly proved the sagacity of the constructors and the stubborn strength of the fabric " [*]

Nor is Mr Bryce less emphatic, although not so brief.   Speaking of the American Constitution, he says —

"After all deductions, it ranks above every other written Constitution for the intrinsic excellence of its scheme, its adaptation to the circumstances of the people, the simplicity, brevity, and precision of its language, its judicious mixture of definiteness in principle with elasticity in details " [†]

It is a notable and significant circumstance that the one statesman who has repeatedly

[*] "Gleanings of Past Years," by W F Gladstone, vol i., p 212
[†] Bryce's "American Commonwealth," vol i p. 27.

directed the attention of the British public to the exceeding excellence of the American Constitution is none other than the Marquis of Salisbury, the Tory Prime Minister. It does not matter that what he admires most in it is the security which it offers against reckless innovation, and the guarantee which it gives to liberty of contract and the right of every man to do what he will with his own. The fact remains that more than once Lord Salisbury has cast a longing eye across the Atlantic to the American Constitution, lamenting that our own Constitution contained no such safeguards as those provided by the wisdom of the Fathers of the American Republic.

Still more remarkable is the declaration of Mr. Cecil Rhodes, who long ago set forth with his accustomed bluntness that for the salvation of the British Empire only two things were needed, "Home Rule and a preferential tariff, and if you ask me why I believe in Home Rule and what I mean by it, I say to you read the American Constitution."

What more need have we of witnesses?

The only consolation that can be offered to the susceptible Briton is that the American Constitution, like the American people, owes its origin to the island which was the cradle of the race. The Americans, in fashioning their Constitution, imported it from England via France, to which country they subsequently re-exported it, in spirit though not in form, with results not even yet fully worked out. Montesquieu, by his eulogistic panegyric upon the English Constitution in his "Esprit des Loix," became the Godfather of the American Constitution. But it was the Puritan principles of free democracy which we exported in the *Mayflower* that fashioned and prepared the founders of the American Commonwealth for their famous achievement. So it may fairly be contended that in the Americanising of the English-speaking world it is the spirit of Old England reincarnate in the body of Uncle Sam.

Chapter III — The Americanisation of Ireland

It is an interesting subject of speculation how the Americanising of the British Empire will be brought about. Many forces are working steadily in that direction, the significance of which is very imperfectly revealed to our eyes. One of the chief of these is seldom realised, for its operation is silent and subtle as the law of gravitation. It is, indeed, no other than the law of gravitation operating in the political

world. Among the heavenly bodies the less revolve around the greater. The mass tells. You cannot build a solar system in which any of the planets is larger and heavier than the sun.

A hundred years ago Great Britain was the sun of the political system of the English world. Her population was sixteen millions, whereas the population of the United States was only five millions. The Americans had torn themselves off from the British connection, but they still felt the pull which a compact mass of sixteen millions exercises continuously upon a body only one-third its bulk. For three-quarters of the century that silent force of gravitation exerted its influence in a continually diminishing degree, until after a time, the two nations being equipoised, the position of the two States was reversed. The United States now began to exert the pull upon the United Kingdom. The operation of this unseen force was for a time obscured, owing to the fact that the smaller nation had taken to itself vast masses of Asiatic and African subjects. But after a time it was perceived that they had not made these men citizens, and it is only citizens who count. The hundreds of millions of dusky subjects in Hindostan add nothing to the intrinsic strength of the British people. They constitute part of "the White Man's Burden." As elements in the problem of political gravitation they only count because they tend to obscure the perception of the real forces governing the situation. The real kernel and nucleus of both States is to be found in their white citizens. The mutual influence of Britain on America and of America on England depends upon the number and the intelligence of their citizens and the intensity of their cohesion. That cohesion is not necessarily geographical. It is in its essence moral, emotional, and intellectual. In the voluntary association of free, self-governing citizens lies the secret of the strength of the State.

Herein we touch upon another element of weakness which tells heavily against Great Britain in comparison with the United States. The citizens of the United States, to the last man, are voluntary citizens. They are proud of their citizenship. There are no unwilling subjects in the whole Republic. There are millions, literally millions, who have been born in other lands, but the foreign born vie with the natives in their exultant pride in being citizens of the United States. When we turn our eyes to the British Empire we are confronted with a very different state of things. Close at our doors lies a country as populous as any but the two largest states in the American Union, the majority of whose inhabitants are in a chronic state of latent rebellion.

HOUSES OF PARLIAMENT, WESTMINSTER.

THE CAPITOL AT WASHINGTON.

The majority of the Irish people acquiesce sullenly in the irresistible logic of *force majeure*. They are not proud of British citizenship. They loathe it. They accept representation at Westminster solely in order that they may use the vote which they are allowed to exercise as the only available substitute for the pike and the rifle, the use of which is denied to them. In this broad survey of the comparative strength of the two great sections of the English-speaking world, it is impossible not to recognise in Ireland the Achilles heel of the Empire. Our failure to win the allegiance of the Irish is the most fatal element in the sum of blunders which are transferring the leadership of our race to our sons beyond the sea.

Less than forty years ago the United States of America were torn in twain by the bloodiest civil war of our time. For nearly five years the whole nation was preoccupied with fratricidal strife. In the end the North conquered. The South, beaten flat, crushed, desolated and despairing, sued for peace. The seceding States were forced back into the Union at the point of the bayonet. But despite all waving of the "Bloody Shirt," despite a million graves of slaughtered men, and the yawning chasm between the victors and the vanquished, the breach was healed by the re-establishment of Home Rule. When the war broke out with Spain no recruits rallied to the defence of the Star-spangled banner more heartily than the sons of the men who, under Davis and Lee, had shed their blood in the attempt to destroy the Union. Uncle Sam has no unwilling subjects, not even in the former stronghold of secession.

The contrast between the complete reconciliation which has been effected between North and South in America and our utter failure to effect even a *modus vivendi* between the English and the Irish, affords a measure of the difference between the political genius of the American Republic and of the British Empire. The secret lies in the fact that the Americans have frankly and fully recognised the principle of government by the consent of the governed, whereas only one-half of the English have ever accepted it. The old virus of absolute government, which was the curse of England in the Seventeenth Century under the Stuarts, came back after the Commonwealth at the Restoration, and was not entirely exorcised in 1688. It revived in the Eighteenth Century under George III., with the result that we lost our American colonies. In the Nineteenth we succeeded in suppressing it everywhere excepting in Ireland. Here, thanks to the House of Lords, we were able to indulge the fatal propensity inherent in our Conservatives of trying to govern a nation without its consent, against its will, and in opposition to its ideas. As a result, we have Ireland and the Irish as an element not of strength, but of weakness. They are as salt in the mortar of Empire, whose weakening and dissolving influence is by no means confined to the United Kingdom. The presence of unwilling subjects, of men made citizens without their consent, is ever a source of weakness to States. But so far are we from having learned that lesson that for the last two years we have been lavishing all the resources of the Empire in a desperate attempt to compel within the pale of our dominions the most stubborn and unwilling set of subjects the world has ever seen. An expenditure of 20,000 lives and £200,000,000 has been incurred for the purpose of forcing the South African Dutch to submit to our dominion. We have killed thousands and devastated their land in order to make them "our subjects." If they had been willing to become our fellow-citizens they would have been a source of strength. As men forced by war to submit to our yoke they will become a source of abiding weakness. We shall have two Irelands on our hands instead of one, and each affords only too tempting an opportunity for those who may use the Americanising trend of our time for the purpose of detaching either or both from the Empire of which at present they form a part.

In view of the possibilities opened up before us by the catastrophe which has destroyed our self-governed dominion in South Africa, it may not be without profit if we were carefully to read and ponder the Declaration of Independence by which, on July 4, 1776, our American colonists formally notified to the whole world their final severance from Great Britain and their determination henceforth to work out their own destinies as sovereign states.

I wonder how many of my British readers have ever perused this famous document. Its reproduction here will probably cause the seizure of this book by the military censors at Cape Town. But, notwithstanding their objection, the Declaration, with its carefully specified statement of the wrongs inflicted upon the Americans by the British Government, may be very profitably read and meditated upon to-day. For here within the four corners of a well-worn placard are set forth in plain terms the reasons why we lost America, and, reading between the lines, we may discover without much difficulty the reasons why we shall lose South Africa and Ireland also if so be that we do not mend our ways. It is doubtful whether one Englishman in a thousand has ever read the Declaration through from end to end. Yet a more fateful document it would be hard to find in the whole of our records. It is the epitaph of our Empire —

In Congress, July 4, 1776

A DECLARATION

BY THE REPRESENTATIVES OF THE UNITED STATES OF AMERICA,

In General Congress assembled.

WHEN in the Course of human Events, it becomes necessary for one People to dissolve the Political Bands which have connected them with another, and to assume among the Powers of the Earth, the separate and equal Station to which the Laws of Nature and of Nature's God entitle them, a decent Respect to the Opinions of Mankind requires that they should declare the Causes which impel them to the separation.

We hold these Truths to be self-evident, that all Men are created equal, that they are endowed by their Creator with certain unalienable Rights, that among these are Life, Liberty and the Pursuit of Happiness. That to secure these Rights, Governments are instituted among Men, deriving their just Powers from the Consent of the Governed, that whenever any Form of Government becomes destructive of these Ends, it is the Right of the People to alter or abolish it, and to institute new Government, laying its foundation on such Principles, and organising its Powers in such Form, as to them shall seem most likely to effect their Safety and Happiness. Prudence, indeed, will dictate that Governments long established should not be changed for light and transient Causes, and accordingly all Experience has shewn, that Mankind are more disposed to suffer, while Evils are sufferable, than to right themselves by abolishing the Forms to which they are accustomed But when a long Train of Abuses and Usurpations, pursuing invariably the same Object, evinces a design to reduce them under absolute Despotism, it is their Right, it is their Duty, to throw off such Government, and to provide new Guards for their future Security Such has been the patient sufferance of these Colonies, and such is now the Necessity which constrains to alter their former Systems of Government The History of the present King of Great Britain is a History of repeated Injuries and Usurpations, all having in direct Object the Establishment of an absolute Tyranny over these States To prove this, let Facts be submitted to a candid World.

He has refused his Assent to Laws, the most wholesome and necessary for the public Good.

He has forbidden his Governors to pass Laws of immediate and pressing Importance, unless suspended in their Operation till his Assent should be obtained, and when so suspended, he has utterly neglected to attend to them.

He has refused to pass other Laws for the Accommodation of large Districts of People, unless those People would relinquish the Right of Representation in the Legislature, a Right inestimable to them, and formidable to Tyrants only

He has called together Legislative Bodies at Places unusual, uncomfortable, and distant from the Depository of their public Records, for the sole Purpose of fatiguing them into Compliance with his Measures.

He has dissolved Representative Houses repeatedly, for opposing with manly Firmness his Invasions on the Rights of the People.

He has refused for a long Time after such Dissolutions, to cause others to be elected; whereby the Legislative Powers, incapable of Annihilation, have returned to the people at large for their exercise; the State remaining in the meantime exposed to all the Dangers of Invasion from without, and Convulsions within.

He has endeavoured to prevent the population of these States; for that Purpose obstructing the Laws for Naturalisation of Foreigners; refusing to pass others to encourage their Migrations hither, and raising the Conditions of new Appropriations of Lands

He has obstructed the Administration of Justice, by refusing his Assent to Laws for establishing Judiciary Powers.

He has made Judges dependent on his Will alone, for the Tenure of their Offices, and the Amount and Payment of their Salaries.

He has erected a multitude of new Offices, and sent hither Swarms of Officers to harass our People, and eat out their Substance.

He has kept among us, in Times of Peace, Standing Armies, without the Consent of our Legislatures.

He has affected to render the Military independent of and superior to the civil Power.

He has combined with others to subject us to a Jurisdiction foreign to our Constitution, and unacknowledged by our Laws; given his Assent to their Acts of pretended Legislation:

For quartering large Bodies of armed Troops among us.

For protecting them, by a mock Trial, from punishment for any Murders which they should commit on the Inhabitants of these States:

For cutting off our Trade with all Parts of the World:

For imposing Taxes on us without our Consent

For depriving us, in many cases, of the Benefits of Trial by Jury

For transporting us beyond Seas to be tried for pretended Offences

For abolishing the free system of English Laws in a neighbouring Province, establishing therein an arbitrary Government, and enlarging its boundaries, so as to render it at once an Example and fit Instrument for introducing the same Absolute Rule into these Colonies

For taking away our Charters, abolishing our most valuable Laws, and altering fundamentally the forms of our Governments

For suspending our own Legislatures, and declaring themselves invested with Power to legislate for us in all Cases whatsoever.

He has abdicated Government here, by declaring us out of his Protection, and waging War against us.

He has plundered our Seas, ravaged our Coasts, burnt our Towns, and destroyed the Lives of our People

He is at this Time, transporting large Armies of foreign Mercenaries to compleat the Works of Death, Desolation, and Tyranny, already begun with Circumstances of Cruelty and Perfidy scarcely parallelled in the most barbarous Ages, and totally unworthy the Head of a civilized Nation

He has constrained our fellow Citizens taken Captive on the high Seas to bear Arms against their Country, to become the Executioners of their Friends and Brethren, or to fall themselves by their Hands.

He has excited Domestic Insurrections amongst us, and has endeavoured to bring on the Inhabitants of our Frontiers, the merciless Indian Savages, whose known Rule of Warfare is an undistinguished Destruction, of all Ages, Sexes, and Conditions

In every Stage of these Oppressions we have petitioned for Redress, in the most humble Terms Our repeated Petitions have been answered only by repeated Injury. A Prince whose Character is thus marked by every Act which may define a Tyrant, is unfit to be the Ruler of a free People.

Nor have we been wanting in Attention to our British Brethren We have warned them from Time to Time of Attempts to extend an unwarrantable Jurisdiction over us. We have reminded them of the Circumstances of our Emigration and Settlement here We have appealed to their native Justice and Magna-

nimity, and we have conjured them by the Ties of our common Kindred to disavow these Usurpations, which would inevitably interrupt our Connections and Correspondence They too have been deaf to the Voice of Justice and of Consanguinity. We must, therefore, acquiesce in the Necessity which denounces our Separation, and hold them, as we hold the rest of Mankind, Enemies in War ; in Peace, Friends

We, therefore, the Representatives of the UNITED STATES OF AMERICA, in GENERAL CONGRESS assembled, appealing to the Supreme Judge of the World for the Rectitude of our Intentions, do in the Name and by the Authority of the good People of these Colonies, solemnly Publish and Declare, That these United Colonies are, and of Right ought to be, FREE AND INDEPENDENT STATES, that they are absolved from all Allegiance to the British Crown, and that all political connection between them and the State of Great Britain, is, and ought to be, totally dissolved, and that as FREE AND INDEPENDENT STATES, they have full Power to levy War, conclude Peace, contract Alliances, establish Commerce, and to do all other Acts and Things which INDEPENDENT STATES may of Right do. And for the Support of this Declaration, with a firm Reliance on the Protection of Divine Providence, we mutually pledge to each other our Lives, our Fortunes, and our sacred Honor.

Signed by ORDER and on BEHALF of the CONGRESS,

JOHN HANCOCK, President.

Attest,

CHARLES THOMPSON, Secretary

The greater part of the offences laid at the door of George III. in his dealing with his American colonists, now lie at our doors in our dealing with the colonists of South Africa Nor need we be surprised if similar causes bring about similar results Human nature is the same in South Africa as it was in Boston and Philadelphia. The Dutch are as stubborn a breed as the descendants of the men of the *Mayflower* If the centrifugal force is certain to make itself felt upon the British Empire, its influence will be earliest perceptible upon those portions of our Empire which adhere most loosely to the parent body The disruption of the Empire or its gradual disintegration under the superior attraction of the United States will begin in those territories where there is nothing to counteract the drawing power of gravitation in the shape of national sentiment or patriotic loyalty. In other words, the United States will have most pull over Ireland and South Africa, for in both of these lands the centrifugal

Mr. JOHN REDMOND, M.P.
(Photograph by Lafayette.)

Mr. JOHN DILLON, M.P.

[Photograph by Frith & Co.]

COLLEGE GREEN, DUBLIN.

Mr. HORACE PLUNKETT.
(Photograph by Chancellor.)

Mr. MICHAEL DAVITT.
(Photograph by Lafayette.)

forces of domestic discontent will reinforce the centripetal forces outside

The majority of the Irish in Ireland have never regarded the British Empire with other sentiments than those of hostility. Under English rule, they have seen their religion proscribed, their lands confiscated, their sons driven into exile. They have been denied the right to make their own laws and mocked with a gracious permission to be in a perpetual minority in an alien Parliament. Again and again they have risen in revolt only to learn on the scaffold and in the felon's cell the rewards which patriotism has in store for the national heroes of Ireland. During last century they have seen their numbers dwindling in the land of their birth, not by the thousand, but by the million. At the same time a tardy confession has been wrung from the predominant partner that for the last fifty years Ireland has been overtaxed in comparison with England by more than two millions per annum. The inevitable result has followed. The majority of the Irish in Ireland regard the British Government not as their friend, but as the ally of their worst enemies, the vampire which preys upon their hearts' blood. To the masses of the South and West, and to a large extent of the North, the United States is more of a fatherland than Great Britain. They are much more interested in what goes on in New York than in London, in Chicago than in Westminster. It is to England that their money goes in rent and in taxes. It is from the United States that their money comes in a pactolean flood of remittances through the post. In the United States there were at the census of 1890 1,870,000 persons of Irish birth. Of those born of Irish parents on American soil who can say how many there are? More, it is safe to say, than are to be found in all Ireland to-day.

If the majority of the Irish race find themselves to-day under the Stars and Stripes, and if the majority of the Irish in Ireland build all their hopes of success upon the support which they can draw from their kin beyond the sea, it is not surprising if Ireland should afford a promising field for the disintegrating influence of American gravitation. It was from the Irish in America that Mr Parnell drew the resources which made the Land League so powerful. It is to the Irish in America that Mr Redmond has gone to solicit support for the United Irish League. It was from the American Irish that Patrick Ford collected the fund for "Spreading the Light." It is in the United States that the Clan na Gael has its headquarters; and it was from Chicago that the dynamitards set out when they undertook their campaign of terrorism which landed most of them in convict prisons.

For the revolutionary party in Ireland America is their base, their banker, their recruiting ground, and their safe retreat. Every year Ireland becomes more and more Americanised, more and more assimilated to the ideas of the democracy of the West.

What America has given to the Irish is something much more valuable than dollars. It is only in the cities of the American Union that the Irish have had an opportunity of displaying those political gifts, the exercise of which they were denied in their own land. It is the fashion to sneer at the way in which the Irish rule New York, Chicago, and half the great cities of the Union. The details of their administration may leave much to be desired, but the extraordinary fashion in which they have succeeded in establishing their authority over the richest, the most energetic, and the most independent communities in the world, is one of the most brilliant and miraculous achievements in modern politics. Everywhere in a minority, they are everywhere in the ascendant. Denied the elementary right of self-government in their own country on the score of political incapacity, they have in the New World afforded mankind one of the most signal illustrations of the art and craft political that the modern world has ever seen. All that may be said in criticism of the way in which they gained or used their power only enhances the wonder of it. Landing at Castle Garden, penniless, ignorant, and despised, they have made themselves in less than half a century the overlords of the greatest cities in the New World. The Anglo-Indian, with all the Empire at his back, has not a firmer grip upon the administration of Calcutta than plain Richard Croker enjoyed for half a lifetime over the commercial capital of America. Men who have done so much with so little, men who have created satrapies out of nothing and constrained the States that expelled the British to submit to their yoke, may be criminals, but they have in them the genius of statesmanship.

This is the more remarkable when we contrast it with the utter failure of the British immigrant to leave any perceptible trace on the political development or the civic administration of the United States. In 1890 there were in the United States of Irish birth 1,870,000, but those of British birth were even more numerous. The figures are as follows:—

England		900,092	
Wales		100,079	
Scotland		242,231	
			1,251,402
Canada and Newfoundland			980,938
			2,232,340

From the British Isles, that *ragina gentium*, came three million persons who in 1890 were resident in the United States Almost another million came from the British American colonies. Four million persons born under the Union Jack were in 1890 living under the Stars and Stripes What influence had this enormous British element upon the politics or the government of the United States, or of any one of them? The only perceptible influence was that of the Irish minority, and that influence has been from the first and still is steadily exerted against the Empire within whose frontiers they were born. Every American politician recognises the Irish vote as a powerful factor in every election Who has ever been heard to speak of the English vote, the Welsh vote, the Scotch vote? There are no such votes. The English, the Welsh, and the Scotch are completely Americanised and lost among the mass of American born The Irish alone remain distinct. The one race immune to complete Americanisation is, nevertheless, the most potent enemy of Great Britain. They only remain unassimilated in order that they may be strong enough to assist their brethren at home in throwing off the English yoke

At present the prospects of the Irish cause are brighter than they have been since the death of Mr. Parnell. Mr. Redmond has carried to his fellow-countrymen in the United States messages of high hope of coming victory. We trust that the Irish may not experience once more that disappointment which has so often dogged their path. But what has been may be, and the confidence excited by the re-establishment of discipline in the Nationalist ranks, may once more be replaced by the gloom and chill of despair. What then?

Is it entirely out of the pale of possible politics that a time may come, if no closer ties of a federal nature are established between the Empire and the Republic, when Ireland may gravitate from the United Kingdom to the United States? The only security against the occurrence of such an event has disappeared The United States, aspiring to be one of the first of naval powers, has begun to realise that it is the sea which unites, the land which divides. It was easier for the *Oregon* to steam round Cape Horn than to pierce the narrow isthmus which unites the Americas Their hold on the Philippines has familiarised the Americans with the possibility of dominion over sea. Dublin is not half as far from New York as Manila is from San Francisco. The Americans no longer rigidly confine themselves within the ring fence of the coast line of the oceans They are spreading themselves abroad. Expansion is in the air.

Several times in the last half century relations between the Empire and the Republic have been somewhat painfully strained Now that the United States is conscious of its superior strength and is venturing more to move out into the open, occasions for friction are certain to be more numerous. If ever—which Heaven forbid—these points of friction should develop actual collision between the two nations, Ireland would at once become an object of supreme interest to the Americans, as formerly it was to the French As for the Irish, their maxim, "England's extremity is Ireland's opportunity," has been too deeply engraved into their consciousness for them not to realise the importance of utilising such an occasion to the uttermost Quite apart from all other possibilities, the never to be overlooked chance that some day Britain may be at war, makes it the imperative duty of every American statesman not to let slip any opportunity that might render more certain and more valuable the support of Ireland in such a quarrel

This is assuming that the cause of dispute may be one altogether extraneous to Ireland But we cannot overlook the possibility that Ireland itself might form the *casus belli*.

The only foreign war which Americans of this generation have waged was fought for the liberation of Cuba. Cuba was the Spaniard's Ireland. The Pearl of the Antilles, like the Emerald Isle, had suffered for centuries from the unsympathetic rule of alien conquerors. The Cubans, like the Irish, were savagely discontented Like the Irish, although not nearly to the same extent, they had friends and sympathisers in all the great American cities. Cuba, like Ireland, was bled to death by the rapacity of the foreigner. At last, after long hesitation, the full cup of Spain's iniquities overflowed, the Americans rose and smote down with one smashing blow the rule of the Dons in the West Indies The war was brief, brilliant, and decisive. As the result the islands which Weyler had wasted with sword and flame are enjoying a prosperity before unheard of. And the American people as a whole are exceedingly well pleased at the result of their first essay as a liberating Power.

All these things render it by no means improbable that a piteous appeal from the Irish after the next famine or, more likely still, after the next abortive insurrection, will find the American ear quick to hear the cry from weeping Erin, "Come over and help us." Probably most of my readers will shrug their shoulders at this speculation, and dismiss it as fantastic nonsense. To all such I will put but one question. Do they imagine for one moment that if British generals were to put in force against Irish insurgents of the Twentieth Century all the pitch-cap devilries of 1798, any power on earth would be able to keep the American people from interposing between our soldiery and their victims? There is not an American city which has not among its most influential men some one who was born in the country which was desolated by our dragoons. The cry of anguish that would rise from the fire-blasted country, in Connaught and in Munster, would reverberate through every American city. The memories of the old blood feud would revive. The shade of Washington would be invoked against the descendants of the men whom he drove from the United States, and the sword of Columbia would not be returned to its scabbard before Ireland had been placed beside Cuba among the proud trophies of the humanitarian and liberating zeal of the American people.

This speculation may seem fantastic to those who have never reflected upon the extraordinary rapidity with which nations discover that they have a providential mission to assist the oppressed when their interests or their passions lead them to desire a pretext for interference. But it is as well to remember that, as far back as 1896, Mr William O'Brien declared in the pages of the *Nineteenth Century* the possibility of American intervention on behalf of Ireland. He even suggested that after the next General Election all the Nationalist members returned for Irish constituencies should refuse to come to Westminster, but should proceed to Washington to formally lay their appeal before the Congress of the United States. The article was entitled, " If Ireland sent her M.P.'s to Washington." It opened with the suggestion that the first business that an Anglo-American Court of Arbitration would have to deal with would be the relations between Great Britain and Ireland. The most notable passage in the article runs as follows "Supposing that the Irish electors should say, ' Enough of idle babble in the English Parliament. We will elect representatives pledged not to go to Westminster, but to Washington to lay the case of Ireland before the President and Congress of the United States with all the solemnity of a nation's appeal, and to invoke the intervention which was so successful in the case of Venezuela ' Eighty-two Irish members, five-sixths of the Irish representation, transferred from the Parliament of England to the Congress of the United States by deliberate national decree, would represent an international event of whose importance the most supercilious Jingo would not affect to make light." Mr. O'Brien thought that if such a pilgrimage took place, the Irish representatives would be received with open arms. He said " the public opinion of the United States could not resist such an appeal from Ireland. I think few will doubt it who

know the depth of American sympathy with Ireland, and the interest that all Americans, and not the least, Irish Americans, have in eliminating the Irish question from their own internal politics Enlightened Englishmen who desire at one and the same time to conciliate Ireland, and to deliver the United States and England from periodical fits of war fever, ought to be the first to welcome the intervention of the new Court of Arbitration in Irish affairs. It would turn a controversy which may easily enough be the beginning of a new and implacable quarrel between the two great English-speaking Powers into a pledge of genuine amity between them. What seems to me reasonably certain," said Mr. O'Brien five years ago, " is that the centre of gravity of the Irish difficulty some time to come is about to shift from Westminster to Washington."

Mr McHugh, who, fresh from a British dungeon, accompanied Mr Redmond this year in his pilgrimage to the United States, boldly proclaimed his belief that Ireland would soon take a greater step forward and would demand admittance into the Union as one of the United States Too much importance need not be attached to such suggestions, which are often thrown out like sparks to dazzle and to expire But in view of the widespread recognition on the part of many English-speaking men on this side of the Atlantic, of the imminent desirability, not to say necessity, of creating a great English-speaking political international trust, these suggestions are not without their significance

Certain persons, who form their estimate of American public opinion solely from the utterances of the wealthy classes in New York, may scout the idea that any sane or statesmanlike American would ever entertain the suggestion put forward by Mr. William O'Brien. If they look a little below the surface, or if they extend their investigations into American public opinion a little further they would modify their conclusion. Nine years ago this very subject was discussed by one of the sanest and most sagacious of American writers in an article published in the *Contemporary Review* of September 1892. In this paper Dr Shaw, who had been asked by the editor to set forth in plain terms what was the American view of Home Rule and Federation, referred to the possible consequences that might result from the refusal of the predominant partner to concede Home Rule to Ireland If England persisted in this course, said Dr Shaw, " Ireland itself might falter in its loyalty at some time of crisis We do not want Ireland, yet obviously we could make her very comfortable and happy as a State in our Union And in the nature of things it is not

easy to see why the American flag might not
float over the Emerald Isle with as much pro-
priety as the British flag in territories contiguous
to our border   Moreover there might be much
moral justification for our reception of Ireland
in the fact that we should at once give that
community a place in a rational system of political organisation, and promote its general welfare
and progress, whereas without Home Rule it
must remain in a distraught condition   Our
mission in Ireland would be the same as England
professes in Egypt—to pacify, restore, and bless.
But we could have no object in undertaking this
expensive annexation of Ireland except the
welfare of humanity and the progress of the
English speaking communities of the world "

CHAPTER IV.—OF SOUTH AFRICA

No phrase has been more frequently used in
the discussion of the South African question
than that the policy of Mr Chamberlain is
creating for us "another Ireland in South
Africa "   Without striking into the forbidden
path of political controversy it suffices to point
out that Mr Chamberlain himself has warned
us that when his war has been brought to a
close we shall require to maintain for an
indefinite time a standing army of 50,000 men
in South Africa in order to enforce the obedience
of the 300,000 unwilling subjects whom we
have determined to compel to remain within
the borders of the Empire   Since that calcula-
tion has been made the British garrison in South
Africa has been steadily maintained at a figure
considerably above 200,000. Even now the
military expert of *The Times* calculates that in
the first six months after all fighting has ceased
it will be only possible to recall 30,000 men,
and that we must contemplate the necessity of
maintaining for a time, to which no limit can be
placed, an armed force of 170,000 men   But
the number of bayonets upon which we shall
find it necessary to sit in our South African
dominions is a detail. Whether they are 50,000
or 170,000 or 200,000, the seat will be equally
uncomfortable, the only difference being one of
expenditure. The fundamental point to be
kept in view is that in South Africa it may be
for years or it may be for generations, we have
deliberately elected to establish our dominion
by reliance upon military force   Before the
war our Empire in South Africa was one of
consent   After the war it will be one of conquest maintained by an armed garrison   The
Dutch of Cape Colony, who were so loyal
immediately before the war as to take the lead
of every Colony in the Empire in voting an

annual subsidy for the maintenance of the
British fleet, are being converted into implacable
enemies of our rule.   But it is probable that
the force which will dislodge the Afrikander
Commonwealth from the position to which we
have destined it in the ' orbit of the British
Empire, and which will convert it into one of
the stars in the constellation of the United
States of America, will not in the first instance
at least be Dutch   We shall lose South Africa,
not by the armed revolt of our alienated subjects, but because we can no longer depend
upon the support and co-operation in maintaining our authority over the much more immediately dangerous and uncontrollable element
which we are doing our best to bring into
existence in Johannesburg
    In order to understand the true inwardness
of this observation it is necessary to go back to
the fatal moment in South African history when
Mr Rhodes decided to enter upon that which
is known in history as the Jameson Conspiracy
    So little is known of the inner springs of
political action, that it is possible most of my
American readers will hear for the first time in
these pages that the present disastrous war in
South Africa is the direct result of a jealousy of
American influence   It is common ground that
this war dates from the Jameson Raid. The
Raid begat the armaments, the armaments begat
Lord Milner's intervention, and that intervention
brought on the war   But what begat the Raid ?
Upon this point I can speak with authority, as I
have frequently heard the whole story of that
most disastrous blunder from the lips of the
man who conceived the conspiracy, and risked
everything in order to carry it out   No mistake
can be greater than the vulgar error of imagining
that Mr Rhodes hatched the Jameson conspiracy out of any animosity or fear of the
Boers. Mr. Rhodes has always been very
partial to the Dutch. Man for man, he knows
that the Boer is a better physical, virile creature
than the city-bred people of Great Britain.
Politically, he had always worked with them.
He never would have been Premier except by ,
their aid, and no man ever formulated more
emphatically the axiom that without the support
of the Dutch you cannot govern South Africa
    Why, then, did he enter into a conspiracy to
overthrow President Kruger? Mr. Rhodes' own
answer to this, which I have heard many times
from his own lips, is that his object was not·
primarily but only incidentally to overthrow
Kruger. His one supreme aim was to capture
the Uitlanders, to secure their allegiance to the
British Empire, and to avert the one thing he
dreaded most of all, the establishment of what
he called an American Republic in the Transvaal, which, in his own vigorous phrase, would

THE RT. HON. CECIL JOHN RHODES.

(From a photograph specially taken for the "Review of Reviews," by E. H. Mills, 19, Stanley Gardens, W.)

have been ten times more a child of the devil for us to deal with than Paul Kruger had ever been

Mr Rhodes was a little too previous in his calculations—a fault on virtue's side, especially in these days, when our Ministers seem congenitally incapable of an intelligent anticipation of events to come. But to understand a miscalculation after the event is easy. It is more difficult to foresee. What Mr. Rhodes thought he saw was the Rand filling up with a heterogeneous conglomerate of adventurous, unscrupulous, unattached mortals, all intent primarily upon making their fortune. These men outnumbered the adult burghers of the Transvaal by four to one. The Boers were practically unarmed, without even adequate supply of cartridges for their rifles, except for protection against the natives. Their artillery was worthless. Although some attempt had been made to construct a fort to overawe Johannesburg, 'they were utterly unprepared for a *coup de main* The previous election for President had shown the existence of a very strong minority hostile to Paul Kruger Mr Rhodes was led to believe by his confidential informants that the Uitlanders were not in the mood to tolerate any longer the authority of the Boers Their leaders were represented as being only one degree less hostile to the British Government than they were to President Kruger, the cause of their complaint being the fact that Mr Rhodes and the High Commissioner had never given them any effective assistance in their campaign against Krugerism.

The Uitlanders were men who had at their disposition the enormous wealth of the Rand, that treasure of the Nibelungs which has drenched the veldt with human blood—they were men of all nationalities and of none—and even those who came from Great Britain and the Colonies held very loosely to the Empire. Conspicuous among those were the Irish and the miners, whom Mr. Rhodes described as the "*Sydney Bulletin* Australians." The *Sydney Bulletin*, it may here be explained, is an extremely able weekly illustrated paper, published in Sydney, which neither fears God nor reverences the King, and which makes British Imperialism the favourite butt of its attacks. German Jews, Frenchmen, Russians, Poles Hollanders, and Americans—it was a motley crowd that the great golden magnet had attracted to Johannesburg—of which one thing at least could be stated without hesitation, viz., that it had as little enthusiasm for the Union Jack or for anything more ideal than dollars and cents as any assemblage of human beings that could be collected on the planet. It was a godless crew, of whom one shrewd observer remarked, that it was too much addicted to

gambling, women, and whisky to have the proper revolutionary fibre But gross mammon worshipper though it might be, Mr Rhodes believed it was the brain as well as the pocket of Africa He knew it was fretfully impatient of the irksome restrictions enforced by President Kruger. He underestimated the resisting force of the Boers, and believed that at any moment the news might come that a bloodless revolution had taken place in the Transvaal, that Paul Kruger had disappeared, and that in his place he would have to deal with a President of a new Republic, flushed with victory, angry at being refused all help, and very much inclined to pay off old scores by being much more anti-British than the Boers had been "In fact," said Mr. Rhodes to me when he was explaining how it was he came to make the one fatal blunder of his career,—"it seemed to me quite certain that if I did not take a hand in the game, the forces on the spot would soon make short work of President Kruger Then I should be face to face with an American Republic—American in the sense of being intensely hostile to and jealous of Britain—an American Republic largely manned by Americans and *Sydney Bulletin* Australians who cared nothing for the old flag. They would have all the wealth of the Rand at their disposal. The drawing power of the Uitlander Republic would have collected round it all the other Colonies. They would have federated with it as a centre, and we should have lost South Africa. To avert this catastrophe, to rope in the Uitlanders before it was too late, I did what I did "

Repeated conversations with Mr. Rhodes, even so recently as last autumn, found him unchanged in the conviction that the danger of that American Republic in the heart of South Africa justified his conspiracy. Kruger was doomed anyhow. It was for England to stand in with the Rising Sun.

Not only will Americans be interested in knowing the true story of the genesis of the Jameson conspiracy, they will be not less surprised to know that its failure was largely due to President Cleveland's message on the Venezuelan Question. The Jameson Conspiracy, as originally planned, based its hope of success upon a revolutionary movement in Johannesburg, in which all nationalities were to take part. Conspicuous among the conspirators were the Americans, Mr. Hayes-Hammond and Captain Mein, and round them were several other Americans whose sympathies were enlisted by the idea that they were in some way emulating the exploits of the fathers of the Revolution in overthrowing a new George III. in the person of President Kruger.

When Mr. Chamberlain made it the condition of his connivance in the conspiracy that Dr Jameson should go in under the British flag, and that the next Governor of the Transvaal should be appointed by the Colonial Office, he hamstrung the one chance of success which the conspiracy had possessed. His condition about the flag was suppressed for a while, but the news leaked out just about the time when the anti-British sentiment among Americans everywhere was excited to fever heat by President Cleveland's message about Venezuela. The immediate result was that the American members of the Johannesburg Conspiracy flatly refused to go on with the revolution. They said they were willing to stake their lives for a bonâ fide revolution, to make a clean sweep of the Krugerites and put up a better Government in its stead, but they point blank and in set terms refused to go another step in what they described as a job to " gobble up " the Transvaal for England

Explanations and disclosures were forthcoming, but the mischief was done. The whole . revolutionary movement had received its deathblow when the Americans discovered Mr. Chamberlain's design. The subsequent effort of Dr Jameson to galvanise the revolution into life need not be referred to here, excepting to say that the responsibility for this fiasco lies primarily at the door of the Colonial Minister, whose " Hurry up " messages were admittedly inspired by a desire to get the revolution over before the Venezuelan-American trouble became acute.

The story how that conspiracy miscarried is ancient history. Dr. Jameson and his men, Mr. Rhodes and all their backers, fared as men usually do who sell the lion's skin before the lion is dead. But the important point is that standpoint of Mr. Rhodes, and the fact that in his opinion the danger point to the Empire in South Africa five years ago was not to be sought among the Dutch but among the Outlanders, and what Mr Rhodes saw then is doubly true to-day. The real danger that threatens the Empire in South Africa is not to be found so much in the sleepless hostility of the Dutch, whose homes have been burned and whose children have been done to death, as one of the humane corollaries of the policy of devastation and farm burning. It is to be found in the cosmopolitan population whom we are summoning back to the Rand. It is a common error to maintain that the Outlanders love us, and that even if they did not love us before the war we have purchased their affection, admiration, and loyalty by the immensity of the sacrifice in the last two years. That, however, is not the way in which the Outlander looks at it at all.

He considers that British incompetence, British short-sightedness, and the insufferable arrogance and ignorance of our military officers, have subjected him for two years to privations which he would never have suffered if we had shown ordinary capacity in the conduct of the war. Between the mining community and the military satraps who act upon their own prejudice and caprice, and are responsible for martial law throughout the whole of South Africa, there is a bitter feud. No Dutchman speaks with such contempt of the British military authorities as do the men on whose behalf the whole of our sacrifices have been incurred. Two years experience in refugee camps in Cape Town and Natal have not sweetened the temper of these quondam political helots who aroused the gushing sympathy of Lord Milner. They will return, and with them will return a horde of political adventurers from all parts of the world. In the next twenty years £300,000,000 sterling will be extracted from the mines of the Rand, and where the carcase is there will the vultures be gathered together. It is confidently calculated that the white mining population that will throng to the Rand will number a minimum of a quarter of a million, and possibly there may be as many as 350,000. The population will be preponderantly male, but it will not be anything like preponderantly British. There will be any number of Americans, the *Sydney Bulletin* Australians will come once more to the front, there will be swarms of Polish Jews, and any number of adventurous Frenchmen, Germans, Russians, and Dutch. These men will go there with one object, and that is to enrich themselves as rapidly as possible, and no community in the world will be more impatient of any restriction upon their liberty or of the imposition of any burdens which in their opinions ought not to be imposed upon them without their consent. Imagine this cosmopolitan community of gold seekers compelled to submit to the arbitrary restrictions of military rule, taxed without their consent, and saddled with a large share of what they regard as the altogether unnecessary expenditure which was caused by the blundering incompetence of the British Government and British military authorities. It is not pretended that for years to come there will be anything in the shape of free Parliamentary government established in any part of South Africa. On the contrary, we are told every day that it may be years or it may be generations before the rule of the sword is replaced.

We are further told by those excellent ministers of the Gospel under whose benediction the war has been waged, that as the result of our sacrifices Downing Street is going to settle the native question in South Africa upon the principles of Exeter Hall. What will be the result? Two years will not pass before we have Johannesburg in a seething mass of discontent, a charged mine to which a match may at any moment be accidentally applied. You only need to move among the leading members of the mining community either in London or in Africa to understand what the future has in store for us "How long do you Outlanders" —I asked an eminent reformer who had done time in gaol for his share in the Jameson conspiracy—"how long do you think you can tolerate Crown Colony government in Johannesburg?'—' Some people,' he said, "say eighteen months So far as my people are concerned I should think that about two days is as much as they could stand" From him, as from another still more eminent authority, I heard the bitterest complaints concerning the ignorance and arrogance of the Colonial Secretary. "President Kruger at his worst," said one whose stake in the Rand is second to none —" President Kruger at his worst was an angel of light compared with Mr. Chamberlain. The man is as pig-headed as he is ignorant, and as unapproachable as the Mikado in old times. Does he think that we are Hottentots, that we can be governed in this fashion? We are not Hottentots, and that he will soon find out." Evidence multiplies on every hand to show that when the mines get to work again, the Outlanders will sigh for the fleshpots of Egypt and the old days of Paul Kruger. I have already referred to the native question as that in which the interests of the mine owner and the philanthropic interests of the British public are likely to come into sharp collision

There are many other questions. Take, for instance, the question of federation. It is always said that we are going to create a new federated Empire in South Africa "If you want federation," said one of the rich men of the Rand to me quite recently, "you had better federate before we get back. You certainly will never federate after we once have felt our strength. Why should we federate? What does federation mean to us. It means first and foremost that you intend to tie round our neck as a millstone the railway debt of Natal and Cape Colony It means that you are going to saddle us with a responsibility for paying interest on £45,000,000 invested in railways which would never earn more than 1 per cent if it were not for us. What have we to do with the Cape lines? Delagoa Bay is our port. Leave us to ourselves and we shall double the line to Delagoa Bay, and that will supply all that we want much more cheaply and rapidly than we could bring anything from Durban or the Cape."

If any one wants to understand exactly the relation that will exist between the returned Uitlanders when the railways get into operation again and the military authorities who must of necessity for a long time be charged with the control of the country, he can see it as in a magic mirror if he will take the trouble to recall the relations which existed between Col Kekewich and Mr Rhodes during the siege of Kimberley. The soldier despises the mineowner, and the latter repays his contempt with interest. On the other hand, the war has created a genuine feeling of respect between the fighting Colonist and the fighting Boer. Upon that basis of mutual respect mutual co-operation could very rapidly be arranged if once a question arose in which they had a common enemy. That common enemy will not be far to seek In any collision that may arise between Downing Street and Johannesburg, Downing Street will be helpless, because Johannesburg can always strike up a fighting alliance with the Dutch, whereas Downing Street can never rely upon Dutch support, at least during the lifetime of this generation. What seems probable, therefore, is that if the war should ever come to an end, and a cosmopolitan population of gold diggers should place 250,000 men on the Rand, the community will insist upon governing itself in its own way. They will form precisely that "American Republic," although probably not under the name of a republic, which Mr Rhodes saw afar off and endeavoured to avert. Any attempt on our part to compel them to pay taxes to which they have not consented would be followed by an African imitation of the Tea Party in Boston harbour. And any attempt to punish such defiance of our authority would immediately precipitate an alliance with the Afrikanders which would leave us powerless, no matter how strong our garrison, and so the British Empire would perish in South Africa, smitten down by the very Outlanders on whose behalf we are supposed to have waged this war

This speculation may seem to many farfetched, but the premisses upon which the calculations are based are indisputable. We are going to try the experiment of governing an adventurous community, accustomed to liberty, by what—however disguised—is in reality a military despotism. We intend to impose taxes upon this community without their consent, we are pledged to secure rights and privileges for the natives, any attempt to fulfil which would afford a common platform for Boer and Outlander These are the difficulties which Mr. Rhodes foresaw in 1895, but at that time England at the worst could always rely upon the support of the Dutch in South Africa in maintaining her authority There was no danger of a revolt on the Rand against the paramountcy of Britain when all the farmers in South Africa could be relied upon to support the Empire against the Rand But to-day we have destroyed the only force upon which we could rely in South Africa, and we shall be reduced to the humiliating alternative of allowing Johannesburg to govern South Africa according to its own sweet will and pleasure, or of precipitating a struggle which could only have the same result If at the end of it all we are permitted to retain Simon's Bay as a coaling-station for our Navy, we may consider ourselves lucky.

The Afrikander Commonwealth may split off from the British Empire It does not exactly follow that it will array itself under the Stars and Stripes. But, on the other hand, there are several influences which may tend in that direction

In the first place very many of the most energetic citizens in Johannesburg will be American citizens. In the second place they will, for some time at least, be in very strained relations with Great Britain What would be more natural than for them to seek support in the sister republic across the seas ?

Great Britain would not be the only Power against which the Afrikander Commonwealth might find that it needed the friendly protection of a first-class fleet German territory marches with that which is now British South Africa, both on the east and west, and German ambition has often marked Dutch South Africa as her natural inheritance Nor is fear the only motive which might drive the Afrikanders under the sheltering wing of the American Eagle. Delagoa Bay, from the point of view of international law, thanks to the unfortunate award of Marshal MacMahon, belongs by sovereign right to Portugal, but the ground around Delagoa Bay is held as real estate by the millionaires of the Rand. They will attempt in the first case to deal with Portugal, but if they fail, it is by no means improbable that if they were assured of the support of a strong navy, they would attempt to secure the right of ownership to what is, after all, the front door of their own house. Add to this the fact that the possibility of a native rising can never be absent from the minds of the white minority in South Africa. Australians may do as they please, their natives are too few and too weak to menace their peace. In Africa it is different. The menacing figure of the Kaffir is never absent from the South African landscape The Afrikanders would feel much more comfortable if they knew that, should the worst come to the worst, they could always count upon reinforcements from beyond the sea in case of a native rising, and where else could they hope to secure

that after the breach with England excepting from the United States ?

But it will be said that the sister republic will have nothing to do with them, and as proof of this we shall be referred to the cold-blooded fashion in which President McKinley left the South African Republics to their fate But many circumstances combined to render it difficult for President McKinley to take any other course. The United States had just emerged from a war in which they believed, rightly or wrongly, that they had been saved from a hostile European combination by the benevolent neutrality and veiled alliance of Great Britain They were also waging a war of their own in the Philippines which rendered it practically impossible for them to pose as the champions of a nation rightly struggling to be free And, in the third place, there is still be a very great difference between an English-speaking republic, largely officered by Americans, appealing to Washington against an attempt on the part of the British Empire to enforce the principle of taxation without representation, and a similar appeal which came to the same republic from Dutch-speaking States popularly believed to be little better than barbarians offering a vain resistance to the onward march of civilisation Fiscal considerations are also likely to pull in the same direction The United States has been diligently preparing to invade the South African market as soon as the war affords them an opportunity. Mr. Roosevelt, in carrying out the policy of President McKinley, and using the tariff as a means of securing reciprocal concessions in the shape of reductions of tariff on American goods, would be able to offer very tempting terms to the Afrikander Commonwealth

The Kimberley mines export every year nearly five million pounds worth of diamonds to all parts of the world Upon these diamonds the American customs duty varies from ten to twenty-five per cent Here is an opportunity of making a reduction in return for a *quid pro quo*. The United States in 1900 exported to South Africa goods valued at twenty million dollars, not including imports for military use or American goods shipped in England This showed an increase of three and a half million dollars over the preceding twelve months, notwithstanding the drop that was occasioned by the war, which practically extinguished the demand for agricultural machinery Supposing that Mr Roosevelt is able to do a deal with Mr Rhodes, cutting the duty on diamonds by fifty per cent in return for a similar cut on duties charged on American imports into the Cape, who could complain ?

Between July 1st, 1899, and January 31st,

D

1901, the Cape Government imported twenty American locomotives, and since then they have been buying extensively in the United States. From the account given by Mr C. Elliott, ex-General Manager of the Cape Railway Administration, the Americans not only supplied the engines on trust, but they returned £450 on six locomotives, stating that the cost of construction had not been so great as was anticipated. The Americans having got hold are not to be shaken off. Mr. Pingree's visit to the seat of war last year, in the joint interest of political curiosity and the promotion of the sale of American boots, was but one among many illustrations of the care and thoroughness with which the Americans are preparing to seize the South African market. They leave to us the cost, the risk, the sacrifices of the war. They reserve to themselves the profit to be made by exporting American goods to the customers who will be left alive at the close of the war.

Few things seem less improbable than that the Afrikander Commonwealth, under the leadership of Johannesburg, if constituted as an independent Republic, might very soon find itself in friendly treaty alliance with the United States.

The experiment, therefore, of attempting to enforce our dominion over unwilling subjects in South Africa is likely to terminate disastrously for the Empire. The fact that what would be a source of weakness to Great Britain would be a source of strength to the United States is due solely to the difference between willing and unwilling subjects.

CHAPTER V.—OF THE WEST INDIES AND
THEREABOUTS

WE now turn from what may be regarded as the diseased members of the British Empire, who being in unwilling and enforced subjection, can be counted upon to lose no opportunity of transferring their allegiance from the King to the President of the United States, to those parts of the British Empire which are most likely to succumb to the operation of the law of political gravitation. In the case of the United States the force of this is likely to be felt most strongly in the case of the West Indian islands.

The British flag at the present moment is flying over a series of archipelagoes of small islands lying in the Caribbean Sea immediately to the south of Florida and at the doorstep of the United States. Of these islands by far the most important is Jamaica, after which come Trinidad and Barbadoes. The others are islets rather than islands, but together they figure conspicuously in the list of British possessions in North America.

Distinct from the West Indian group, lying farther to the north-east are the Bahamas, and still farther away lies the island of Bermuda. The Bermudas are coming more and more to hold the relation to the United States which the Channel Islands hold to France. Although lying close at her doors, they are under a foreign flag, and they attract every year an increasing number of visitors from the mainland. The West India islands, these "summer isles of Eden set in azure seas," which excited the enthusiasm of Charles Kingsley, and many another traveller before and since, have long been the despair of our Colonial Office. Mr. Chamberlain has been engaged, ever since his accession to office, in a desperate endeavour to restore some semblance of prosperity to our unfortunate possessions which have been ruined by the sugar bounties. Jamaica possesses an exceptional interest, for it was the only colony founded by Oliver Cromwell. Like many another colony, it came into existence by accident rather than design. The great naval expedition which he launched to attack the power of Spain in San Domingo miscarried and picked up Jamaica as a kind of consolation prize. For nearly 200 years after its annexation Jamaica prospered. It survived the emancipation of the slaves. But it received a deadly wound when the imposition of the sugar bounties in the interests of beet sugar ruined the cane sugar plantations of the West Indies. Mr Brooks Adams, in a remarkable and very sombre paper on "England's Decadence in the West Indies," republished by Macmillan in "America's Economic Supremacy," attributes the destruction of the West Indies to the policy of Germany. He says 'Taken in all its ramifications this destruction of the sugar interest may probably be reckoned the heaviest financial blow that a competitor has ever dealt Great Britain." Towards 1880 the British West Indies made a profit calculated at about £6,500,000 per annum. Germany ruined the West Indies by adherence to Napoleon's policy of attack. For nearly three generations the chief Continental nations with hostile intent paid bounties on the export of sugar. In August, 1896, Germany and Austria doubled their bounties, and the following spring France advanced hers. The English got their sugar cheaper at the cost of the taxpayers of the Continent, but the cane sugar industry was practically destroyed; the islands of Dominica and Santa Lucia have become almost wildernesses, the whole archipelago has been blighted. Our consumption of sugar has enormously increased. In 1869 every Englishman consumed 42 lb. of sugar as against 35 lb in the United States   The other countries varied from the Italian minimum of 7 lb per head to a maximum of 28 lb in France   As the result of artificial cheapening of sugar by means of subsidies the English consumption per head rose in 1897 to 84 lb, that is to say, while the price of sugar was reduced by one-half the consumption of sugar doubled. Our sugar bill remained the same, but every man, woman, and child of us doubled his consumption.   Mr. Brooks Adams thinks that we acted unwisely in accepting the bribe offered us in the shape of cheap sugar   In his opinion we should have fought the bounties by countervailing duties, and so have warded off the blow that was levelled against the prosperity of our own colonies

Be that as it may, there is no doubt as to what is the opinion of the West Indian planters. They maintain that the bounty system was not fair competition, and that they have been sacrificed on the altar of a doctrinaire Free Trade   The subsequent efforts which have been made by Mr Chamberlain to restore the prosperity of these islands have not been remarkably successful.

For a long time past they have been sinking from bad to worse until in the last decade of the Nineteenth Century it became evident that something must be done, and done at once, if our West Indian Colonies were not to go bankrupt   Mr Chamberlain appointed a Commission, of which Sir Edward Grey was the most important member.   It issued a report, and Mr Chamberlain has ever since been more or less strenuously endeavouring to carry out its recommendations   So far the activity of the Colonial Secretary does not appear to have been fraught with much benefit to the Colony   The impoverished inhabitants are much more painfully conscious of the immediate increase in taxation which the changes have involved than the more or less remote and hypothetical advantages which they are promised in the future   A subsidy to a line of cargo steamers has not been sufficient to bring the up-country negro into immediate touch with Covent Garden market, and discontent seems to be rife in the island which in some districts resembles nothing so much as a huge pauper warren

There are some Jamaicans, indeed, who complain bitterly that Mr Chamberlain's method of promoting the prosperity of Jamaica bears too much resemblance to the time-honoured expedient of feeding a dog with a piece of his own tail.

It will be admitted even by the greatest optimist that the state of Jamaica and of the other West Indian Colonies still leaves much to be desired, and it is equally indisputable that West Indians themselves attribute their disasters to the fiscal policy of the Empire to which they belong. Not only so, but the fact that the inhabitants did not suffer even worse things they attribute to the enterprise of a Boston man who established a flourishing trade in bananas with the United States   A writer in the *Daily Telegraph* of Jamaica says " Poor impoverished Jamaica should never be ungrateful to America for making markets for our sugars and bananas during a period when in England the policy was, ' Oh, cut the painter, and let the colonies go ' '

It is not so long since the United States admitted West Indian sugar free of duty, and that fact is not forgotten in Jamaica   Mr Chamberlain has no doubt endeavoured to develop trade between Jamaica and the Mother Country, but so far with singularly little success Lord Pirbright, writing in the *National Review* for December, 1896, declared that Mr Chamberlain's policy was foredoomed to failure, and that the refusal to adopt a policy of retaliation for the purpose of fighting the sugar bounties would inevitably result in the loss of the sugar colonies   He wrote "We cannot strengthen the bonds of loyalty which hold the West Indies to the Mother Country by the promise of eleemosynary doles which are to compensate them for the loss of their flourishing industry, and keep them from bankruptcy. If they were to accept this grant in aid, which must become a permanent grant, they must inevitably degenerate.   The loss of independence would certainly beget a feeling of distrust in the Mother Country to whose inaction they would attribute their dependent position Geographically much nearer to America than to Great Britain, they might seek and would certainly receive from the United States not alone the commercial facilities which we deny them, but other inducements of far greater importance.   Trade would follow the flag That flag would no longer be ours, and we might have to deplore not only the ruin, but also the loss of our West Indian possessions '

When Mr Chamberlain was beginning his experiments in the act of resuscitating a perishing colony by the time-honoured method of increasing the import duties on British goods, the United States, abandoning the policy of abstention from all interference in the affairs of other nations, suddenly stepped forth armed from head to heel as the avenger of the wrongs of Cuba   Spain was driven from the Western Main, Cuba was freed, and Porto Rico was annexed by the conquering Power   The advent of the United States as a colonising power in the midst of the West Indian Archipelago could

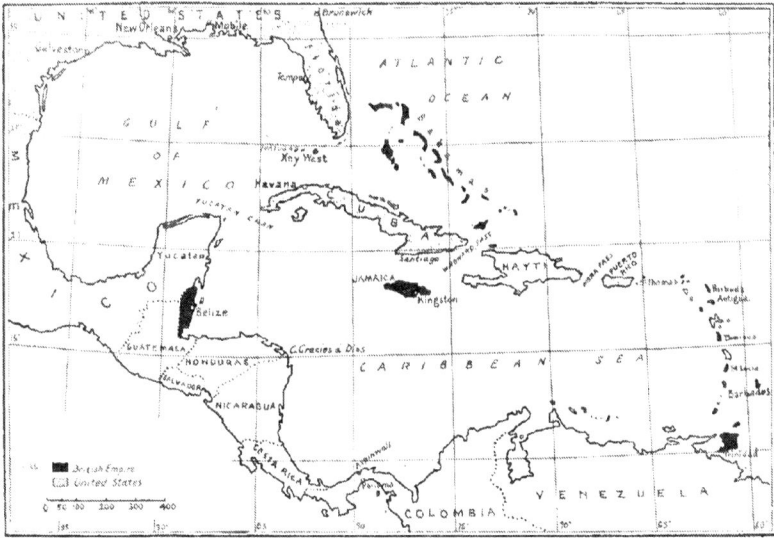

BRITAIN AND THE UNITED STATES IN THE WEST INDIES.

[*Journal.*] CUBAN ANNEXATION. [*Minneapolis.*

CUBA.—"It seems the only way over the Tariff Wall."

Journal.] [*Minneapolis.*

LIKELY TO CATCH THE WHOLE WEST INDIAN GROUP.

not but thrill with excitement even the lethargic imagination of the Lotos eaters of our Colonies For the United States is more than a political federation of forty-three Sovereign Republics It represents 76,000,000 human beings, each of whom has probably a more toothsome appetite for the delicate products of the West Indies than the men of any other race now living on the planet

The immediate result of the annexation of Porto Rico was to give an immense stimulus to the production of sugar When the island was wrenched from the nerveless hand of Spain, her annual export of sugar was only 40,000 tons Last year she exported 100,000 tons In 1901 it is expected that her export will reach 150,000 tons The production of coffee is also going up with leaps and bounds It is obvious that, if this is not a mere spurt, annexation by the United States is proved to be like the touch of an enchanter's wand causing a flood of wealth to spring up in these West Indian Islands, there is not a sugar island now under the Union Jack that will not be clamouring to be transferred to the United States. Whatever we may try to do the fact remains solid as granite, and unalterable by all that we can do, the United States, with its enormous masses of would-be purchasers of all manner of sweetstuffs and tropical fruit, is and always must be the best market for the West Indian producer After the decision of the Supreme Court on the 27th of May, 1901, when the legality of the Foraker Act imposing special duties on goods imported from Porto Rico was affirmed by five voices against four, there is nothing to hinder the United States taking over any number of West Indian Islands *

* As this case is of great historical and political importance, I quote here Mr. Wellman's lucid summary of its purport —

"1 The Constitution does not follow the flag *ex propria vigore*— of its own force

"2 The United States may enter upon a colonial policy—has already entered upon it—without violation of the Constitution

"3. This nation has all the powers that rightfully belong to a sovereign international state and may acquire territory without incorporating such territory as an integral part of itself

"4 The simple act of acquisition by treaty or otherwise does not automatically bring about such incorporation, and incorporation is effected only by the will of the States acting consciously through Congress

"5 Porto Rico is not a part of the United States, but 'a territory appurtenant and belonging to the United States' Tariffs established by Congress upon goods coming from or going to Porto Rico are valid and collectible The Foraker Act is constitutional

"6 Congress has full power over the territories, may regulate and dispose of them, may at its discretion extend the Constitution to them, may admit them as states, or may hold them indefinitely as territories, colonies, or dependencies

"7 Porto Rico is not a 'foreign country,' and the e-

It is as yet too soon to pronounce upon the net economic result of the annexation of Porto Rico But should the first promise be realised, the economic pull towards the United States will be irresistible

It would seem from the most recent statistics that Mr Chamberlain's policy has failed to check the progress of the movement which tends to place Jamaica more and more under the economic ascendency of the United States Geographical position counts for much. Jamaica is within a few hours' steam of Cuba, which is in turn only a few hours' steam from Florida, and "nearest neighbours best customers" seems to hold good in the West Indies as elsewhere In 1896 50 per cent. of Jamaican exports went to the United States, and only 27 per cent to Great Britain. After four years of Mr. Chamberlain's policy the share of the United States had risen to 63 per cent, and that of the United Kingdom had shrunk to 19 per cent The figures are not quite so bad as far as relates to the purchases made by Jamaica in American and British markets, but even here there has been no improvement In 1896 41 per cent of her imports came from the United States, and 48 per cent. from the United Kingdom. In 1900 the share of the United States had risen from 41 to 43 per cent, and that of the United Kingdom had fallen from 48 per cent to 47 per cent The attempt to foster a trade between Jamaica and Canada does not seem to have been very successful. Her exports to the Dominion stood at 1 6 per cent in 1896, and at the same figure exactly in 1900 Her imports from Canada, which were 7 5 per cent. in 1896, had dropped to 7·1 per cent. in 1900 The *Boston Journal*, commenting on the 6th of last September on the significance of these figures, remarks :—

"We take nearly nine-tenths of Jamaica's sugar, nearly all her fruit, much of her coffee and cocoa, a great share of her logwood, almost all her cocoanuts. The famous Jamaica rum is the only one of the island's products which is consumed chiefly by Great Britain

"Jamaica is so near the United States and stands so closely related to our continental system, that this steady drift of her trade away from Great Britain and toward us is not strange. It is wholly natural and intelligible. But it is obvious that it makes the British connection increasingly difficult and expensive

"With Porto Rico enjoying absolute free trade

fore the Dingley law, which levies duties upon goods imported 'from foreign countries,' does not apply to Porto Rico Nor yet is 'Porto Rico a part of the United States' It is a domestic territory, over which Congress has 'unrestricted control'" with the United States, and Cuba almost its equivalent under reciprocity, the British West India possessions in the Antilles will have either to be given up or maintained at a cost out of all proportion to their real value to the Imperial Government."

The question whether the movement towards annexation to the United States will acquire an impetus which will make it irresistible depends upon the results which will follow the American annexation of Porto Rico and the American protectorate established over Cuba. If the value of real estate in Porto Rico goes up by leaps and bounds, and if the Colony becomes as prosperous as Jamaica is the reverse, the sentiment of loyalty to the Union Jack will not long stand the dissolvent of such a contrast. Cuba is not annexed to the United States—at least, not yet—but the advantage of being within the Union and so avoiding the tariff wall which at present limits the access of the products of Cuba to the American market will be certain to operate with steady pressure in favour of annexation. The United States will not annex Cuba, but Cuba will annex itself to the United States. That is to say, she will do so if the Americans convince the Cubans that annexation will put more money into their pocket and will deprive them of no essential liberty. The force of gravitation is continuous, and the example of voluntary incorporation is apt to prove contagious. When General Gomez, the Cuban patriot, left the United States after a tour through the Union last summer, he expressed his conviction that, after a period of absolute independence, Cuba would do well to throw in her lot with the United States. It is usually the case that if once a country tastes the delights of absolute independence she will never seek to merge her destiny with any neighbour, no matter how great and powerful that neighbour may be. But the Americans may reverse this. The spectacle of a well-governed and prosperous Porto Rico may prove potent enough to overcome the desire of the Cubans to fly their own flag outside the Union. General Gomez declared that not only did he contemplate the merging of Cuba in the Republic, but that many other West Indians believed that San Domingo and Hayti would be glad to accept the protectorate of the Stars and Stripes.

In discussing the probable economic forces which tend to add these outlying English-speaking Colonies to the great American Republic, it should not be forgotten that the Americans would bring to such new possessions much more than mere prestige and capital. There is a certain lethargy in these lotus-eaters' Paradises which it would take all the Americans' energy to overcome. "If any influence and energy,"

said Dr Shaw, very truly, some years ago, "can ever be effectively applied to lift the West Indies out of the political, social, and industrial quagmire into which they have sunk, such rescue must come from the United States. It is difficult to see what answer there is to this. Sir Wemyss Reid has just told us that an American Cabinet Minister at Washington spoke to him as if the absorption of our West Indian Colonies by the United States was a forgone conclusion.

All the arguments which apply to the West Indian Islands apply *mutatis mutandis* to the only two tracts of territory which we possess in South and Central America. British Guiana, the delimitation of whose frontiers nearly involved us in trouble with the United States a few years ago, is forbidden to extend its frontiers by virtue of the Monroe Doctrine. The English-speaking men who live under the Union Jack in the British Colony of Guiana are rigorously confined within the existing frontiers of the province. If they were to transfer their allegiance to the United States that interdict would immediately be repealed. They could then extend the outposts of their territory as far inland as they pleased. At present they are handicapped by the Union Jack. They are as much Americans as any of the citizens of the United States. But because they are in organic relation with the Mother Country they are denied all rights of interior expansion. They have no hinterland, and they are made to feel at every turn that, so far as the development of their Colony is concerned, it would be better to be an independent republic than to belong to the vast system of the British Empire.

However much we may regret the loss of our West Indian Colonies, our regret will be tempered by satisfaction at the thought that we have had ample opportunity to see what the monarchical section of the English-speaking race can do in making these communities happy, prosperous, and contented. If we fail so completely that they are anxious to try whether better results would not follow if they are placed under the control of the republican half of the race we have no reason to complain. Nay, if the squalid poverty of many of our fellow-subjects could be permanently relieved by allowing these islands to become the colonies and dependencies of the United States, it would be our duty, not to retard, but to expedite the transfer. If Britain wishes for no unwilling subjects, neither does she wish to have any citizens in the Empire who are reminded at every turn that they are suffering in body or in estate from their connection with the Mother Country.

CHAPTER VI.—OF NEWFOUNDLAND AND CANADA

IT is always hazardous to prophesy, but it would not be surprising if England's oldest Colony were to be the first to desert the Empire in order to throw in her lot with the Republic

The justification for this somewhat audacious forecast is the fact that Newfoundland alone, of all our Colonies, finds its vital interests sacrificed to the interests of the Empire. None of our other Colonies have such a grievance as that which troubles the Newfoundlanders None of our other Colonies are subjected to the daily temptation which confronts them in the shape of the self-evident proposition that their material interests would be benefited by a transfer of their allegiance from the Union Jack to the Stars and Stripes.

The facts of the case lie in a nutshell. When Newfoundland was first settled, it was not regarded as a Colony in the proper sense of the term It was only looked upon as a kind of pier or landing-stage on which the hardy fishers sent out from Bristol could land and dry their nets Newfoundland, in other words, was not regarded as having any existence other than that of a mere appendage to the cod fishery For the first two centuries after its discovery no one at home seems to have dreamed of the possibility of making it the seat of a British Colony. Colonisation, indeed, was, if not actually forbidden, at least discountenanced rather than encouraged, and even so late as the beginning of the eighteenth century, the original idea that Newfoundland was little more than a coast-line which was convenient for the watering and refitting of the fishing fleet continued to dominate the minds of our statesmen. But for this, it is impossible to believe that the men who negotiated the Treaty of Ryswick would ever have made over to the French Government the exclusive use of the French shore This arrangement, which was subsequently confirmed at the Treaty of Utrecht half a century later, was based upon the supposition that the only thing worth considering in Newfoundland was the use of its shores as convenient and indispensable appurtenances of the fishing banks.

Whatever may have been the explanation of this surrender to the French of a region stretching about three hundred miles from north to south on the west coast, the arrangement was solemnly ratified by a treaty which still remains in force Hence the cause of most of the evils which afflict Newfoundland For nearly a hundred years after the signature of the Treaty of Utrecht the arrangement which gave the west shore to the French worked fairly well, but in the last fifty years Newfoundland, from being a mere fishing station, became a thriving Colony. It attracted emigrants from the other side of the Atlantic, notably from Ireland; they increased and multiplied, and at last succeeded in gaining recognition as one of the hardiest and most industrious of all the Colonies under the Crown.

But no sooner was the colonisation of Newfoundland begun than the colonists fell foul of the French shore The more they increased and multiplied, the more intolerable did it seem to them that they should be deprived of the right to use three hundred miles of their own coast

In virtue of a treaty the original terms of which had been strained to such an extent as to convert the right conceded to the French to land and dry their nets into a right of veto by them upon the erection of any factories or similar buildings along the whole length of the coast, there sprang up the agitation against the French shore—an agitation which has increased in vehemence with years, and although it may be for the moment lulled, it may at any time revive and rage with all the more fury because it has been quieted for a time

Some years ago I had an opportunity of discussing the whole matter at length with the representatives sent over by the Newfoundland Government in order to impress upon Downing Street the urgent importance of extinguishing the French rights on the west coast They made no hesitation in declaring that, if the British Government finally refused to clear out the French, they would be compelled as a mere matter of self-preservation to look to the only other Government from whom they could obtain relief For some years the question whether Newfoundland had not better secede from the Empire and appeal for the protection of the United States had been in the air, although it did not figure much in public debate either on platform or in the press.

It is very easy to understand how it was that the Newfoundlanders should turn a wistful and longing gaze towards Washington A combination of economic and political motives may strain severely the allegiance of Newfoundland to the mother country At present the American market is practically closed to the product of the Newfoundland fishery Of the million pounds worth of cod caught off these banks half goes to British ports and the other half to Portugal and Brazil But Newfoundland imports goods from the United States of the annual value of £300,000 It is, however, less for the sake of opening the American market than for

Mr. GOLDWIN SMITH.
(Photograph by Elliott & Fry.)

RT. HON. SIR WILFRID LAURIER.
THE CANADIAN PREMIER.

Photograph by Jarvis, Ottawa.]   THE PARLIAMENT BUILDINGS AT OTTAWA.

the gain of getting rid of the French shore difficulty that annexation might come to be desired by our Colonists

The question of the French shore is very simple France has certain undeniable rights dating from the eighteenth century, secured by a formal treaty to which England was a party. Circumstances have changed since that treaty was negotiated A state of things has sprung up which renders the provisions of that treaty intolerably irksome to a third party which was practically not in existence when the treaty was signed, namely, the self-governing Colony of Newfoundland. The maintenance of the provisions of the Treaty of Utrecht entails hardship upon the Newfoundlanders, from which they ask our Government to relieve them France is by no means irreconcilable upon this question She recognises the difficulty of our position and says, in effect, that she is quite willing to surrender her rights under the Treaty of Utrecht—for a consideration. The question is what that consideration shall be. For the last twenty years the matter has been discussed between London and Paris without any conclusion being arrived at. Our offers have never been regarded as satisfactory by the French, and we have hitherto been unable to offer what the French would accept as an adequate equivalent for the abandonment of their rights under the treaty The British Government has given too many hostages to fortune in all parts of the world to dare press too urgently for a settlement of the question The Newfoundlanders understand perfectly well that we cannot squeeze France in Newfoundland without exposing ourselves to a retaliatory squeeze in Egypt. Hence they say that the local interests of Newfoundland have been and are at this moment being sacrificed to the general interests of the British Empire That is the truth, and there is no gainsaying it

Suppose one fine day that the Union Jack was hauled down, and that the United States was suddenly invested with the complete sovereignty over Newfoundland, what would happen? There would probably be a Commission appointed to take evidence about the French shore question That evidence would be presented to both Houses of Congress, when it would appear that the growth of the Colony was hampered and its permanent interests injuriously affected by the maintenance of the provisions of the Treaty of Utrecht. It would further be reported that, in order to give the Colony a fair chance and to relieve the United States of a constant source of irritation threatening the general peace, the rights of France must be terminated. After that report had been received and taken into consideration, the

American Secretary of State would be instructed to write to the French Government to the effect that the provisions of the Treaty of Utrecht relating to the west coast of the recently-acquired United States territory of Newfoundland were inflicting an intolerable grievance upon the inhabitants of Newfoundland; therefore the United States Government must formally give notice of their decision to terminate the treaty, but would be very glad to enter into negotiations with France as to the compensation which France might claim for the loss of her rights If the two Governments were unable to arrive at an amicable understanding as to what compensation was adequate, the United States would be willing to refer the question for adjudication to a court of arbitration constituted under the rules of the Hague Conference.

France might sulk, and a good many angry articles might be written in the French papers, but the position of the United States would be unassailable. The Americans have given no hostages to fortune which would compel them to think twice and even thrice before incurring French resentment Their demand for the removal of the restrictions which were throttling the development of an American territory would be morally sound, and their willingness to refer the question of compensation to arbitration would place their action upon an incontestably legal footing The United States, in short, could in one day liberate the Newfoundlanders from the presence of the French on their shores without danger of war and without sacrificing American interests in any quarter of the world The Newfoundlanders have for some time past been slowly and reluctantly arriving at the conclusion that this is what England cannot do On the day when they arrive at the final decision that it is no use looking any longer to Downing Street for help, the movement in favour of American annexation may sweep all before it

There are two other considerations which should not be forgotten. One is that a large proportion of the colonists are either of Irish birth or Irish extraction There are no more enthusiastic supporters of the Irish National cause than many of the leading Irish citizens of St John s Nothing would give them greater joy than in this way to avenge the wrongs of Ireland upon a Unionist Government

That, it may be said, is but a sentimental consideration. It is likely to be strongly reinforced by the very material argument of an appeal to the breeches pocket It is not so many years ago since the Newfoundland local legislature negotiated a reciprocity treaty with the Government of Washington for the purpose of securing for their fish access to the American market Rightly or wrongly, the British Government refused to ratify that treaty, and it fell through If the British connection means not only the maintenance indefinitely of the French on the west coast, but also of a barrier between the Newfoundland Fisheries and the immense market of the United States, is it unreasonable to think that the drift towards the centre of gravity may become irresistible ?

Such a secession would be serious indeed. Newfoundland has hitherto refused to cast in its lot with the Dominion of Canada. It has jealously preserved its own independence Like a great advanced bastion of the American Continent, it lies right across the great ocean roadway which leads from Liverpool to the St. Lawrence In the hands of a hostile power the harbour of St. John's would be a deadly menace to the whole of our Canadian trade. Both from a naval and commercial point the loss of Newfoundland would be so serious a blow to the Empire that it is probable an attempt would be made to prevent it by force of arms The right of secession which Mr Chamberlain has publicly acknowledged is enjoyed by the "independent sister nations" of Canada and Australia, would probably be denied to the smaller Colony of Newfoundland , but, if so, it would only mean annexation at two removes, because the wit of man is unable to devise or the resources of the British Empire are inadequate to provide means whereby we could hold down unwilling subjects in all parts of the world

When Englishmen discuss the possible pull of the gravitation of the United States upon their Empire, they usually confine their remarks to Canada. They do not realise that Canada, being by far the largest and most important of the British American possessions, would probably be the last to succumb to the continually increasing force of gravitation exercised by its southern neighbour. Canada alone of all the British Colonies in the Western Hemisphere is large enough and strong enough to render its independent existence even thinkable if the protecting ægis of Great Britain were withdrawn All the other Colonies would probably drop like ripe plums into Uncle Sam's hat but for their connection with Great Britain The Dominion of Canada, however, has ambitions of its own, and is rather inclined to believe that, if annexation is to take place, it would be better for the world if the United States were annexed by Canada rather than Canada by the United States Mr Evans, Secretary of the Hamilton Canadian Club, maintained that the future belonged to Canada, and he quoted words said to have been uttered by the late Secretary Seward to the following effect :—

" Having its Atlantic seaport at Halifax, and its Pacific depot near Vancouver Island, British America would inevitably draw to it the commerce of Europe, Asia, and the United States Thus from a mere colonial dependency it would assume a controlling rank in the world. To her other nations would be tributary , and in vain would the United States attempt to -be her rival." *

Mr. Evans does not think the fulfilment of this prophecy at all improbable. He maintains that whereas since 1760 the population of Canada has increased eighty-fold, for then it was only 60,000, the population of the United States, which was then 3,000,000, has only increased twenty-five-fold. In his opinion the United States would have more need of Canada than Canada of the United States, for, as their territories are being filled up, and their forests destroyed, in the not far future they would be largely dependent upon other countries for their raw material, while Canada has more undeveloped wealth than any other country in the world.

The Canadians are the Scotch of the Western Hemisphere, and have just as good an opinion of themselves as our neighbours in North Britain, who to this day resent bitterly any suggestion that the union which merged -Scotland and England in Great Britain was the annexation of the smaller country by the larger Scotland and England were united first by the golden circlet of the Crown when James I. and VI. crossed the Tweed, and founded an ill-fated dynasty in Great Britain Such monarchical contrivances are not available in the New World. It is probable that the Union, if it is to be effected, will be due, not to any golden circlets of the Crown, but to the much more prosaic but not less potent agency of the almighty dollar If the Canadians decide to throw in their lot with the United States, John Bull

---

* It is somewhat difficult to believe that Mr Seward actually said this, for he appears to have made a remark in a very different sense in the year 1860 He said " Standing here and looking far off into the North-West, I see the Russian as he busily occupies himself in establishing seaports and towns and fortifications on the verge of this continent as the outposts of St Petersburg, and I say, ' Go on, and build up your outposts all along the coast, even to the Arctic Ocean they will yet become the outposts of my own country—monuments of the civilisation of the United States in the North-West ' So I look off on Prince Rupert's Land and Canada and see there an ingenious, enterprising, and ambitious people occupied with bridging rivers and constructing canals, railroads, and telegraphs, to organise and preserve great British provinces north of the Great Lakes, the St Lawrence, and around the shores of Hudson's Bay, and I am able to say, ' It is very well , you are building excellent States to be hereafter admitted into the American Union ' '

will not spend one red cent in thwarting their wishes As an "independent sister nation," Mr Chamberlain has publicly declared they have unrestricted liberty of secession from the Empire, for the British Empire is much more loosely compacted together than the American Republic, which welded its States into one organic whole by the great Civil War But it is also true that, though no one in the United Kingdom would raise a finger to prevent Canada acting as she thought best for her own interests, any attempt on the part of the United States to annex the Canadians against their will would be resisted by the whole force of the British Empire This is so clearly understood on both sides that no one on the American Continent dreams of taking by force that which could only be valuable if it was tendered by consent Hence, in discussing the future of Canada, we may dismiss altogether from our minds all question of a solution by armed force

The frontier which divides the Dominion from the Republic is unfortified on either side, but exists by consent of both Nevertheless, although it is not guarded by soldiers or protected by cannon, it is infested with custom-houses, the disappearance of which would be so great and so palpable a gain that the desire to get rid of them may be regarded as one of the influences which tend in favour of annexation I remember the late Mr Bayard, just as he was leaving the American Embassy in London, describing to me what he regarded as the unpardonable mistake which was made by the Protectionists of the United States at the close of the Civil War " No one," he said, " has ever rendered adequate justice to the service which the Union received from the Canadians during the whole of that tremendous struggle. With the exception of one or two ridiculous raids by Confederate sympathisers, we were able to leave the whole of our northern frontier without a garrison Not only so, but we used Canada as an inexhaustible source of supplies throughout the whole war. Yet when at the close of the war a deputation from the Canadians went to Washington to plead for free access to American markets, they were told not to expect to have the privileges of American citizens unless they came under the American flag. Now the Canadian can be led, but he cannot be bullied The deputation, instead of applying for the privileges of American citizenship, went home, federated the Dominion, constructed the Canadian Pacific, and postponed for many years the inevitable union of North America under one flag. A little less selfishness and a little more statesmanship would have brought them all in long ago "

Whether Mr Bayard was right or wrong in his account of the genesis of what may be called Canadian Nationalism, there can be no doubt that since that date the Canadians have resolutely turned their gaze from Washington to Westminster. There is something almost pathetic in the anxiety of our Canadian fellow subjects to emphasize their loyalty to the Empire. No one does them the injustice to believe that they really were swept off their feet by any passionate feeling against the Boers when they sent their contingents to assist the mother country in South Africa They had been waiting for their chance to demonstrate their affection, and they seized it not caring very much about the merits of the quarrel in which they shed their blood Sir Wilfrid Laurier, it is true, made eloquent speeches, putting the best face upon the cause in which Canadian blood had been shed, but in order to do so he found it necessary to make protestations as to the liberties and privileges to be extended to the Boers, the realisation of which has been postponed to the Greek Kalends All that they knew, or cared to know, was that England, Mother England, was calling for their help So for England, Mother England, they poured in thousands to South Africa, where they shed their blood without stint in defence of the flag. Last autumn they gave the Heir to the Throne and his wife a welcome as enthusiastic as that which they received in Australia. More than that it would be impossible to say Surely then Canada is in no danger of succumbing to the Americanisation which is sweeping everything into the arms of the United States?

The same spirit of loyalty led the Canadian Parliament to take the initiative in establishing the principle of preferential terms for British goods They could only do this by a sidewind, as it were, offering a reduction of from 25 to 30 per cent upon imports from countries which did not tax Canadian goods —a provision which had the practical result of reducing the import duty on British goods from 25 to 30 per cent below that levied upon goods imported from the United States At the same time, the majority of American imports come in free, so that if an average is taken on all the goods imported from the United States and on those imported from the United Kingdom the average tax is still somewhat higher on British goods than on American The Canadians, however, did their best, and have borne submissively their exclusion by Germany from the most favoured nation treatment as the penalty of their attempt to draw closer the ties which link them to Great Britain

Down to the year 1887 there was a Secession Party in Nova Scotia, but since then there has been no party in any province of the Dominion that has advocated annexation to the United States Here and there there are annexationists, and those who are in favour of Canadian independence are even more numerous But, taking it as a whole, Canadians are passionately loyal to the old flag, and I think it is extremely probable that there is no part of the King's dominions in which this Annual will be read with more profound disapproval—I might even say indignation—than in the Dominion of Canada. Nevertheless this loyalty, although very vehement and very sincere, can hardly be regarded as a sufficient barrier against the all-pervading Americanism, which will inevitably bring the Dominion and the Republic into a much closer union than that which at present exists

The first great force which operates increasingly with potent force is economic Despite all the efforts of the Laurier Cabinet to encourage British trade at the expense of America, Canada remains the best market of the United States. Every Canadian, man, woman, or child, spends on an average £5 a year in the purchase of American goods The German average is about a guinea a head, while the average sale of American goods in Great Britain is below 7s. a head. Two-thirds of the American goods purchased by Canadians consist of American manufactures The total value of American imports into Canada amounted to £22,000,000 sterling Not only is it large in itself, but it is increasing. In 1875, of all Canada's purchases abroad, 50 per cent. came from Great Britain As this percentage began to drop, the experiment of the preferential duty was tried, but failed to arrest the decrease. In 1897 the proportion of British imports had dropped to 26 per cent, and in 1900 to 25 per cent. In 1875 the United States sold to Canada 42 per cent. of her total imports; in 1897 this had risen to 55 per cent., and in 1900 to over 60 per cent. The United States, therefore, notwithstanding the preferential duty, has more than taken the position which we occupied with the Canadian purchaser in 1875. It was inevitable that this should be so The United States is close at hand; the Canadians are American in their tastes, and goods prepared for the American market find a ready sale across the frontier. It is a remarkable fact, in view of all that is being talked to-day about the value of the Central and South American markets, that the Canadians, who are only 5,500,000 in number, buy more goods from the United States than are purchased by all the inhabitants of all the Central and South American Republics that are to be found between the Rio Grande and Cape Horn. The bulk of the Canadian exports to the United States consists of raw materials, lumber, and the

like, in return for which she takes the goods manufactured in American mills and factories

The Americans are keenly alive to the importance of developing this trade, and one of the first deputations which President Roosevelt had to receive was that organised by the Boston Chamber of Commerce in favour of reciprocity with Canada What the Boston business men fear is that unless something is done in the way of reducing American taxes on Canadian imports the Canadians will either increase the duties upon American goods, or redouble their efforts to induce Great Britain to adopt the principle of a preferential tariff in favour of Colonial and against foreign and American goods The only three interests in the United States that appear to be offering any serious opposition are the lumber interests of the North-West, the bituminous coal miners of Maryland and West Virginia, and the fishermen of Gloucester

President Roosevelt returned a sympathetic but non-committal answer to the deputation

The Canadians, apparently, have grown tired of expecting any concessions from the United States Sir Wilfrid Laurier this autumn made a definite declaration that the Canadian tariff was to remain as it was, and that any overtures on the subject of reciprocity would have to be made from Washington to Ottawa, and not from Ottawa to Washington The slump in Protection, so long foreseen, is no doubt on its way, but for the moment it tarries.

It should never be forgotten that the Irish element in Canada is very strong, how strong may be inferred from two facts In 1887, when Mr Balfour introduced his Coercion Bill for Ireland, the Canadian Parliament, despite the strongest opposition from the Canadian Conservative Ministry then in power, passed a resolution by a majority of nearly four to one strongly condemning the Irish policy of Mr. Balfour, and affirming their devotion to Home Rule. That the Canadians have not changed in their sentiment may be inferred from the second fact that when Mr John Redmond visited Canada in 1901, Sir Wilfrid Laurier and other Ministers were present at a banquet, by which the Irish Nationalist leader was welcomed into the Dominion Sir Wilfrid's presence gave great scandal to our Unionists at home, who profess to be utterly unable to reconcile his support of Mr Redmond and of Home Rule with his devotion to the Empire In reality if they but opened their eyes, they would see that the two things are inseparably connected.

The interchange of commodities between two communities speaking the same language, and living on either side of an imaginary line, is only one of the economic forces that would make for Union. For many years past there has been a steady stream of immigration from Canada to the United States There are very few Canadian families who have not one or more relatives who have gone to seek their fortunes in the great American cities, or on the fertile prairies of the United States There are more emigrants from Canada in the United States in proportion to their population than from any other country The richer and more developed lands to the south have an irresistible attraction for the more enterprising and ambitious Canadians When Mr Dryden, the Minister for Agriculture in Ontario, invested his money in farming he put it into a ranch in Dakota Of late years a growing tendency has been observable for the tide of immigration to flow the other way. In the North-West there are still vast areas of good land to be had for next to nothing Naturally as the land to the south fills up settlers will cross the frontier, and the process of colonisation from the States will steadily Americanise the North-West.

There is little or no difference in the social and political conditions of the settlers, so it is as natural for them to cross and recross the frontier as it is for people in Sussex to cross into Hampshire, or *vice-versa*. Thus there are being woven across and across, from side to side of the invisible frontier line, ties which tend to weave the two communities into one

In addition to the influence of commerce and of emigration there is another force which may be still more potent. I refer to the fact that the great American capitalists, ever on the look-out for fresh fields in which to invest their millions, have begun to develop on a great scale the immense mineral resources which are as yet practically untapped in the Canadian Dominion American capital is pouring into the country. Few things have attracted more attention in recent industrial development than the extent to which American capitalists are investing their money in the exploitation of the immense and almost virgin resources of Canada The industrial annexation of the Dominion is in full swing The Vanderbilt railway combination has taken in hand the development of the enormous coal and iron district of Nova Scotia, proceeding in the campaign with that combination of restless energy and methodical preparation that characterises the great American Trusts Further west, the Dominion Iron and Steel Company, under an American President, with a capital of over twenty million dollars, has established one of the most gigantic steel works in the world at Sault St. Marie on Lake Superior In this exploitation of Canadian resources by American capital, the Parliament of the Dominion has interested itself actively. A land grant of over five million acres, a subsidy of £200,000 for real construction, and contracts for a million pounds worth of rails to be delivered in the next five years, have given the Company confidence. It is going ahead Americans are setting the pace in the Dominion.

Rumours from time to time appear in the newspapers that this or the other combination of American millionaires have decided to acquire a controlling interest in Canada's one great railway, the Canadian Pacific, but although these remain rumours there is every reason to expect that the men who have engineered the great combinations which exist in order to bar out competition, will not long abstain from an attempt to control the great interoceanic railway by which the Canadians have linked together the Atlantic and the Pacific.

But dismissing this as a mere possibility of the future, we have sufficient evidence to prove that American capital is ever tending to acquire more and more interest in the development of Canadian resources. Commerce, emigration, and investments all tell in the same direction with an automatic and persistent force which is not materially affected by political agitation. Sir Hiram Maxim told me the other day that, when he was last in Canada, he had been approached by some owners of valuable deposits and water privileges to assist them in placing their property upon the British market. They expatiated upon the intrinsic value of the property which they had to dispose of, and, finally, by way of a crowning inducement, they said to him, "This property is worth two hundred million dollars, but when annexation comes it will be worth two hundred million pounds sterling" "What," said Sir Hiram, "I thought you were all enthusiastic loyalists" "We are loyal to the Empire, but we," was the reply, "all know that annexation will come some day, and, when it comes, it will much more than double the value of our property."

We now pass to consider the influences, which are partly economic and partly political, which point in the same direction There are at least two—one at each extremity of the Dominion The first is the long-standing and almost insoluble dispute about the fisheries on the Atlantic seaboard The quarrels between the fishermen of Nova Scotia and the fishermen of Massachusetts have been for many years a fertile source of friction The Canadians bitterly resent any poaching by American fishermen in Canadian waters Collisions between the Canadian and New England fishermen have created so much ill-feeling in the past that the fishery dispute has been one of the standing dishes at every Anglo-American repast For some years now a *modus vivendi* has been in existence, which avoids any of the old irritating incidents of the capture and confiscation of American ships within the three-mile limit, but the difficulty is not settled It has only been postponed So acute was the trouble at one time that Mr Edward Atkinson, in 1887, brought before the New York Chamber of Commerce a proposal that the United States should purchase from the Dominion of Canada New Brunswick, Nova Scotia, and Prince Edward Island, for the sum of £10,000,000 which he estimated was about the share in the Canadian debt for which these provinces were responsible. The suggestion came to nothing, but that it was made is significant. It shows that the Americans who bought Alaska from Russia are quite capable of attempting to settle other territorial difficulties in the same commercial fashion.

The other difficulty resulted from the discovery of gold on the Klondyke. The Canadians naturally wished to have access to their goldfields without passing through an American Custom House. The Americans, on the other hand, maintained that until gold was discovered the Canadians themselves recognised that Skagway, which may be regarded as the ocean gate of Klondyke, was part and parcel of the United States, and they resent the attempt of Canada to possess herself of an open door to the sea as an infraction of the Monroe doctrine, and an attempt to aggrandise the British Empire at the cost of the American Republic The proposal to settle this dispute by arbitration miscarried, owing to the short-sighted objection taken by our Foreign Office to the American proposition that in such arbitration the umpire should be chosen from the New World, which means that he should be either a Central American or a South American The proposal was one which told altogether against the United States, for the natural bias of the Spanish Americans is by no means in favour of the United States The proposal, however, dropped through, and the Skagway question remains among those unsettled questions which have small regard for the peace of nations.

In considering the probable future of Canada one salient fact can never be overlooked. Canada is not a homogeneous English-speaking community. The province of Quebec is essentially French in speech, Catholic in religion, and although loyal to the Empire this loyalty is the result of the Liberal policy adopted as the result of Lord Durham's mission, yet it jealously preserves its essential French nationality. It is indeed a foreign nation within a British Dominion, and its existence materially complicates the question under consideration. As Mr. Goldwin Smith said, "When there is a solid mass of people of one race inhabiting a compact territory, with a language, religion, character, laws, tendencies, aspirations and sentiments of its own, there is *de facto* a nation " But the curious thing is that authorities, both Canadian and American, differ entirely as to whether the existence of this French nation will tend to accelerate or retard the union of Canada and the United States. When the Duke of Argyll returned from Canada after serving his term as Governor-General, he told me that he regarded the French Canadians as one of the great obstacles in the way of annexation The French priests had got everything the way they wanted it in Quebec, they could not possibly improve their position, and might easily mar it if they exchanged the Union Jack for the Stars and Stripes. Further, they could not hinder a great and continuous emigration of their young people to the mills of New England, though they regarded such an exodus with profound uneasiness. The French habitant once settled in New England was exposed to the taint of heresy. Even if he preserved the faith he became lax and was no longer as strict in the observance of his religious duties as he was in the old home of his childhood. They did not become Protestant so much as indifferent or freethinkers Thus, in the opinion of this excellent authority, the ultramontane ascendency which prevailed in Quebec indirectly operated as a powerful bulwark of British Dominion

On the other hand, this very element appears to some stout Imperialists as one of the greatest dangers confronting us in the future. Mr. T. W Russell some eight or nine years ago visited Canada, and came back filled with horror at the state of things in Quebec. Mr Russell is an Ulster Protestant, and it is evident from his report that he regarded the state of things which prevailed in Quebec as a disgrace to the Dominion. "Quebec," he said, "was controlled by a rich, arrogant and powerful church. Cardinal Taschereau was infinitely more powerful than the Prime Minister and his Cabinet, and the British element was being squeezed out although the Englishry paid five-sixths of the taxation " Mr Russell did not on that account propose to expel French Canada from the Dominion, but the sentiments which he expressed represent probably with only too much fidelity the conviction of the majority of fervent Protestants in Ontario, and reveal a snag upon which the Dominion might be wrecked. There is no doubt that the dominant idea of Lord Durham in proposing his scheme of settlement was that it would be possible gradually but steadily to convert French Canada to the universal use of the English language. His scheme produced political contentment largely because it failed utterly to realise his hope about the language. Any attempt to interfere with the French language or impose secular education upon the French Catholics would produce an agitation which in the opinion of many competent judges would have as its effect the annexation of French Canada to the United States.

There are some who advocate annexation on the ground that the French are too large and too compact a mass of non-English-speaking men to be assimilated or absorbed by so small a community as that which inhabits the Canadian Dominion. If they were cast into the Continental crucible of the United States instead of being a separate nationality their cultivation of French would be a mere local peculiarity of no more importance than the obstinacy with which some German and Norwegian Colonists in Minnesota persist in refusing to use the English tongue. On the other hand, there are those who argue from a precisely opposite point of view and maintain that the United States carries already as many foreign elements as are compatible with the maintenance of its English-speaking character of its people, and they object strongly to add a clotted mass of a couple of millions of French habitants to the other indigestible lumps with which the digestion of Uncle Sam has to grapple. In the midst of all this conflict and confusion of even expert opinion it seems to be tolerably clear that whether the priests like it or not the industrial districts of New England continue to draw the more adventurous and enterprising youth of French Canada across the frontier. Recognising this as inevitable, the hierarchy have made more than adequate arrangements for the spiritual supervision of their migrating flock. The net result is that French Canada is no longer confined to the districts north of the St Lawrence. If an ethnographical map of the North Eastern States were to be published it would appear that Boston has almost as much claim to be considered a French city as Quebec and Montreal.

The question as to the effect which the participation of Canada in the South African War is likely to have upon the loyalty of the French Canadians is a matter that has been a good deal discussed. It is a curious fact that the first time Canada sent her sons to fight in an Imperial quarrel it was the Protestants who were enthusiastic, while the Catholics hung back, although the war was one not with a Catholic but with a Protestant people. Sir J. G. Bourinot strongly opposed the war, but found himself in a small minority, owing to the ascendency of Sir Wilfrid Laurier. He expressed a very strong conviction as to the grave peril to the Empire which was created by putting this new strain upon the loyalty of the French Canadians. The Boer War did not interest them on either side, but they dreaded the precedent. If Canada could be dragged into an English war with the Boers, how could they hope to escape the still more urgent appeal which would reach them if Great Britain were to be involved in a war with France? In such a case the French Canadian would find himself in exactly the same position as the Cape Dutch find themselves to-day, and it is not surprising that they shrank from being committed to any close co-operation with the Imperial arms.

Even before the Boer War arose to alarm French Canadian susceptibilities, one well-known French Canadian, M. Louis Frechette, at one time a member of the Dominion Parliament and a well-known Canadian poet, published an article which was almost a manifesto, under the title of "The United States for French Canadians." According to M. Frechette, French Canadians regarded Imperial Federation with unfeigned alarm. In an Imperial Parliament they would find themselves in a hopeless minority, in face of a majority inevitably hostile. He continued :—"The idea of Annexation has during the last few years made rapid progress with Canadians of French origin; the fact is that even to-day, were they consulted on the question under conditions of absolute freedom, without any moral pressure from either side, I am certain that a considerable majority of Annexationists would result from the ballot And this majority cannot but increase . Alliance with the States of the Union would with one sweep of the pen settle all those thorny questions which now embarrass us At one stroke . we should have no more hatred or rivalry of faith or race ; no longer conquerors ever looking upon us as the conquered , no longer any joint responsibility with any European nation . no longer any frontiers . no longer any possible wars , a single flag over the whole of North America, which then would be, not the holding of any particular nation, but the home of Humanity itself, the Empire of Peace, the richest and most powerful dominion of the earth, under a democratic government."

That the Canadians, French and English alike, are loyal is the fortunate result of the commonsense and resolution of our Whig statesmen who, by the display of those qualities of statesmanship which have been so conspicuously lacking in South Africa, converted a French-speaking Roman Catholic province, steeped in sedition and seething with rebellious discontent, into one of the most devoted Colonies of the

Empire The secret is simple We left them
alone allowing them to do for themselves as
they thought best. But even now the appointment of such a Governor-General as Lord
Milner would drive the whole of Quebec wild
with alarm and suspicion Sir Wilfrid Laurier,
the Liberal Prime Minister of the Dominion, has
never lost a chance of emphasising the fact that
Canada is not only a Colony and a Dominion,
Canada, he says, is a nation, and, as such, claims
the rights of nationhood.

How sensitive and easily jarred are the nerves
of our Canadian fellow-subjects may be seen
from the storm of dissatisfaction which has been
occasioned by the disrespect showed to the
French language by the Duke of Cornwall, who
of course acted on the advice of Lord Minto.
Why the genius of discord should have been
allowed to mar the loyal festivals that attended
the Royal tour no one but the Governor-General
can tell. But the refusal to allow the Heir to
the Crown to reply in French to loyal French
addresses seems to savour of the arrogant and
intolerant spirit which has of late poisoned the
atmosphere of the Colonial Office. Taken together with other incidents, some of which were,
perhaps unavoidable, this slight to their language
has led to protests which somewhat beclouded
the closing scene of the Royal tour. The
Canadians are very loyal, but we cannot pre-
sume upon their loyalty As the *Avenir du
Nord*, an influential organ of the French at
Montreal, took occasion to remind the Duke —

¹ The French and English people of Canada greet in
the Duke of Cornwall and York the son of their sovereign,
but do not intend thereby to furnish the Imperialists with
the illusion that Canada aspires to be stifled by tighter
and tighter British ties The respect that we profess in
a large measure, the marks of sympathy that we manifest
—even in a too exaggerated manner—for the King of
England and his son, will be changed into enmity and
energetic struggle if ever it is sought to erase from our
Constitution the clauses that make us almost independent,
with a view to replace them by Imperialistic obligations
such as are dreamed of by Mr Chamberlain and a few
others ¹

This may be dismissed as worthy of no importance because it is "only French talk." So
our loyalists at the Cape ignored the protests
and complaints of the Dutch *Absit omen*

It may be said that the French Canadians
may be very enthusiastic to be annexed, but
that the citizens of the United States would be
much less eager to welcome Canada within the
pale of the Union What Americans think on
the question of the future of Canada is not
difficult to discern One and all would disclaim
any attempt to annex Canada against her will;
but one and all regard absorption as her inevitable destiny, and while they would not hasten
the hour when the frontier-line disappears,

they would rejoice to see the Union Jack disappear from the Western Continent

President Roosevelt's words are worth quoting
in this connection Before he was President or
even Vice-President, he wrote —"The inhabitants of a colony are in a cramped and unnatural
state .   As long as a Canadian remains a
colonist he remains in a position inferior to that
of his cousins both in England and in the United
States. The Englishman at bottom looks down
on the Canadian, as on one who admits his
inferiority, and quite properly, too The
American regards the Canadian with the good-
natured condescension felt by the freeman for
a man who is not free."

"Every true patriot, every man of statesmanlike habit, should look forward to the day when
not a single European Power will hold a foot of
American soil. At present it is not necessary
to take the position that no European Power
shall hold American territory, but it certainly
will become necessary if the timid and selfish
peace-at-any-price men have their way, and if
the United States fails to check, at the outset,
European aggrandisement on this continent."

But it will be said that Mr. Roosevelt is a
representative of the extreme Expansionist
school. It may, therefore, be well to quote the
testimony of one who belongs to the other
extreme. With the doubtful exception of Mr
Atkinson, there is probably no more thorough-
going anti-Expansionist than Mr Andrew
Carnegie No one can accuse him of animosity
to the land in which he was born, and in which he
spends his summers. He has passed immune
through the Jingo fever which laid so many of
his compatriots low But, upon the subject of
Canada, Mr. Carnegie expressed sentiments even
more uncompromising than those of Mr. Roosevelt In the year 1895, when tariff questions
were to the fore, Mr Carnegie came out strongly
in favour of imposing heavy duties upon all
imports from Canada without regard to the
doctrine either of Free Trade or Protection,
but as a matter of high politics. The following
passage is a very significant but perfectly frank
and sincere expression of the sentiments of a
great number of the friendliest Americans upon
the question of our position in Canada —
"I think we betray a lack of statesmanship in
allowing commercial advantages to a country
which owes allegiance to a foreign Power
founded upon monarchical institutions, which
may always be trusted at heart to detest the
republican idea. If Canada were free and
independent, and threw in her lot with this
Continent, it would be another matter. So
long as she remains upon our flank, a possible
foe, not upon her own account, but subject to
the orders of a European Power, and ready to

be called by that Power to exert her forces against us even upon issues that may not concern Canada, I should let her distinctly understand that we view her as a menace to the peace and security of our country, and I should treat her accordingly She should not be in the Union and out of the Union at the same time if I could prevent it. Therefore, I should tax highly all her products entering the United States, and this I should do, not in dislike for Canada, but for love of her, in the hope that it would cause her to realise that the nations upon this Continent are expected to be European nations, and I trust, finally, one nation, so far as the English-speaking portion is concerned. I should use the rod, not in anger, but in love, but I should use it She should be either a member of the Republic or she should stand for her own self, responsible for her conduct in peace and war, and she should not shield herself by calling to her aid a foreign Power."

I have quoted the opinions of President Roosevelt and Mr. Carnegie. To them I would add a third, much less distinguished, but not less typical man Mr W. M Hazeltine, discussing in 1897 the probable policy of President McKinley, declared that if Mr. McKinley were mindful of the pledge embodied in the platform to which he subscribed, he would apply his influence and his ability in all lawful ways to further the movement for the voluntary incorporation of Canada with the Republic :—" He may not hold that extension of territory is desirable for its own sake, but he cannot but recognise that in the case of Canada there would be also an extension of market, and an extension of the field of American investments over Canadian mines and enterprises. Nor can he shut his eyes to the fact—that the annexation of the Dominion of Canada would mean the final exclusion of war, with all its burdens and horrors, from this Continent, and the secure dedication of North America to industry and peace "

Mr. Hazeltine's expectations were not fulfilled President McKinley did nothing to promote the incorporation of Canada with the United States, and on the whole it was probably just as well. American sentiment was slightly, very slightly, ruffled by the outbreak of Jingoism across the border, and some observations were let fall which showed that American opinion might take alarm if the Dominion were to be permanently inoculated with the spirit of militant Imperialism. Of that, however, there is little danger. At the same time it would not be wise to ignore the fact that Canada's growing sense of nationhood, and our sense of the obligations under which we lie to the Dominion for the help it rendered to us in the

South African war, will not tend altogether to facilitate the negotiations which are about to be resumed for the settlement of the few outstanding questions which still remain to be settled.

The permanent factor which always occasions irritation on the part of the Americans is the fact that they can neither deal with Canada alone nor with Great Britain alone. The influence of the British Government is almost invariably exercised in favour of a compromise The Canadians are, however, very stiff at a bargain, and are very quick to declare that their interests are being betrayed by the mother-country if we do not back them up to the uttermost in the claims which they make upon the American Government. Americans, it may be quite erroneously, are of opinion that if Great Britain were out of the way and they had to deal with Canada alone they would very soon come to terms, but they resent the Spenlow and Jorkins arrangement by which one of the partners always takes shelter behind the other. Canada, however, absolutely refuses to be left out of the negotiation of questions which primarily concern her own interests. Upon this subject Mr Carnegie, writing in the *Contemporary Review* in November 1897, said :—

Ambassador Pauncefote and Secretary of State Blaine, years ago, agreed upon a settlement of the Behring Sea question, and Lord Salisbury telegraphed his congratulations, through Sir Julian Pauncefote, to Mr Blaine. The two nations were jointly to police the seas and stop the barbarous destruction of the female seals. Canada appeared at Washington and demanded to see the President of the United States upon the subject Audience was denied to the presumptuous colony, nevertheless, her action forced Lord Salisbury to disavow the treaty No confidence here is violated, as President Harrison referred to the subject in a message to Congress Britain was informed that if she presumed to make treaties in which Canada was interested without her consent, she would not have Canada very long It will be remembered that Canada took precisely the same position in regard to international copyright It is this long desired treaty-making power which Canada has recently acquired for herself, at least as far as concerns fiscal policy, so that she need no longer even consult her suzerain She can now appear at Washington, and insist upon being received when new tariff measures are desired, having suddenly become a "free nation," according to her Prime Minister There are surprises in store here for the indulgent mother

Our permanent difficulty, that of inducing the Canadians to accept what we consider a legitimate compromise, but what they are apt to regard as an indefensible sacrifice of their vital interests, will certainly not have been diminished by recent events The Canadians will feel and say that they did not storm Paardeberg in order that Great Britain should give away their right to Skagway, or their fishery monopoly, for imperial considerations in which they have very remote interest If we insist they will sulk, and

Mr Carnegie's foreboding prophecy may be realised There will be no rupture, but the silken tie will be strained, and in proportion as it is weakened the pull of the economic forces making for union will be increased

The Canadians are at present smarting under a severe disappointment The party in power, after having for some years fostered emigration and developed trade relations with the mother country, confidently expected that the census would reveal a great increase in the population In 1891 the census figures were 4,823,875. In 1901 it was hoped that they would report a population of 6,000,000. Imagine the dismay occasioned by the discovery that there were only 5,338,833 residents in the Dominion. The whole Dominion in ten years has only added to its population about the same number of citizens as were added in the same period to the single State of Minnesota Of the 513,000 added to the population of Canada, 306,000 are to be found west of Ontario The population of Ontario itself is virtually stationary, an increase of 2 per cent being neither here nor there.

Professor Henry Davies, of Yale University, recently summed up his conclusions arrived at after an interviewing tour in the Dominion as follows —

" Much of Canada's stagnation is due to the inability of her leading men to see that the great assimilating power on this hemisphere is American, and not English This the people have already begun to learn. England has practically capitulated, so far as Canada is concerned, as recent futile parleyings have shown The situation, therefore, wants nothing but better trade relations with this country to perfect conquest "

What is to be hoped for is that, when the inevitable union takes place, it will be brought about with the hearty consent and concurrence of the mother-country, even if the mother-country herself does not set the example to Canada by taking the initiative in promoting that race alliance towards which everything seems to point. Should such an union take place it is probable there would be considerable simplification of the somewhat complex arrangements now existing in the Canadian Dominion. Decentralisation and Home Rule are very good things, but they may be carried too far, and eight separate Parliaments with eight separate executives seem a somewhat excessive allowance for a population that is not much in excess of the population of Greater London.

Although both the American and Canadian constitutions are based upon the federal principle, there is considerable difference in the way in which this principle is applied In the United States the federal power is strictly defined. The Congress at Washington has no power to legislate except on certain specified subjects All others not specially reserved for the central power are left to be dealt with according to the sovereign will of each of the federated states. In Canada the problem is approached from the other end. The powers of the provincial parliaments are strictly defined, while the undefined residue is left to the Parliament of the Dominion The Canadian judiciary is federal throughout the whole Dominion, and the judges are not elective. In the United States the judiciary is both federal and local, and the local judges are elected by popular vote. Laws of banking, of commerce, and of marriage are federal in the Dominion, and are left to the States in the Republic It is extremely difficult to amend the American Constitution, whereas the Canadian Constitution can be amended without much difficulty. When there is a dispute between the local authorities or between the provincial governments and the Federal Government, there is an appeal in the last instance to the Judicial Committee of the Privy Council in London In the United States the Supreme Court at Washington is the final authority.

In many respects the Canadian administration, especially that part which concerns the welfare of Indians, compares favourably with that of the United States. The contrast between the administration of justice in mining districts in Canada and in the United States has frequently been commented upon by the Americans themselves. There is none of the free shooting in the Canadian mining camps which used to be so characteristic of California The same men who were ready to shoot at sight in Denver and Colorado no sooner crossed the 49th parallel of latitude than they recognised that free shooting was contrary to the law of the land, and that no one had a pull which was good for anything with the Canadian justices.

These questions of detail, although interesting and important, are not vital, except in so far as they tend to show that if the Dominion and the Republic are ever to be merged in one greater union, both parties to the marriage will bring an ample dower, both moral and material, to the common stock.

It is not impossible that the Nemesis which follows the South African war may tend to operate against the unity of the Empire The Canadians, especially those who served in Strathcona's Horse, did not carry back with them to Canada a very high appreciation of the military genius of the British officer or the organising capacity of the British War Office Like all the Colonials engaged in this war, they felt themselves to be far and away better men than the Regulars whom they were sent to assist. Some of them came home convinced that the Boers were in the right, and that England had enlisted their services in a bad cause. They said nothing, but waited. They are waiting still. The spectacle which the British Army offers to the Empire to-day is not conducive to the development of Imperial pride. The Colonists were willing enough to help the mother country out of a temporary scrape, it being understood that the said mother country was still a going concern, that dry rot had not sapped her strength, that her statesmen were not dotards, and her administrators amateur dilletanti, and that, in short, there was honour and glory in being connected with what was believed to be the greatest, the wisest, the strongest of the Empires of the world.

But with the whole British army lying foundered month after month in South Africa, what are they to think of it? Has the mother country then become only a toothless old granddame, whose faculties have all gone to fat, and who has neither the wit to make peace nor the skill to make war? They do not say so as yet, nay, they are even preparing to send out another contingent to her assistance, but some such conviction may be forcing its way home to the Colonial mind. How much longer is it to last? And if Britannia is in her dotage, if her people are decadent, and if a piano and cook-stove mobility is all that her officers are capable of, then how long will it be before the cry, "To your tents, O Israel," or its modern equivalent, 'Hail, Columbia," is raised in the Dominion? It is a question of considerable interest just now to many people, of whom President Roosevelt is not the most considerable.

CHAPTER VII.—OF AUSTRALIA

ONE of the great events of the year 1901 was the opening of the first Parliament of the Australian Commonwealth by the heir to the British Crown. The event was hailed with immense enthusiasm throughout the Empire, as a public ceremonial demonstration of the closeness of the tie which binds the island continent of the Southern Seas to the motherland of the race. It may seem, therefore, singularly out of place to discuss at such a time the question whether even at the Antipodes the pull of the American Republic will be felt by the Australian Commonwealth. It must be admitted, of course, that the force of gravitation diminishes according to the distance at which it is exercised, and Australia is by no means subject to the same continuous temptation to throw in her lot

with the Americans to which the West India Islands and the Canadians are subject. Nevertheless, even in this first year a good many things have happened to give us cause to think, if not furiously, at least seriously, as to whether the net effect of the Federation of the Australian Colonies will tend so much to the consolidation of the Empire as we all wish to believe.

To begin with, the very first result of the Constitution of the Australian Commonwealth has been to put up a tariff wall between Great Britain and the independent sister nation at the Antipodes that is more of a barrier than a bond of union. To take only a small illustration of this. The *Australasian Review of Reviews,* which was founded in the interests of the Empire, and for the purpose of promoting the Union of the English-speaking peoples, is an off-shoot of the parent *Review of Reviews.* At least half of the contents of each number are printed from proofs sent from London. The immediate effect of the new tariff has been to increase the cost of the production of the *Australasian Review of Reviews.* A 10 per cent duty has been imposed upon paper, and 25 per cent upon the ink with which it is printed. All magazines printed in the mother-country and exported ready-made to Australia must pay a duty. It is a very small matter, but it illustrates the point that the new order of things at the Antipodes has had some results not altogether promoting the realisation of the King's ideal that Australia should be regarded as as much part and parcel of the United Kingdom as Kent or Sussex. In framing the Australian tariff, the Government refused absolutely to follow the example of Canada. No preference whatever has been allowed to British goods.

The Germans and the Americans, who bear none of the expense and undertake none of the responsibility for defending Australia, are as free to send in their goods as the British taxpayer who has to bear the whole burden of Imperial defence. I am not complaining of this, only mentioning it as an indication that the Australian Commonwealth has shown no sympathy with those Imperialists who think that the unity of the Empire can best be attained and maintained by an Imperial Zollverein.

Not only have the Australians imposed new taxes upon British goods, but their attitude on the question of the appeals to the Privy Council showed a sensitive jealousy in relation to the mother-country. Mr Chamberlain, in the very heyday of his popularity, found himself pulled up sharply by the refusal of the Australians to accept any settlement of the question of the Court of final appeal except the one which they liked. Right or wrong, they insisted upon

[Photograph by] EXHIBITION BUILDINGS, MELBOURNE, WHERE THE FIRST FEDERAL [G. W. Wilson, Aberdeen. PARLIAMENT ASSEMBLED.

THE AUSTRALIAN COMMONWEALTH.

having their own way, and, as usual, they got it There is now no right of appeal to the Privy Council or to any English Court for the decision of any questions as to the interpretation of the Constitution or of the merits of conflicting claims of the separate States, unless the Australian High Court itself should certify that the question should be determined by the Privy Council At the same time any appellant can appeal from the State Court direct to the Privy Council, without going through the Federal High Court —a provision which we owe to the wisdom of Mr Chamberlain, and which will almost certainly result in conflicting decisions upon points of law. In the main, however, the Australians carried their point, and barred any appeal from the decision of their own High Court excepting by permission of that High Court itself.

A third point which is worth remembering and discussing in the question of the possible merging of Australia into the greater federation of all the English-speaking peoples, is the fact that in framing the Australian Commonwealth the Australians on one vital principle elected to follow the example of the United States rather than that of the Canadian Dominion In Canada, it has already been stated, the Canadians defined the powers of the Provincial Assemblies and left all other powers to the Federal Parliament. In Australia they followed the American precedent As Sir John Cockburn told the International Commercial Congress that met at Philadelphia in October, 1899, the United States Constitution for the last ten years had been well-thumbed and well-read in the Australian Colonies "Our problem," he said, "has been throughout almost identical with yours", and it is not surprising that he should go on to say "In the fundamental characteristic of our constitution we have followed the example of the United States, and have placed only enumerated powers in the hands of the Federal authority, reserving all unenumerated powers for the State. Our cardinal condition is that only enumerated powers are placed in the hands of Federal authority."

Those enumerated powers differ somewhat from those of the United States, in that the questions of marriage and divorce are reserved for the Federal Parliament, whereas in America each State has its own law of marriage and divorce. On the other hand, they followed the American example in calling the two Houses of the Federal Legislature, the Senate and the House of Representatives, and, as is the case in the United States, each State enjoys equally inalienable rights of representation in the Senate, no matter whether its population be large or small, and no matter whether its area be extensive or limited. They have, however, departed

from the American precedent by constituting the Senate by direct election, and also by making it easier to amend the Constitution A constitutional amendment in Australia must first be passed by an absolute majority of both Houses in the Federal Parliament, or by one House on two occasions if rejected by the other. The amendment has then to be referred to the people of the several States, and a double majority, of States and of people, is necessary before the amendment takes effect It is probable that if a plebiscite of the citizens of the United States could be taken to-day, the majority would declare in favour of thus modifying their own constitution Except these three points, namely, a Federal law for marriage and divorce, direct election of senators, and greater elasticity in readjusting the provisions of the altered needs to the new time, the Australian Constitution does not much differ from the American

Australia is following in the steps of the United States in other matters besides the fashioning of its Constitution. The new Parliament is not yet a year old, but it has already formulated a demand pregnant with great consequences for the adoption of a Monroe doctrine for the Pacific The question arose in the debate upon a New Guinea Protectorate, and the demand that the Australian Government should press for the adoption by the Empire of a Monroe doctrine for the Pacific met with unanimous support The Prime Minister undertook to carry out the wishes of representatives of the Commonwealth, and thus at a bound Australia has leapt into the international area, with a demand, avowedly fashioned upon the American precedent, which will be regarded as a direct challenge by all the States which have possessions in the Pacific The policy may be right or it may be wrong, but it has at least the excellent quality of precision It is an unmistakable proclamation on the part of the new Commonwealth that no European or Asiatic Power is to be allowed to extend its dominions in the Pacific Ocean It does not yet appear whether the doctrine is to be expanded so far as to include the United States of America Probably not * Neither is it quite

* In this connection it is interesting to remember that Senator Proctor suggested some two or three years ago that in Asia, Britain and the United States should replace the waning Imperialism of old Rome by a new Imperialism destined to carry the world-wide principles of Anglo-Saxon peace and justice, liberty and law The measures which he suggested as necessary to achieve this end are the following :—

(1) A Treaty of Arbitration which all nations should be invited to join, but which in the first case should be negotiated between the United States, Great Britain and Holland

clear from the brief telegram which is all that has yet reached this country, what are the limits of the area within which the Australian Monroe doctrine is to apply. As the demand arose out of a debate on the question of New Guinea, it is probable that the area covered by this new interdict includes all the islands on this side of the Straits of Malacca, even if it does not also include the great island of Sumatra, where the Dutch for many years past have been at war with the Atchinese

Following the precedent of the Monroe doctrine, there will be no immediate demand that the Powers which have already seated themselves on the islands in the seas adjacent to Australia should haul down their flags and depart, for which mercy we may well express our thanks But as there is a tendency among the Americans to expand the Monroe doctrine so far as to convert it into a reserved notice to quit to all European Powers whose flags are temporarily tolerated in the New World, so we may be pretty certain that the Australian Monroeists, if encouraged, will intimate pretty plainly that the presence of the Dutch in Java and Sumatra, the Germans in New Guinea and Samoa, and the French in New Caledonia and Tahiti, is only tolerated during good behaviour, and that any manifestation of a desire on their part to extend the area of their territories will be held to be good and sufficient reason for bundling them out bag and baggage over the seas which are now ear-marked and exclusively reserved for Australians or at least for English-speaking men

What the European Powers will think of this, it is easy to imagine. The "Spectator," some time ago, intimated, not obscurely, that nothing was more likely than that the Australians, casting covetous eyes on Java, would endeavour to eject the Dutch , but although there are no limits to the fantasies of the "Spectator," there are some limits to the resources of the Imperial Government

Of course, any attempt to enforce the Australian Monroe doctrine for the Pacific would be futile unless the Australians could wield, not only the small squadron which they maintain in Australian waters, but the war fleets of the

(2) That those nations should count coal as much contraband of war as gunpowder

(3) All countries acquired by the United States should be thrown open to the commerce of the world on equal terms

(4) The United States, Great Britain and Japan should proclaim a new Monroe Doctrine applicable to China , and co operate with that country in preventing acquisition of territory there by European Powers

(5) The United States, Great Britain and the Netherlands should proclaim and maintain a new Monroe Doctrine applicable to the vast islands of the Indian Archipelago

Empire It is easy to see what dangers the adoption of such a policy by the Empire would entail upon us in the four quarters of the world. It is equally easy to see the angry disappointment which will be occasioned in Australia if an unsympathetic answer is returned from Downing Street. One thing is quite certain, and that is that if the Empire were to attempt to put a ring-fence round the unoccupied lands of the Pacific, it would in a very short time be compelled to undertake the duty of occupying and administering them all This might not be difficult with the smaller unappropriated islands, which would not pay the expense of administration, but it would be very different with the islands which lie between the Straits of Malacca and the Gulf of Carpentaria. Sir Julius Vogel long ago proposed to proclaim a protectorate on behalf of New Zealand over all the Pacific islands—a bold step which, if it had been taken then, might have averted many of the dangers which would have to be faced if a similar policy were adopted to-day. Since Sir Julius Vogel's time, Germany has entered into the Pacific, and there will be small disposition on the part of the other Powers to recognise a mere paper protectorate. For the moment, however, we may dismiss the subject, merely noting the fact as one more point in which Australian policy is more in accord with that of the United States than that of the United Kingdom

We now approach the subject which of all others is most likely to strain to breaking point the ties between the Commonwealth and the Mother Country Australia is an undeveloped continent, the northern half of which lies within the tropics, that is to say, there is a region as large as the whole of Europe without Russia, which it is practically impossible to develop without coloured labour Opinion is divided on this point The colony which lies within the tropical zone speaks with two voices. The Queensland delegates in the Federal Parliament assert that white men can do all the work that is needed in the sugar plantations, while the Queensland Government holds exactly the opposite opinion, and maintains that any interdict upon coloured labour will be fatal to the Colony. When doctors disagree, the people decide, and when Queensland herself speaks with a double voice, the uninstructed outsider must draw his own conclusions Of one thing there is no doubt, and that is that whether white men can or cannot live and thrive while performing arduous manual labour under a tropical sun, the white man won't. It is equally certain that the brown and the yellow men are only too anxious to have an opportunity to earn their living by converting the wilderness into a garden. There are more millions of Indian coolies,

Chinese labourers, and Japanese husbandmen ready to open up and develop the immense agricultural and mineral resources of Northern Australia, than there are white men in the whole continent But, again, following the example of the United States, the Federal Parliament is absolutely opposed to the introduction of coloured labour The cry of a White Australia has carried all before it, and the members have shown an almost fanatic zeal in fencing round the Island Continent with a high wall for the exclusion of Chinese, Japanese, and Indian coolies. They have even gone the length of refusing to pay a subsidy for the carriage of mails to any steamship company which employs Lascars. Mr. Chamberlain objected to any strong measure of exclusion against Asiatics But he had no objection to their exclusion by means of an educational test which, as it will be administered, many members of the Federal Parliament themselves would find much difficulty in passing In regard to the question whether coloured labour should be employed, Mr. Chamberlain vetoed this on the two fold ground that it was impossible for the Imperial Government to sanction the exclusion of the King's own subjects from a British Colony, and that such an interdict might involve the Imperial Government in complications with other Powers, possibly with Japan

All the arguments which are now being used in America to secure the renewal of the Chinese Exclusion Bill are brought out and urged in order to lock and double-lock the door of Australia against any influx of Asiatics Here, again, Australia is proclaiming a policy which can only be enforced by the aid of the Imperial fleet One of the great achievements of which the civilised Powers were very proud in the Nineteenth Century was the success with which they battered in the gates which the Japanese had locked and double-locked against the invasion of Europeans Having battered down the front door of the Japanese house, and hailed it as a great triumph of civilisation, the Australians are now calling upon us to keep the Japanese from battering down the barrier which has been built up to prevent the ingress of Asiatics into Australia Yet in the latter case there is admittedly ample room to spare for millions of Japanese, and unless their labour is employed, vast tracts of territory exceeding in extent the whole of the area of the Japanese islands will remain practically useless to mankind The Japanese Conservatives, whose resistance we overcame by the summary persuasion of our cannon, could at least claim that they had filled up their own country, and that there was no waste land for settlers Such considerations, however, do not weigh for much with the rulers

of the new Commonwealth They have made up their mind that Australia is to be reserved for white men No yellow, brown, or black man need apply, not even although it should be a demonstrable fact that without his labour hundreds of thousands of square miles of fertile land must remain unreclaimed from the wilderness

It is obvious from this brief survey of some of the points upon which possible friction may arise that the Australians may demand from the Home Government that which the Home Government cannot concede The new Commonwealth, in the pride of its youth, will find it very difficult to confine its enthusiasm within limits necessary for the welfare of the Empire

There will be a very strong party in the Commonwealth in favour of independence The *Sydney Bulletin*, a weekly serio-comic journal, which has done much to preach the gospel of the Australian Commonwealth, and is the only weekly paper which circulates throughout the whole colony, is the most uncompromising advocate of Australia for the Australians that could be found anywhere in the Empire. It deserves great credit for the unflinching intrepidity with which it opposed the South African War, but it has to be reckoned with as a permanent force against the maintenance of the Imperial tie

Apart from these political points on which the Australians resemble the Americans, there are others obvious to everyone who has visited the Antipodes

When Mark Twain visited Australia he found the Australians in many respects exceedingly American For instance, in his " More Tramps Abroad,' he said —

" Sydney has a population of 400,000 When a stranger from America steps ashore there, the first thing that strikes him is that it is an English city with American trimmings Later on, in Melbourne, he will find the American trimmings still more in evidence There even the architecture will often suggest America The photograph of its stateliest business street might be passed off for a picture of the finest street in a large American city "

He did not, however, see any need for Australia following the example of the American Colonies He said —

" There seems to be a party that would have Australasia cut loose from the British Empire, and set up housekeeping on her own It seems an unwise idea They point to the United States but it seems to me that the cases lack a good deal of being alike Australia governs herself wholly There is no interference If our case had been the same, we should not have gone out when we did But the Americans are welcomed in Australia One of the speakers,' he said, "at the Commemoration Banquet at Adelaide, the Minister of Public Works, was an American born and reared in New Zealand There is nothing narrow about the province, politically or in any other way that I know of Sixty four different religions and a Yankee Cabinet Minister No amount of horse-racing can damn this community "

Where the Australians differ from the Americans is in the absence of any element corresponding to the ethical leaven of the Pilgrim Fathers In the whole of their history the Australians have never passed through the hard experiences which discipline nations They have been the spoiled children of the human race. War, pestilence and famine, the three scourges of mankind, have never compelled them to realise the sterner realities of existence They have never experienced any deeper emotions than those engendered by the vicissitudes of the South African War. They are splendid cricketers, matchless horsemen, and devoted to all manner of sport. Sport, indeed, may be said to be the Australian religion, and with them the chief end of man is to have a good time A self-indulgent and undisciplined race which is suddenly called upon to cope with the delicate and dangerous problems of international policy is certain to be wilful, impulsive, impetuous, not to say reckless in the pursuit of its ideals.

The late Mr. Francis Adams, who for some time was on the staff of the *Sydney Bulletin,* gave a very sombre account of the citizens of the New Commonwealth. He said —

"Educated in a secular manner, even in the denominational grammar schools, our New World youth is a pure Positivist and Materialist Religion seems to him at best a social affair, to whose inner appeal he is profoundly indifferent. History is nothing to him, and all he knows or cares for England lies in his resentment and curiosity concerning London Sunday is rapidly becoming Continental, more and more the characteristics of a careless, pleasure-loving race are developed, that is secularly educated The true Gallio gets his own way History is identified with religion, and as such excluded from the curriculum, so that the sense of the poetry of the past and the solidarity of the race is rapidly being lost to the young Australian To the next generation England will be a geographical expression, and the Empire a myth in imminent danger of becoming a bogey "

Mr D Christie Murray declared that the Australians were the rowdiest and most drunken population in the world —

"Parental control, as we know it, in England, has died out entirely There is no reverence in the rising generation, and the ties of home are slight Age and experience count for little, the whole country is filled with a feverish and restless energy Everybody is in a hurry to be rich "

Sir Gavan Duffy eleven years ago, before Federation had been accomplished, thus described Australia and the Australians —

"There are six States which possess more natural wealth, wider territory, a better climate, and richer mineral deposits than the six great Kingdoms in Europe, where a new England, a new Italy, a new France, a new Spain, and a new Austria are in rapid process of growth, and are already occupied by a picked population They are no insignificant handful of men—these Australian colonists , they are more numerous than the people of England were when they won Magna Charta, or the people of the United States were when the Stars and Stripes were first hoisted to the sky—resolute, impatient men, not unworthy to follow such examples on adequate occasions."

When the late Henry George visited Australia, he was much impressed with the fact that the English characteristics of Australians were only on the surface —

"It seemed to me that in spite of the retention of English ways and habits, the Australian type that is developing is nearer to the American than to the British The new country, the fresher, freer life, the better diffusion of wealth, are telling in the same way on the English that have taken root in Australia as on the English that took root in America There are, I think, in the people, and especially in the native-born, evidences of the very inventiveness, the same self-reliance and push, the same independence, the same quickness of thought and movement, the same self-satisfaction and spread-eagletiveness as are supposed to be characteristic of our own The Australian States are only nominally colonies They are in reality in all things of practical importance self-governing Republics. With the political connection with Great Britain, which under present conditions combines security with freedom, there is no restiveness, neither do I think there is any loyalty more than skin deep The tariff legislation, in which Great Britain is treated as any other foreign country, is a more substantial declaration of independence than any mere formal declaration could be As for the feeling towards the United States, it is fully as good and as warm as we deserve I am inclined to think that the Australians would be quick to respond to any proposition from us for reciprocity We could virtually annex Australia, as we could virtually annex Canada and Great Britain by the simple process of abolishing our tariff and raising our revenues by means not in themselves corrupt

Henry George's suggestion as to reciprocity may bear fruit. President Roosevelt received from his predecessor as an inheritance the adoption of a policy of reciprocity. The connection between Australia and the Pacific Coast is very close. Even now mails sent from London *via* San Francisco reach New Zealand a fortnight earlier than mails sent by any other route

The Americans, eager for new markets, will find a better opening for their manufactures in Australia than in the Philippines. Nor will they have any set-off in the shape of military charges or cost of administration. Should the Australians ever declare for independence, the strain of the rupture will lead them naturally to seek for support where it can be found, and the history and traditions of the United States render it impossible that they should look in vain for the sympathy and support of the American Republic.

One of the most interesting questions of the future is whether the Australians of the future

RT. HON. EDMUND BARTON.
THE FEDERAL PREMIER.

RT. HON. C. C. KINGSTON (Framer of the First Tariff Bill).
(Photo by Elliott & Fry.)

RT. HON. SIR JOHN FORREST.
FEDERAL POSTMASTER-GENERAL.
(Photo by Elliott & Fry.)

RT. HON. R. J. SEDDON.
PREMIER OF NEW ZEALAND.

will speak English or German. At present all the odds are in favour of English, but the chance that the majority of men who would people Australia at the end of the century may speak German and not English is greater than most English people have yet realised   According to the last census returns, the total population of the Australian Commonwealth was under four millions, the exact figures being 3,777,212, or less than the population of London. In the previous decade the total increase was 593,975   There was practically no gain by immigration   The increase from that source was only 5,328, most if not all of whom were either Japanese, Hindus, or Kanakas   The Australian legislators and journalists have sounded an alarm over the extent to which the Australian parents have adopted as a rule of life the preventive limitation of the family   According to Mr Coghlan's recently published book entitled " A Study in Statistics," between 1895 and 1898 the average birth-rate in New South Wales has declined by one-third, and there are fewer children under ten years of age in Victoria than there were ten years ago   In New South Wales in 1885 546,000 women between the ages of eighteen and fifty produced as many children as 665,767 women of the same ages in 1898. The number of children born to wives of Australian birth is 3·5 , in France it is 3·4   Thirty years ago the average in Australia was 5·31. The birth-rate has fallen in the United Kingdom, but nothing like to the same extent.

The average number of children per marriage in the United Kingdom was 4·36 ten years ago   In 1900 it had fallen to 3·63, a reduction of nearly 7 per cent   A population which has ceased to increase and multiply, and has arrived at a birth-rate almost identical with that which has for several years past arrested the increase of population in France, cannot count confidently upon controlling the future of the continent upon the rim of which it has squatted

Australia in geographical extent is large enough to include the whole of the United States, with the exception of Florida and Alaska   It is, with the exception of Siberia, the one vast unoccupied habitable expanse left on the world's surface   If the Australians are ceasing to increase and multiply and replenish the earth, and are confining themselves merely to keeping up their numbers with a small annual increase, they need not expect to be able to monopolise the possession of the vast hinterland which could afford homes for the overflow of Europe for the next hundred years

If the Australians are ceasing to breed, the Germans are not. For the last ten years the great development of manufacturing industry in

Germany has practically arrested the outflow of emigrants from the Fatherland   But the present financial crisis in the German Empire will turn on the tap once more   Even without any such distinct impetus to emigration, it is obvious that Central Europe must again begin to pour out a steady stream of her surplus population for which there is no room at home   Hitherto the great stream of German emigrants has been directed to the United States of America   But there the English-speaking people have got too much start   They are too numerous and too powerful for the Germans ever to hope to destroy the English-speaking character of the United States.   It is different in Australia   It is by no means beyond the pale of possibility that German emigration, if directed to the Antipodes, might reach a quarter of a million a year   In ten years, one-half of the population of Australia would be of German origin   If Germans breed and Australians will not, the future will unquestionably lie with the most prolific race   Australia to the German offers every advantage of a German colony, and none of the disadvantages   Every German settler is as free to take up land in Australia as if he were born in the United Kingdom. The Germans have already effected a lodgment in the Antipodes.

Mr. Sutherland, who contributed to the *Centennial* of May, 1900, an article on the German Villages, declared that there were few Colonies in which a Continental European nation had left so distinctly its national and racial mark   At that time there were from 30,000 to 40,000 German colonists in Australia   They were chiefly to be found in South Australia. For many miles north and south of Port Mannum the country is dotted with German farms, and the farmers are developing vine-growing   Mr Sutherland says —

" The stream of German emigration to South Australia never ceases   It is not a matter of fits and starts ; it goes on quietly from year to year, and the proportion of German colonists steadily keeps pace with the growth of the population   The affinity of kinship, religion, and language has proved more powerful than any disintegrating influence   At the present time there is reason to believe that the flow of German colonisation is largely on the increase   By the last census it appeared that the number of colonists who owned Germany as their birthplace was almost exactly equal to the sum total of those who were born in all the other Australian Colonies   Some of the finest steamers in the Australian trade are now engaged in bringing passengers direct from Bremen and Antwerp to the chief cities of Australia   Adelaide receives a large proportion of this influx "

The Germans make good colonists   They do not crowd to the towns as the Australians do   They abide by the Lutheran religion, and, although they cherish their own language, they become good Australian citizens   There is not much probability that even if Australia became a German-speaking land, it would place itself under the domination of the German Empire But at the present moment, taking a wide look-out over the world there seems to be much better chance of creating a Greater Germany beyond the sea in Australia than anywhere else on the world's surface

I have said nothing in this chapter about New Zealand, which appears to be developing her destinies quite independently of Australia At present it would seem as if New Zealand had a greater attraction for the United States than the United States for New Zealand There is no country in the world whose social experiments are watched with greater interest by the younger school of American economists and politicians than those which have been carried out by that Colony Should the industrial development of the United States take a trend in the direction of State socialism, it is to the experiments of New Zealand that the American legislators will look for guidance as to what to do and what to avoid doing But whether the attraction is exercised by New Zealand upon the United States or by the United States upon New Zealand, it cannot fail to unite the two countries more closely together by ties of common interest, although there is little trace of American influence in New Zealand at present

Writing on the question of the future relations of the United States and New Zealand in the *Nineteenth Century* in 1890, Mr. Bakewell, a very intelligent resident in Auckland, New Zealand, expressed an emphatic opinion as to the readiness of the New Zealanders at that time to transfer their allegiance from the British Empire to the United States of America. He said —

"If Australia became independent, Canada would follow suit, and the probability is that a great federation of English-speaking Republics would be formed, including the United States. In that case New Zealand would join as a separate State, as Texas did If the question of annexation as a State to the United States of North America were put to the vote to-morrow, there would not be a thousand votes against it "

That was eleven years ago. Mr Bakewell would not repeat it to-day In 1890 there was very little Imperial feeling in New Zealand. Loyalty was chiefly confined to those colonists who were British-born The younger generation sat very loosely to the Empire

"If you want to keep us from Republicanism,' said Mr Bakewell, "you must let us see something of Royalty "

The hint has been taken, and the recent tour of the Duke and Duchess of Cornwall and York has been exploited to the uttermost in the interests of the Empire Nevertheless, there is no more independent community on the world's surface than New Zealand, nor any which would more angrily resent any attempt to cross its will. It is impossible to repress a somewhat sardonic smile at the thought of Mr Seddon beating the war-drum and sending forth contingent after contingent of New Zealand youth in order to suppress the independence of the South African Republics, when everyone knows perfectly well that he and all the New Zealanders would have rushed to arms long before if Mr Chamberlain had interfered one-tenth as much with the internal affairs of New Zealand as he did with those of the Transvaal President Kruger was a much less independent potentate than Mr Seddon, and New Zealand as an "independent sister nation " is much more independent of control from Downing Street than the Transvaal would be if its independence were restored to-morrow, with such treaty limitations as even President Kruger is now willing to accept

———

CHAPTER VIII.—A CRUCIBLE OF NATIONS.

THE United States of America owes no small portion of its exuberant energies to the fact that there has poured into that Continent for the last fifty years a never-ceasing flood of emigrants recruited for the most part from the more energetic, enterprising and adventurous members of the Old World The United States has taken the place of the United Kingdom as the natural refuge of the political refugee. There is not a country in Europe which has not contributed of its best to build up the American people. The tradition of the *Mayflower* has been maintained to this day It is true that most of those who have migrated to the United States have not gone thither to seek freedom to worship God so much as to seek opportunity to earn a decent livelihood, but there has never failed a goodly proportion of those who were driven from the Old World by the lash of the persecutor But whether they have emigrated for conscience' sake, or whether they came in search of filthy lucre, they have always been above the average Sometimes the motive which drove them westward has been a desire to escape from justice or to evade the obligations of citizenship, but whether the motive in itself was respectable or disreputable, the fact that it sufficed to transfer so many human bodies across 3000 miles of ocean to new homes in a new world showed at least that the souls which gave mobility to these human bodies were capable of taking risks, of facing the unknown, and of submitting to the sacrifice entailed by severance from the environment of their childhood

In other words, the nineteen millions of

emigrants who have crossed the Atlantic in this century to find homes in the United States, have been men of faith They believed in themselves , they believed in the future , and, although it was only in a material sense, they sought a better city than that into which they had been born , they were masters of their destiny The crowded millions of the Old World who are born and live and die in the district in which they happen to be born represent the *vis inertiæ* of Europe The nineteen millions who crossed the Atlantic represent its aspirations and its energy. Many of them, no doubt, were driven westward by the scourge of starvation. But many millions, who suffered as much as they, remained behind, lacking the energy necessary to transport them to another hemisphere
The emigrant population, therefore, possesses pre-eminently this characteristic—that it has sufficient life to have motion, sufficient faith to face the future, under the unknown conditions of a new world, and sufficient capacity to acquire the means requisite to transport them across the Atlantic This emigration, which is often regarded by Americans as an element of danger, has probably contributed more than any other, except the Puritan education of New England, to the making of the Republic.

The American, it is evident, is no mere English-man transplanted to another continent. In his veins flows the blood of a dozen non-English races. The English, some say, can claim only an antiquarian interest in the new race which has emerged from the furnace pot into which all nationalities have been smelted down in order to produce that richest ingot of humanity, the modern American * But there is surely no need for this vehement repudiation of the nation which first colonised Virginia and equipped the *Mayflower*. As for the foreign element in the human conglomerate, that troubles us little. We English are a composite race. It is no small part of the secret of our greatness If the North American Continent may be compared to a mammoth blast furnace, in which the crude ores quarried in many diverse mines are being smelted into a human compound quite distinct

* I hope that this may not bring a blush to the cheek of any American, for, as Mr W D Howells wrote in 1897, " Whatever Europe may think to the contrary, we are now really a modest people " But when I read the speech of Mr Cummins, the Governor elect of Iowa, at the New York Chamber of Commerce dinner, I was reassured For Mr Cummins declared that " In the depth and breadth of character, in the volume of hope and ambition, in the universality of knowledge, in reverence for law and order, in the beauty and sanctity of our homes, in sobriety, in respect for the rights of others, in recognition of the duties of citizenship, and in the ease and honour with which we tread the myriad paths leading from rank to rank in life, our people surpass all their fellow-men "

and diverse from any of its constituents, these islands of ours may be described as a crucible in which the same process has been going on for ages We are emphatically a mixed race. The process which we witness on a great scale and with immense rapidity in Chicago and New York has been going on for centuries in Britain Aboriginal Briton, conquering Roman, marauding Pict, devastating Saxon, piratical Dane, plundering Norseman, and civilising Norman, were all used up in the blend labelled English. Long after the English stock emerged from the crucible of war, it was continually improved by the addition of foreign elements. French Huguenots, German emigrants, fugitive Jews, Dutchmen and Spaniards, all added more or less of a foreign strain to our English blood It has been our salvation The mixing of Welsh and Irish, Scotch and English, Celts of the Highland and Danes of Northumberland, which has gone on for centuries and is going on to-day, has produced a type which is being reproduced on a gigantic scale and with infinite modifications across the Atlantic That they are not the same, but diverse, is a matter of course. Even the American Constitution, fashioned, as its founders believed, on the lines of the British, differs notably from its model. There is no such thing as a common race even in England, let alone in the United States We are all con-glomerates, with endlessly varying constituents But we have at least a common language, and we all own allegiance to Shakespeare if to no other man of woman born. As Professor Waldstein pointed out, the English-speaking nations possess seven of the elements which go to constitute a nationality, viz , a common language , common forms of government , common culture, including customs and insti-tutions ; a common history , a common religion, and, finally, common interests.

But the United Kingdom was a crucible the size of a tea-cup In the United States we find a crucible of Continental dimensions A pro-cess which in England has spread over centuries has been carried on in the United States within the lifetime of generations But, notwithstand-ing all this vast influx from beyond the seas, it has failed to submerge the distinctively English-speaking American The New Englander is still on top, and likely to remain so, although in many of the great cities he has been dethroned for a time by the Irish and their bosses.

The greatest thing which the Americans have done, much greater than the conquest of the Philippines or the invasion of the English market, or even than the suppression of the Great Rebellion, has been the superintendence of this vast crucible. The greatest achieve-ment was the smelting of men of all nationalities into one dominant American type, or—to vary the metaphor—weaving all these diverse threads of foreign material into one uniform texture of American civilisation. It has been done very largely in great cities, and the work has been taken in hand by men who are very far from conscious artificers of providential designs. Tammany and its related political organisations have done a work, the full value of which is still far from being adequately appreciated either at home or abroad. These political organisations, impelled solely by their own political ambitions, were nevertheless the most efficient agencies for grafting this multitudinous myriad of foreign emigrants upon the American trunk. The Italian or Polish emigrant who arrives in New York and Chicago with a couple of dollars in his pocket and with no word of English on his tongue would have perished, had it not been that in the Ward Heeler and the Captain of the precincts into which he had drifted, he found a friend who, in return for political service to be rendered in future, was a very present help in time of need. He found him lodgings in a tenement house, he often found him work, he found him an interpreter. When he got into trouble with the police, he bailed him out or paid his fine, or used his pull with the magistrate to enable him to escape unwhipped of justice; when he was ill, he put him in the hospital, when he was dead, he buried him; and, above all, before election day came, he naturalised him, and secured his vote. No man is naturalised in America according to law, unless he can declare that he has read and accepted the principles of the American Constitution. Millions of foreigners have been naturalised and vote every day, who know about as much of the principles of the Constitution as the Russian soldiers who thought that the Constitution was a woman and the wife of one of their Grand Dukes. Nevertheless, it was by this means, in the first instance, that the foreign emigrant was enabled to take the first step towards the acquisition of the American nationality.

The school to which his children were sent completed the operation. In one generation, or at most in two, the foreign emigrant became thoroughly Americanised, for the Americanisation of the world is nowhere gaining ground more rapidly than in the Americanisation of the citizens of the world, who from love of adventure, from sheer misfortune, or from any other cause, have transferred their residence from the old world to the New.

When the Republic was founded, Mr Bancroft estimated that only four-fifths of the population of the revolted colonies used English as their mother-tongue. According to Mr. Carroll Wright, the United States Commissioner of Labour, the population to-day is half rather than one fifth. This, of course, does not imply that Mr. Wright's half is made up of persons of foreign birth. At the census of 1900 not more than 10,000,000 of the population of the United States had been born outside the Union. Of the 19,000,000 who emigrated to the United States since 1821, 9,000,000 are dead; but before they died they multiplied amazingly.

It is characteristic of the foreign emigrant that, even when he speaks French, he has been much more obedient to the ancient precept to multiply and increase and replenish the earth than the native born English-American. The tendency to limit families, which is most conspicuous in France, and is now only one degree less conspicuous in the Australian colonies and the United Kingdom, has long been remarked as one of the dangers menacing the maintenance of an English-speaking civilisation in the United States. The well-to-do American family of old standing will have two, three, or four children, while the German, Irish, or Polish emigrant who works in the mill or the mine or the factory, will have litters of children to the number of fifteen and under. It may be said that it does not matter, as they all learn to speak English, but it matters a great deal in estimating the influence of the various foreign strains upon their ultimate product, the American race. Professor Starr recently startled the world by maintaining that, if it were not for the continuous influx of foreign emigration with its resultant prolific families, the genuine American would approximate to the type of the Red Indian, and, I suppose, like the Red Indian, would dwindle and disappear. A recent traveller in the United States declared, on returning to Britain, that the American continent was like nothing so much as one of the great refuse-destroyers which exist in every large town. The climate seemed to burn up the vitality of the settlers, producing nervous exhaustion, which, if not recruited continuously from without, would use up the race. These estimates are great exaggerations, but they testify to a tendency which should not be lost sight of. The European American seems to run too much to nerve and brain. He lacks the beefy animalism of his British and German progenitor, and living at a great pace stands in perpetual need of nerve tonics, medicines, and pills of all sorts. The Americans, judging by many of the foremost specimens of the race, have developed their brains at the expense of their stomachs. They have great calculating apparatuses, but their digestive organs leave much to be desired. You will often find men who are standing the heavy strain of a long day's work in commerce or in journalism who are compelled to diet themselves upon milk and crackers.

It is very curious to note the various ingredients which have been contributing to this international crucible by foreign nations The German percentage was highest between 1850 and 1860, when it reached 36·6 per cent In the last decade this had fallen to 13·7. The Irish percentage was 42·3 per cent. in the period from 1821 to 1850, but between 1851 to 1860 it fell to 35·2, and in the last decade it had dropped to only 10·5 per cent

Great Britain reached its maximum between 1861 and 1870, when the percentage was 26·2 In the last decade it had fallen to 7·4 The emigrants from Scandinavia, Germany, Great Britain and Ireland, including those from Canada and Newfoundland, amounted to 74·3 per cent. of the nineteen millions of emigrants who settled in America in the last eighty years, but between 1850 and 1860 they contributed 91·2 per cent. to the total, and in 1890-1900 their proportion had fallen to 40·4 per cent

The emigration from Southern and Eastern Europe may be said only to have begun in 1880. But the number increased so rapidly that in the last decade Austria-Hungary, Italy, Russia, and Poland contributed 50·1 per cent of the total number of emigrants The number of emigrants arriving in the United States has shown a tendency of late to decrease It reached its maximum in the year 1882, when no fewer than 788,992 emigrants entered the Union From that year the figures dropped until 1886, when they numbered only 334,203. The fluctuations were very great In 1892 they had risen to 623,084, in 1898 they had fallen to 229,299 Since then they had begun to climb up again, and in the year ending June 30th, 1900, the total number of emigrants was 448,572 Of this number only 2,392 belonged to the professional classes, 61,443 were skilled labourers, 163,508 were labourers, while the remainder, chiefly women and children, 134,941, had no specified occupation

Almost all these emigrants go to the North and West At last census the proportion of foreign-born in the Southern States was less than 5 per cent This contrasts very much with the returns from other States Rhode Island had 31·4, North Dakota, 35·4, Montana, 27·6, Colorado, 16·9, and Nebraska, 16·6 of the foreign-born.

Of the 448,000 immigrants into the United States last year, 300 000 came from Austria-Hungary, Italy, and Russia Of the total number of immigrants, one quarter came from Germany, one-fifth from Ireland, 15 per cent from England, 6 per cent from Sweden and Norway. It is estimated that the number of Germans in the United States was close upon ten millions, of whom three millions were born in Germany, and the rest are of German parentage It sounds like a far-away dream of the past to recall the fact that sixty years ago, at the time when the future destiny of Texas was not finally fixed, German dreamers maintained that it might be possible to build up a German state in Texas which might permanently divide North America from the dominant Anglo-Saxon.

The most difficult ingredient in the crucible, the one which has hitherto proved most refractory, is the black population of the south The census of 1900 showed the coloured population to number 9,312,585 Of these 8,840,789 were negroes, the others being about 250,000 Indians, 119,000 Chinese, and about 86,000 Japanese. The increase of the negroes did not quite keep pace with that of the white population, which is probably due entirely to the fact that there were no negro immigrants into the United States since the suppression of the slave trade In 1890, the blacks were 12·5 per cent. of the population, in 1900 they were 12·2 These refractory substances often contain within themselves elements of great value necessary for the formation of a perfect blend. The American recoils from the thought of miscenegation. But if the tendency of the climate and the habit of life is to attenuate the physical frame and burn up the nervous vitality of the race, it is obvious that the nine million negroes afford an element of robust animal vigour which may yet stand in good stead if the process of assimilation could be rendered less unpleasant. The education of the negro race, taken in hand so admirably by Booker Washington, who, in founding Tuskegee College, has shown a rare combination of science and common sense, will render the process less intolerable than it appears at present. But the outcry by the Southern press when President Roosevelt invited Booker Washington to dine at the White House was an unpleasant reminder of the intensity of race prejudice, while the continual occurrence of lynchings shows that considerable progress has yet to be made before the Americans can see their way to a satisfactory solution of the negro problem. In the last twenty years over 3000 lynchings have taken place in the United States, the highest total being 236 in 1892 In 1900 the figure had fallen to 115. It is not true, as is generally asserted, that the majority of lynchings occur to avenge assaults or outrages by black men upon white women. In the last sixteen years 2516 lynchings were reported. In fewer than 800 of these was an assault upon women alleged as the excuse. The chief cause for which negroes were lynched or murdered was attempted murder, but 115 were lynched for horse stealing and

9; for arson. However painful these crimes of violence may be, they are comparatively few in number, 100 lynchings among 9,000,000 negroes is a blot on the sun, no doubt, but it is not an eclipse.

The political effect of this vast foreign element, whether black or white, in the United States, upon the race alliance of the English-speaking peoples has naturally attracted considerable attention. The present Duke of Argyll regarded it as one of the features which would tend to promote such an alliance Writing in the *North American Review* in October, 1893, he laid considerable stress upon the advantage which it would be to the United States to have the sympathy of a sound, strong English confederation in league with the Union He wrote —" As the foreign element, Italian or German or French-Canadian, gets stronger and more segregated in special states in the Union, it is quite conceivable that race or national questions under some specious name may cause trouble, and that the 'national' population may live to hoist the tricolour or some other foreign flag in preference to the Stars and Stripes. The French in the north-east might well form such a national cave of Adullam Then how about the foreign elements in the South, half Congo, half Creole ? These things may be out of sight for the present, but the present becomes the distant past very soon in politics, and an English Bund is not a bad antidote to certain schemes and dreams which are very un-English, using that adjective in its best sense."

The tendency of foreign populations to become centred in certain districts is probably a temporary phenomenon There are quarters in New York and Chicago where the English language is hardly known There is an anecdote told of a foreign immigrant who, having settled in New York, applied herself diligently to learning what she imagined to be the language of the country in which she had settled, and it was only after she had removed to another precinct that she learned to her chagrin that she had wasted all her pains in learning a Bohemian dialect, which, as it was the only language spoken in her street, she had mistaken for the American tongue In all the States, however, the work of fusing the various nationalities into one homogeneous whole is carried on steadily, though not at such high pressure, even in the country districts where it is still possible for aliens to preserve the language, religion, and customs of their fatherland Mr. Rodney Walsh, who contributed an article to the "Forum" for February, 1891, on "The Farmer's Changed Condition," declared that in entire counties in Illinois and Wisconsin the English language is scarcely ever

heard outside the great towns. The church services are conducted in a foreign tongue, and instruction is given in it at the schools Mr Babcock, writing on "The Scandinavians in the North West ' a year later, said "You can travel 300 miles across Wisconsin, Iowa, and Minnesota without once leaving land owned by Scandinavians " In Minnesota one-seventh of the legislators are Scandinavians, and there are thirty-seven Scandinavian newspapers. But one of the most remarkable testimonies as to the extent to which the United States have been Europeanised reached me in the shape of a letter from Galveston, in Texas, in 1891 The writer, Mr E. J. Coyle, wrote —

" Don't believe for a moment that twenty-five per cent. of our citizens are of British or Saxon origin, or of English-speaking sympathies, for they are not Take for example this Latin-American province, Texas, or California, Arizona or any of the new lands ceded by the Guadaloupe-Hidalgo treaty, and has the Englishman a foothold ? Thank God, no New Braunfells, Comal County, one of our most successful German Colonies, located in 1840, has never recognised an English journal in its midst The children of the second generation speak the language of Goethe I can take you to five thousand post offices, schools, and courts of justice in our state where Spanish, German, and Bohemian are exclusively used—in fact, the official language Galveston, with a population of fifty thousand, cannot muster a corporal's squad of Americans of English-speaking origin , the same can be said of all our great western cities The day of the English-speaking people here is gone, and it will never re dawn."

It would be interesting to compare this confident prediction of ten years ago with the present state of things in Texas. That there may be in various parts of the American Union communities which preserve their ancient language with the zeal of the Welsh or of the Scottish Highlanders may be true, but the only effect of this will be to increase the number of bi-lingual people in the United States. It is even possible that a nationality which has allowed its language to fall into disuse in its native land may regain its vigour and vitality by being transported to the United States The movement for reviving the use and the study of the ancient Irish language is much more vigorous in the United States than in Ireland itself Newspapers printed in Irish are produced, circulated and read in America to a much greater extent than any similar publications in Ireland The attempt to boycott the English language in some American schools has been carried to considerable lengths, but even in places like Milwaukee and other foreign settlements in the North West, it is found impossible to prevent the children learning English. They pick it up in the playground, and as English is, and is likely to remain, the *lingua franca* of the continent, the commercial advantages of acquiring the English tongue are far too great not to be appreciated by the shrewd citizens of the Republic.

What type will ultimately issue from this crucible of the nations it is yet too early to predict. Into the crucible all the nations have cast of their best, and it would be a sore disappointment if this vast experiment in nation-making did not yield a result commensurate with the immensity of the crucible and the richness of the material cast therein.

Richard Croker

PART II.

THE REST OF THE WORLD

Chapter I.—Europe.

IF we in England, who from the point of view of politics and religion are much more American than we are Anglican, contemplate with satisfaction and even with enthusiasm the Americanisation of the world, the process is naturally regarded with very different sentiments in other quarters Even Anglican Englishmen can hardly refrain from a certain feeling of national pride when they see all the nations of the earth subjected to the subtle and penetrating influence of ideas which are at least conveyed in English speech, and which may in some cases be traced back to the days of the English Commonwealth As Macaulay pointed out, even the Cavaliers themselves could hardly refrain from exulting at the thought of the pinnacle of greatness to which the armies of the Ironsides and the exploits of Blake and his captains raised the reputation of England in the days of Cromwell And so in like manner even those Anglican Englishman who find themselves reduced from a position of pre-eminence to that of a minority, swept irresistibly forward by the strong democratic currents which sway the English-speaking world, cannot altogether repress a sense of exultant pride that the men who have sprung from the loins of the Commonwealth should be so powerfully moulding the destinies of the world. The Anglicans are in the movement, they are not of it Nevertheless, after all, blood is thicker than water, and the men

> " Who speak the tongue that Shakespeare spake,
> The faith and morals hold which Milton held,"

can never be severed by difference of political allegiance from the common stock of our common race

No such consolation, however, is vouchsafed to the nations of Europe, who find themselves subjected, against their will and without their leave being asked or obtained, to the process of Americanisation That the process is beneficial, that they will be better for the treatment, may be true, but they do not see it. At the same time it is well to discriminate between Europe and the Europeans that therein do dwell To the majority of the Europeans the American invasion is by no means unwelcome, while a very large section would delight to see a much greater Americanisation of Europe than anything which is likely to take place.

It is otherwise with the sovereigns and nobles who represent feudalism and the old world monarchical and aristocratic ideas which have as their European centre the Courts of Berlin and Vienna In Europe, France and Switzerland are already republican Belgium, Holland, and the Scandinavian countries, while monarchical in form, are republican in essence. The Spanish Government may be regarded as a kind of annexe of the Hapsburgs, while the Italian monarchy is a southern buttress of the Austro-German Alliance Russia stands apart, a world in itself, perhaps the most democratic country in Europe, consisting as it does of one vast congeries of communes, which are little republics under the supreme direction of a central autocracy. The Emperor of Russia, however, the monarch of right divine, solemnly consecrated to be guide and governor of his people when crowned at the Kremlin, has, no doubt, many sympathies in common with the other sovereigns of Europe, but the Tsars of to-day do not aspire to fill the *rôle* of the Tsars at the beginning of the Nineteenth Century. In those days first-Alexander and then Nicholas believed that the defence of the monarchical principle was one of the most sacred of their duties—a conviction to which the Holy Alliance gave vigorous expression The Holy Alliance has long since passed away, leaving behind it as its chief result the Monroe doctrine, the promulgation of which was suggested by Canning to President Monroe as the most effective answer to the pretensions of the allied sovereigns of Central Europe.

The centre of resistance to American principles in Europe lies at Berlin, and the leader against and great protagonist of Americanisation is the Kaiser of Germany. There is something pathetic in the heroic pose of the German Emperor resisting the American flood It is Canute over again, but the Kaiser has not planted himself on the shore, passively to wait the rising of the tide in order to rebuke the flattery of his courtiers, he takes his stand where land and water meet, and with drawn sword defies the advancing tide. And all the while the water is percolating through the sand on which he is standing, undermining the very foundations

F

HIS FORESIGHT.

Europe.—"You're not the only rooster in South America."

Uncle Sam.—"I was aware of that when I cooped you up."

upon which his feet are planted, so that he himself is driven to Americanise, even when he is resisting Americanisation. There are no more Americanised cities in Europe than Hamburg and Berlin. They are American in the rapidity of their growth, American in their nervous energy, American in their quick appropriation of the facilities for rapid transport. Americans find themselves much more at home, notwithstanding the differences of language, in the feverish concentrated energy of the life of Hamburg and of Berlin than in the more staid and conservative cities of Liverpool and London. The German manufacturer, the German shipbuilder, the German engineer, are quick to seize and use the latest American machines. The American type-writer is supreme in Germany as in Britain, and what is much more important than this, the American farmer continues to raise bread and bacon in increasing quantities for the German breakfast table.

Nor is it only in material things that the substance of American manufactures enters into the fabric of modern Germany. The constant flow of German emigration to the United States of America has created a German-American, whose influence upon the relatives whom he left behind in the fatherland is somewhat analogous to the influence of the American-Irish upon the Irish in Ireland. The German-Americans, like the American-Irish, are passionately patriotic, with a dual patriotism. They are intensely Republican, the hyphenated American, as he is called, has shown a readiness to shed his blood and sacrifice himself in the service of his adopted country equal to that of any native born of the States. But at the same time his romantic devotion to the country from which he sprang is not impaired by his allegiance to the State in which he has found a home. But this intense and idealised devotion to a motherland is quite compatible, as the experience of the Irish shows, with an absolute indifference to and even positive dislike of the political system which, for the time being, afflicts the old folks at home. The German-American differentiates between the Fatherland and the Kaiser, and therein in the eyes of the Court commits unpardonable sin. To identify the Emperor with the Empire, to render it impossible for any German to think of Germany without at the same time doing homage to the German Emperor, is one of the preoccupations of William II.

But the German-Americans have escaped beyond the glamour of his personality. They are the men of Germany, but they are not the men of the Kaiser. Their influence on the German electorate is an American influence, which tells much more in the direction of the Social Democrats than of the Junker Party, who constitute the stern men-at-arms of the Prussian Monarchy. It would be an interesting study to investigate how far the Social Democratic movement in Germany is fed as by secret springs from across the Atlantic. The connection is not by any means so obvious as that which binds together the Irish-Americans and the Irish National League, but there is a constant movement of men and of ideas between the Social Democratic Party in Germany and the German electorate in the United States.

Against all these influences the Kaiser wages desperate but unavailing war. In resisting the Americanisation of Germany, his first aim has naturally been to prevent the Americanisation of the Germans who leave Germany. The ceaseless tide of emigration which sets westward from German shores flows for the most part to New York, the European gate of the American Continent. When once the German passes Bartholdi's statue of Liberty Enlightening the World, he is lost to the German Empire. He may remain a German for a generation or two, cherishing his language, cultivating the literature of his country, but in ten years his children have picked up English, and in fifty years nothing but the name and family tradition remain to connect them with the Fatherland. Their descendants are no more Germans than President Roosevelt is a Dutchman.

To arrest this process of the thorough Americanisation, appropriation, and from his point of view the absolute effacement of German citizens, the Emperor has sought to deflect the tide of German emigration to German colonies which he has acquired, and which he has subsidised regardless of expense in various parts of the world. But the German who has once made up his mind to turn his back upon the home of his race, is singularly impervious to the charms of Damaraland or the fascinations of German East Africa. The Kaiser can export officials where he pleases, but the tide of German emigration, like the wind, goeth where it listeth.

A despairing attempt is now being made to turn the tide of German emigration from North to South America. The German Colonial Party imagine that by creating great German colonies in Brazil, it may be possible to build up a greater Germany in the Southern Continent, where the German Empire may preserve intact from Americanism millions of German citizens. The experiment has not yet been abandoned, but South Americans say that the process of Americanisation is not less speedy in Brazil. The German shows the same readiness to adapt himself to his local environment and to acquire the language of his adopted country whether that environment is English or Portuguese. The only result which has so far attended the attempt to deflect German emigration to Brazil has been to give a sharper edge to the Monroe doctrine, and to strengthen the determination of the Government at Washington to build an American navy adequate to enforce the American veto upon European conquest in the Western hemisphere

Compelled to admit failure in his attempt to prevent the Americanisation of Germans outside Germany, the Emperor has redoubled his efforts in order to prevent the Americanisation of Europe. This has been a fixed idea with him ever since he came to the throne. On his first visit to the Tsar of Russia, he propounded to him his favourite thesis, and endeavoured to enlist the Tsar's support in the holy cause of anti-Americanism Nicholas II. listened with a sympathetic interest, which is natural to him in talking to all men, whether moujiks or Kaisers, but he did not see his way to fall in with his guest's idea

The Kaiser, behind his apparent impulsiveness, is tenacious in pursuing his objects. Foiled in his first essay to win over the Tsar to a great European combination to organise the Old World against the New, he did not on that account abandon his favourite project The duty of first publicly proclaiming in the hearing of the world the doctrine which the Kaiser had privately endeavoured to impress upon the Tsar fell upon Count Goluchowski, the Foreign Secretary of Austria-Hungary Addressing the Parliamentary Delegations in November, 1897, he pleaded strongly in favour of the adoption of a pacific policy in Europe if for no other reason than that the very existence of the European peoples depended upon their power to defend themselves, fighting shoulder to shoulder, against Transoceanic competition He foreshadowed the adoption of counteracting measures, which he declared must be prompt and thorough in order to protect the vital interests of the European nations. Count Goluchowski's alarming summons to the Old World excited considerable discussion, but led to no definite result for some years.

Meantime the Kaiser continued to look with grave misgiving upon the increasing dependency of his people upon American foodstuffs In the year 1900 the exports from the United States to Germany were larger than those of any other country, the figures being in round numbers, from the United States $243,000,000 , from Great Britain, $200,000,000 , from Russia, $171,000,000 , from Austria, $172,000,000 ; from South America, $115,000,000. In 1891 the United States were third on the list, but in ten years she had distanced all competitors, and was easily first Germany can no longer feed her own population with her own foodstuffs—a

fact which is of vital importance from the point of view of a possible war. In 1900 she had to import close upon 1,000,000 tons of wheat and 800,000 tons of rye The population of Germany stands now at about 60,000,000. Taking, therefore, the staples of life, wheat and rye alone, nine millions of Germans would starve unless the insufficient yield of German farms were supplemented by the importation of foodstuffs, which in the next twelve months it is estimated will entail an expenditure of $100,000,000 , or, in other words, all Germany would be without food for fifty-five days in the year but for imports from abroad.   This dependence upon the foreigner, especially upon American food, is very distasteful to the Kaiser Of the $1,438,000,000 worth of goods imported into Germany in the year 1900, $287,000,000 came from Great Britain, $243,000,000 from the United States, and $115,000,000 from South America So that very nearly one-half the total imports into Germany came either from the New World or from the British Empire The dependence of Germany for her daily bread on shipments from over-sea contributed greatly to strengthen the Kaiser's decision to double the German navy. "Our future," he declared, "lies upon the sea." The decision to double the strength of the German fighting fleet was significantly proclaimed in the ears of the world immediately after the three-fold defeat of British arms in South Africa had severely shaken our prestige That the new shipbuilding policy then announced by Germany was aimed against Great Britain was generally recognised abroad ; but when the German Emperor visited London shortly afterwards he had a very different explanation to give of the increase of the German fleet. So far from being a menace to Great Britain, he is said to have protested, he regarded every new ship added to the German navy as an addition to the fighting force of the British fleet. For, he argued, it was inevitable that the United States, sooner or later, would endeavour to grasp the supreme position on the sea at present held by Great Britain. When that day came Great Britain would find in the German Fleet her most potent ally. The nations of the Old World, representing culture and civilisation, would have to stand shoulder to shoulder in resisting the contemplated attack of the new barbarians of the Western World, who, swollen by prosperity and pride and unweighted by any of the responsibilities which enforce caution on other States, would inevitably come into collision sooner or later with the present Mistress of the Seas

Whatever may be said of this pretext, it was an ingenious piece of special pleading, and it helped him to gloss over the ugly significance of his naval programme. After the departure

PRESIDENT JAMES MONROE.
Originator of the Monroe Doctrine.

Mr. OLNEY.
Mr. Cleveland's Secretary of State.

PRESIDENT CLEVELAND.

EUROPE AND AMERICA COMPARED.

of the Kaiser from England little was heard of his anti-American views until last July, when M. Pierre de Segur was entertained by the Kaiser, along with other French tourists, on board the _Hohenzollern_ when it was in Norwegian waters. The interview seems to have been purely accidental M de Segur and his _compagnons de voyage_ were visiting one of the Norwegian fiords when they came across the Imperial yacht, _Hohenzollern._ The Emperor asked them to dine on board, and after marshalling his guests, as a Commander-in-Chief would marshal an Army Corps, with the voice and gestures of an officer on the parade-ground, he entered into animated conversation with them, in which he appears to have expressed himself with a degree of freedom unwonted even for him. His conversation with his French guests, wrote M de Segur in the _Revue de Paris,_ was chiefly about the United States of America He evinces but slight enthusiasm for that country To him there is a menace for the future in the colossal Trusts so dear to the Yankee millionaire, which tend to place an industry or an international exchange in the hands of a single individual or a group of individuals. "Suppose," he said, in substance, "that a Morgan succeeds in combining under his flag several of the oceanic lines He does not occupy any official position in his country outside of the influence derived from his wealth. It would, therefore, be impossible to treat with him if it should happen that an international incident or a foreign power were involved in his enterprise. And neither would it be possible to have recourse to the State, which having no part in the business could decline any responsibility. Then to whom could one turn? To obviate this danger the Kaiser foresees the necessity of forming a European Customs Union against the United States on similar lines to the Continental blockade devised by Napoleon against England, in order to safeguard the interests and assure the freedom of Continental commerce at the expense of America's development. And he declared to us without circumlocution that, in such an eventuality, England would be forced to choose the alternative of two absolutely opposite policies either to adhere to the blockade and place herself on the side of Europe against the United States, or else to join the latter against the Powers of the Continent."

So remarkable a declaration, even when published in a literary and political organ of the importance of the _Revue de Paris,_ was naturally received with scepticism, and the _New York Herald_ despatched a commissioner to Berlin to ascertain whether or not the German Govern-

ment was prepared to disclaim, contradict, or explain away the report of M. de Segur The American Ambassador in Germany, Dr. Von Helleben, professed confidence that the German Foreign Office could easily explain away the alleged utterances of the Kaiser, but when application was made to the Foreign Office, the officials could only say that the matter was one entirely personal to the Kaiser. A somewhat interesting interview seems to have taken place between the representative of the Foreign Office and the _Herald's_ commissioner, the latter naively remarking that the German official gave him the impression that he did not grasp the importance of public opinion in the United States, but did deem it important to lay down with some emphasis the right of Germany to interfere in South American affairs should occasion arise. Whenever any of the southern republics gave offence to Germany, said the Foreign Office official, that country would send her warships there to exact justice, and would insist upon her right so to act Being reminded that this was not the question under discussion, he answered that the reply would probably be forthcoming from higher quarters The answer came in the shape of an official communication by the German Ambassador on his return to Washington when he was authorised to declare that "All talk that his Majesty" (the Kaiser) "desires to bring the European nations together in a challenge of America's progress in the commercial world is without foundation. My sovereign," the Ambassador said, "has the most frank admiration for America's progress and the most cordial and friendly feelings for the United States. His Majesty has shown once more how he appreciates American skill and workmanship in having a yacht built in the United States" Nevertheless what M de Segur says coincides too much with what the Emperor is known to have proposed to the Tsar, and the general tenor of his conversation in this country, for us to have much reason to regard the French author's report as incorrect

The reference to Mr. Morgan and the consolidation of industries under the Trust system only indicates that the Emperor is keen to snatch at any and every development of American enterprise or American ambition in order to emphasise the reality of the American danger, to insist upon the necessity of concerted European action. When he was in London the talk was not of offering England the alternative to join in the European blockade of the United States, or to be herself subjected to the pains and penalties of a financial war. When he was here his talk was all about the probable attack by the United States upon the naval supremacy of Great Britain. But in his conversation upon the

Hohenzollern he appears to have harped back to the idea which he propounded in St. Petersburg, and which inspired Count Goluchowsky with the idea of taking counteracting measures to safeguard the vital interests of European industry. Since that time the Germans and Austrians have been busily engaged in discussing what measures they ought to adopt. That something should be done seems to be taken for granted. On the 23rd of October, 1901, the representatives of industry and agriculture in Austria held an important meeting, under the benediction of the Austrian Government, for the purpose of considering the most effective means of averting the danger of American competition in all branches of production. Dr Peetz declared that the United States were aiming at universal economic supremacy, that Austria-Hungary must, therefore, in all circumstances secure the home market for native industry and agriculture, while maintaining as far as possible the openings for export. After a good deal of vigorous oratory, in which American economic methods were somewhat severely denounced, a resolution was unanimously adopted which contained the following four specific recommendations — "(1.) That there should be a complete revision of the Austro-Hungarian Customs tariff on the lines laid down by Germany, in order to afford equal, effective, and permanent protection to industry and agriculture. (2.) That a reciprocity arrangement should be substituted for the general application of the most-favoured-nation clause in future commercial treaties. (3.) That while treaties for longer periods may be concluded with other countries when they afford adequate protection to native production and export trade, those with the United States and the Argentine Confederation should only be for short terms. (4.) That the Central European States should enter into an agreement for mutual protection against transoceanic competition."

Austria, it was declared by the semi-official *Fremdenblatt*, was the youngest and weakest of the industrial States, and as such suffered more from American competition than any of her neighbours. The watchword "America for the Americans" must be answered by the rallying cry "Europe for the Europeans," said the *Fremdenblatt*. "Africa and Asia constitute the European reserves, and we shall know how to defend ourselves, but we must set about it in time and make a beginning."

In Berlin the German Industrial Union have expressed through their Secretary, Dr Wilhelm Vendlandt, their views upon the subject. He declared that the time had come for some Bismarck to rise up and assemble the nations of Europe and throttle the American peril.

Europe, he argued, could perfectly well be independent of the American market. Russia, by developing her cotton plantations in the Caucasus, had finally liberated the Old World from dependence upon the New. "I believe," he declared, "in fighting America with the same weapons of exclusion which America herself has used so remorselessly and so successfully. We propose to work for an all European Union. The commercial interests of the hour are paramount, and a discriminatory alliance of all European Powers, including England, will be the inevitable result of the American invasion."

This is all very fine and large, but what does it come to? So far it has come to nothing. The self-sufficing State which produces everything within its own frontiers has become an anachronism in the modern world. Chinese walls of prohibitive tariffs are futile expedients. No doubt America will find that several of the nations of the Old World will follow her example and quote it as ample justification for an attempt to discriminate against American goods. Nothing can be done before 1903, when the commercial treaties will come up for revision, and before 1903 a good many things may happen. But although the Governments of the Old World may compel their subjects to pay high prices for goods which the Americans, if left unhindered, would supply more cheaply, they will thereby increase discontent and dissatisfaction, which will facilitate the Americanisation of Europe. For the higher the tariff, the dearer will be food. Dear food means misery in the home. Misery in the home means discontent in the electorate, and discontent in the electorate means the increase of the motive force which will seek steadily to revolutionise the Old World governments on what may be more or less accurately described as American principles.

Thus the action of the Kaiser and the Mrs Partingtons of Vienna is even more futile than the conduct of the wise men of Borrodaile, who built a wall across the mouth of their pass in the belief that they could thereby prevent the cuckoo flying away with the summer. Their policy exercised no influence upon the procession of the seasons. But the action of the anti-American pan-Europeans will directly accelerate the process which they wish to retard.

Reciprocity, said President McKinley, in the speech which he delivered on the day before he was assassinated, "reciprocity is the natural outcome of the wonderful industrial development of the United States under the policy now firmly established. If perchance some of our tariffs are no longer needed for revenue, or to encourage or protect our industries at home, why should they not be employed to extend

COUNT A. GOLUCHOWSKI.
AUSTRIAN FOREIGN MINISTER.

BARON D'ESTOURNELLES DE CONSTANT.

KAISER WILHELM II.

PRINCE HILKOFF,
RUSSIAN MINISTER OF RAILWAYS.

and promote our markets abroad?" Three days previously Mr Roosevelt, then Vice-President, speaking at Minneapolis, declared that through treaty or by direct legislation it may, at least in certain cases, become advantageous to supplement our present policy by a system of reciprocal benefit and obligation. Now there are only two kinds of reciprocity As the Reciprocity Commissioner-General Kasson remarked "there is no novelty in reciprocity The principle has prevailed in human relations since the beginning of intercourse among men. Between individuals and among nations it is an exchange of some right or privilege or favour in exchange for some right or privilege or favour which the other controls and is willing to grant in consideration. It has developed in two ways, reciprocity in favours, and reciprocity in burdens and prohibitions The former is accomplished in the form of mutual agreement in the form of treaties and the latter by legislative retaliation "

The remarkable thing about the present situation is that while the trend of opinion in the United States is in favour of the adoption of reciprocity in favours, the cry on the Continent of Europe is entirely in favour of reciprocity by burdens and prohibitions The chief safeguard which has hitherto protected the exporters of the United States from exclusive duties on the part of the European nations has been the existence of a series of commercial treaties containing the most favoured nation clause which expires in 1903. At that date the Austrians and the Germans, possibly the Italians, with such other of the European nations as they can induce to join them, intend to see what can be done in protecting their own industries by applying a European equivalent of the Dingley tariff to American goods. Under these circumstances it is evident that it will be somewhat difficult to carry out the policy recommended by Mr. McKinley. As President Roosevelt said, we must remember that in dealing with other nations, benefits must be given while benefits are sought, But if one side offers benefits while the other is seeking only to inflict injuries, negotiations are not likely to progress very rapidly.

There seems to be no doubt that the American invasion has somewhat scared Europeans, nor is the scare confined to Germany and Austria When Prince Albert of Belgium returned from his American trip in 1898 he was said to have exclaimed to an American friend "Alas! you Americans will eat us all up." Admiral Canevaro, formerly Italian Foreign Minister, speaking at Toulon last April, remarked that "the Triple and Dual Alliances taken together had given Europe thirty years of peace, and he added that this fact would perhaps lead the European nations to consider the possibility and the necessity of uniting against America, as the future of civilisation would require them to do "

There are few publicists so intelligent and so liberal as Mr. Paul Leroy-Beaulieu, but he is so far under the influence of the menace from the New World as to have declared himself specifically in favour of endeavouring to realise a European Zollverein. As Mr. Sydney Brooks pointed out in an interesting article upon America and Europe, which he contributed to the *Atlantic Monthly* for November, he would not abolish customs duties between the different States, but only reduce them considerably by clearly defined commercial treaties concluded for a long period. With few exceptions, he wrote, the maximum should be 12 per cent, and a permanent European Customs Union should be appointed with the task of providing for successive reductions of the duties, and of establishing the closest possible relations between the European nations. There can be no doubt, he declared, as to the possibility of such an arrangement. It is an ill wind that blows nobody any good, and it would be a welcome result of the present scare as to the American invasion if it were to force reluctant and jealous nations to take so long a stride in the direction of federation. To defend themselves against the United States of America these thinkers advocate the creation of what, from a fiscal point of view, would be the United States of Europe.

Chapter II.—The Ottoman Empire.

Three years ago, when I was in Constantinople, I excited considerable astonishment by declaring that nothing was more probable than that the United States might be driven to solve the hitherto insoluble problem of the ownership of Constantinople The facts were simple and the deduction obvious, but there is nothing that many people are so slow to recognise as the salient facts of a political situation To-day, thanks to the operation of a band of brigands on the Bulgarian frontier, the eyes of the public have been opened, and both in Europe and America the man in the street is talking of possibilities in the Ottoman Empire which then seemed to be outside the range of practical politics

The incident which has produced so sudden an awakening was the capture of Miss Stone, an American missionary On the 2nd of September, 1901, Miss Stone, when on her way from the little town of Bansko, in Bulgaria, to Djumaia in Turkey, crossed the frontier of Bulgaria into Macedonia, when she was waylaid by a band of brigands dressed in Turkish uniforms, with the red fez, and carried off into the mountains together with a Bulgarian lady who was one of the party. They were kept in captivity in order to extort a ransom of £25,000. The incident of an American lady being held prisoner in the Macedonian mountains created a great stir in the United States. Newspapers took it up, and subsequently a subscription was raised to provide the money demanded as a ransom. The machinery of diplomacy was set in motion, and Europe and America found themselves face to face with a question which, before it was settled, threatened to involve the United States in armed intervention in Turkey. In view of such a contingency people began to ask how Miss Stone found herself in such a position, and then the great Republic of the West for the first time began to realise the extent to which the American missions had advanced since 1858. Their first centre was Adrianople, which lies outside Macedonia. The mission has now three stations in Bulgaria The American church has 1500 members, they have churches also at Sofia, the Capital of Bulgaria, at Salonica and at Monastir. Altogether the Americans have nine missionaries in Bulgaria and Macedonia, and seven American lady teachers. In Northern Bulgaria the American Methodists have eleven American and native missionaries. In Bulgaria, the American Board of Missionaries have established three schools, for the higher education of both men and women, and one Kindergarten They have organised fifteen churches where services are held regularly, besides twelve places of worship, and about 1500 communicants The church at Bansko, from which Miss Stone started on the journey which ended so disastrously, has 150 members, and the building cost £1000 In 1872 the Americans translated the Bible into Bulgarian, they established a printing-press, book-stall, and a free public reading-room in Sofia, and they published a weekly newspaper. This propaganda of the Americans is not very popular among the Bulgarians, who are Greek Orthodox, but the theological propaganda is condoned on account of the excellent results from it.

The Russians, of course, dislike it even more than the Bulgarian Government, but here again the American element intervenes in an unexpected quarter. The Russian agent at Sofia, M. Bachmetieff, is married to an American wife, and Mme. Bachmetieff is a great personal friend of Miss Stone's, so that although from a high political point of view M Bachmetieff would be expected to oppose Miss Stone's actions, from a domestic point of view the influence of Mme.

Bachmetieff, exercised constantly at home, has made the Russian agent a very good friend and warm supporter of the American missionary. It is indeed difficult for any intelligent person not to sympathise with the excellent work which the American missionaries are doing in those regions, for the Americans have not only done the work themselves, they have stimulated the Bulgarian people to emulate their deeds, and to establish similar institutions. As Mr W. E. Curtis says in the admirable series of letters which he has contributed to the *Chicago Record-Herald*, they have laid the foundation of a general education system, they have inspired a temperance movement; and wherever their influence extends you will find a radical moral and social change from the conditions which existed when independence was proclaimed twenty-three years ago.

The most influential woman in Bulgaria, Mrs. W B. Kossuroth, was a pupil of Miss Stone's. She is the first woman who ventured to carry on business on her own account She was educated according to American ideas, and after the death of her husband, she took charge of the business he had left. Mrs Popoff, the wife of the pastor of the Protestant church at Sofia, was educated at an Ohio seminary. Hence it was not at all surprising that Miss Stone should have sallied forth at the head of a party of village students, among whom were three young Bulgarian women whom she was going to place in charge of schools in Macedonia. The brigands, who assumed Turkish costume to avoid suspicion, are declared to have been Bulgarian brigands, belonging to the Macedonian insurrectionary movement. They did not molest the women teachers, but they carried off both Miss Stone and Mrs. Tsilka, whom they held for ransom.

The immediate result of this outrage was that the attention of the Americans was aroused. Negotiations were at once begun, in which menaces and bribes alike failed to secure the immediate relief of the captives October and November were consumed in abortive attempts to secure the release of Miss Stone and her companion. At the beginning of December she was reported to have died in the hands of her captors. This rumour was contradicted, but up to the time of going to press Miss Stone was still in the hands of the brigands.

The incident naturally directed American public opinion to the state of the Balkan Peninsula. It familiarised the citizens of the United States with the permanent condition of the Turkish provinces, and it reminded the world of one of the worst crimes perpetrated by European diplomacy. The cry of the men of Macedonia, "Come over and help us!" met with no response from the British Government of 1878. The Russians had helped them. By the treaty of San Stefano the whole of what is known as "Big Bulgaria," from the Danube to the Ægean, was liberated from the blighting despotism of the Turks. At the Berlin Congress, at the instance of Britain and Austria, Macedonia was cut off from free Bulgaria and thrust back into slavery to enjoy the uncovenanted mercies of the Turk. Of all the crimes perpetrated at the Berlin Congress, this was the worst. A sop was given to the conscience of Europe by inserting Article 23 into the treaty of Berlin, to secure to the populations of Macedonia and other Balkan provinces the right of self-government. Unfortunately, as usually happens in such cases, the article remained a dead letter. The European Powers agreed what ought to be done, and even went so far as to draw up an organic constitution for the government of Macedonia, but nothing effective was done to carry out the provisions of the Treaty.

What the result of the capture of the American lady missionary will be it is impossible to predict. Miss Stone may be liberated before these pages see print, or, on the other hand, she may be sacrificed, owing to the alarm excited in the minds of her captors at being punished for their crime. In either case the Americans will be compelled sooner or later to take the matter up seriously. If the brigands get their money, the profit that they have made upon this transaction will encourage them to develop and extend the kidnapping business. More American missionaries will be caught, and held prisoners to be ransomed, and thus the American Government may be forced to take action. If, on the other hand, Miss Stone is killed, the Macedonian question will at once be raised—who can say with what consequences?

It is not necessary in this survey of the Americanisation of the World to speculate further upon the part which the citizens of the United States have played in the recent history of the Ottoman Empire. I described this at some length in the book which I wrote in 1899, entitled "The United States of Europe." I take the liberty, however, of reproducing here its salient passages.

Thirty years ago a couple of Americans, Christian men, with heads on their shoulders, settled in Turkey and set about teaching on American methods the rising youth of the East in an institution called the Robert College. They have never from that day to this had at their command a greater income than 30,000 dols. or 40,000 dols. a year. They have insisted that every student within their walls shall be thoroughly trained on the American principles,

MISS STONE.

which, since they were imported by the men of the *Mayflower,* have well-nigh made the tour of the world. That was their line, and they have stuck to it now for thirty years.

With what result? That American College is to-day the chief hope of the future of the millions who inhabit the Sultan's dominions. They have 200 students in the college to-day, but they have trained and sent out into the world thousands of bright, brainy young fellows, who have carried the leaven of the American town meeting into all provinces of the Ottoman Empire.

The one great thing done in the making of States in the last quarter of the century was the creation of the Bulgarian Principality. But the Bulgarian Principality, the resurrection of the Bulgarian nationality, although materially achieved by the sword of the liberating and avenging hordes of Russia, was due primarily to the Robert College. It was the Americans who sowed the seed. It was the men of Robert College who took into Bulgaria the glad news of a good time coming when Bulgaria would be free. And when the Russian Army of liberation returned home after the peace was signed it passed down the Bosphorus, and as each huge transport, crowded with the war-worn veterans of the Balkan battlefields, steamed past the picturesque Crag of Roumeli Hissar, on which the Robert College sits enthroned, the troops one and all did homage to the institution which had made Bulgaria possible, by cheering lustily and causing the military bands to play American airs. It was the tribute of the artificers in blood and iron to the architects on whose designs they had builded the Bulgarian State

But the influence of the American College did not stop there When the Constitutional Assembly met at Tirnova to frame the constitution for the new-born State, it was the Robert College graduates who succeeded in giving the new constitution its extreme democratic character, and when, after the Russians left, the Bulgarians began to do their own governing, it was again the American-trained men who displayed the spirit of independence which baffled and angered the Russian generals. From that time to now—when I visited Sofia one Robert College man was Prime Minister of Bulgaria and another was Bulgarian Minister at Constantinople, while a third, one of the ablest of them, was Bulgarian Minister at Athens—the Robert College has been a nursery for Bulgarian statesmen. So marked indeed has been the influence of this one institution, there are some who say that of all the results of the Crimean War nothing was of such permanent importance as the one fact that it attracted to Constantinople a plain American citizen from New York.

The influence of the United States in the East is by no means confined to Robert College. There are other institutions founded by Americans at Constantinople which are working quite as well as the Robert College ; but as they educate girls instead of boys, they will not make their political influence felt until the sons of the students come to man's estate. But it is not only in Constantinople Americans are at work. They are at the present moment almost the only people who are doing any good for humanity in Asiatic Turkey.

How many American citizens are aware, I wonder, that from the slopes of Mount Ararat all the way to the shores of the blue Ægean sea American missionaries have scattered broadcast over all the distressful land the seeds of American principles? The Russians know it, and regard the fact with anything but complacency When General Mossouloff, the director of the foreign faiths within the Russian Empire, visited Etchmiadzin, in the confines of Turkish Armenia, the Armenian patriarch spread before him a map of Asia Minor which was marked all over with American colleges, American churches, American schools and American missions. They are busy everywhere, begetting new life in these Asiatic races. They stick to their Bible and their spelling-book, but every year an increasing number of Armenians and other Orientals issue from the American schools familiar with the principles of the Declaration of Independence and the fundamental doctrines of the American constitution And so the leaven is spreading throughout the whole land.

Of course, such new wine could not be poured into the very old bottles of the Turkish provinces without making itself felt. The Armenians, a thrifty and studious race, soon became "swell-headed" What Bulgarians had done they thought Armenians could do As the Robert College men had created an independent Bulgaria, they, in turn, would show that they could create an independent Armenia So they set to work, but, alas' though they did their part of the work bravely enough, Russia, this time, was in no mood to come to their rescue So the Sultan fell upon them in his wrath and delivered them over to the Bashi-Bazouk and the Kurd What followed is written in letters of blood and fire across the recent history of the East.

But the end is not yet The American missionaries, who took no part in the abortive insurrection, were not as a rule much molested. They are working on, teaching, preaching, sowing the seed day by day, creating the forces which will in time overturn the Turkish Government and regenerate Armenia. The Turk knows it, and is longing for the time when he may have it out with the giaour from beyond the sea But behind the American missionary stands the British consul, and the Sultan fears to give the signal for extirpation. Long ago, when I was a boy, I remember being much impressed with a passage in Cobden's political writings, in which, after describing the desolation that prevailed in the Garden of the East owing to the blighting despotism of the Turks, he asked whether it would not be enormously for the benefit of the world in general, and of British trade in particular, if the whole of the region now blighted by the presence of the Turk could be handed over to an American syndicate or company of New England merchants, who would be entrusted with the administration of the country, with instructions to run it on business principles. "Who can doubt," said the great free-trader, "that if such an arrangement could be made, before long the desert would blossom as a rose? Great centres of busy industry would arise in territories that were at one time the granary and treasury of the world" This beatific vision of Manchester-dom has never ceased to haunt my memory. But until recent times, I have never seen how this excellent American syndicate was to get Turkey into its pocket Gradually, however, with the decay of Turkish authority, with the expansion of American ambitions and above all, with the development of the American fleet, Cobden's dream seems to me to be in a fair way of being realised.

It seems to me the most natural thing in the world that some fine day there will be one of those savage outbreaks of religious or imperial fanaticism which will lead some unhanged ruffian who has been decorated by the Sultan, or some Kurdish chief, to take it into his head to avenge the wrongs of Islam on the nearest American mission station He will sweep down at the head of his troops upon a school or manse. The building will be given to the flames, the American missionary will be flung into the burning building to perish in the fire, while his wife and daughters will be carried off to the harem of some pasha Nothing could be more natural or more in accordance with the ordinary practice in these savage regions. There is no available force to defend the American settlers from their assailants In these remote districts it is often possible to conceal a crime for months by the very completeness with which the victims have been extirpated. But, of course, after a time, whether it be weeks or whether it be months, the fate of that mission station would be known The story of the great massacre, when the missionary was burned alive in his own flaming school-house, would leak out, and then, in the natural course of things, some enterprising newspaper man would make his way to the scene of the outrage, would verify the facts, would ascertain the whereabouts of the unfortunate American women, and possibly return to the outside world bearing with him a pathetic and urgent appeal from the captives for rescue from a Turkish harem

This outrage, after all, is nothing more than the kind of thing to which the Christian races of the East have had to submit from generation to generation The victims have been as white, as Christian, and as wretched as those whose imaginary doom at the hands of the Turk or Kurd I have been describing. But in the latter case the girls, with their devoted mother, who may be subjected to the worst outrage at the hands of their captors, would differ from the Armenians in that they speak English That one difference would be vital On the day on which that smart newspaper man wrote out his story of the fate of those American women—wrote it out in vivid characters, bright and clear before the eyes of the whole English-speaking race—the doom of the Ottoman Empire would be sealed.

There are eighty millions of human beings in the United States, most of whom speak English, and each one of whom would feel that the imprisoned women were even as his own sisters On the day on which the news of their incarceration and outrage reached the Christian Republic of the West, the whole of the eighty millions who inhabit the invulnerable fortress which Nature has established between the fosses of the

Atlantic and the Pacific would start to their feet as one man, and from the whole continent would rise but one question and one imperative command. The question would be : Where is Dewey ? Where is Sampson ? Where are our invincible ironclads, which in two battles swept the flag of Spain from the seas ? Why are our great captains roosting round upon their battleships, while such horrors are inflicted upon women from America ? " And after that inquiry would come quick and sharp the imperious mandate " To the Dardanelles ! To the Dardanelles ! "

In three weeks the commanders who shattered the Spanish fleet at Manila, and drove the ironclads of Admiral Cervera in blazing ruin upon the coast of Cuba, would appear off the Dardanelles to exact instant and condign punishment for the outrage inflicted upon American women.

Nor would they stop at the Dardanelles The Stars and Stripes would soon fly over the waters of the Sea of Marmora, and the thunder of the American guns would sound the death-knell of the Ottoman dynasty No power on earth would be able to arrest the advance of the American ships, nor, indeed, is there any Power in Europe that would even attempt to do so The patience of Christendom has long been almost worn out, and Europe would probably maintain an expectant attitude while the death-blow was struck at the crumbling relics of the Ottoman Power

When the Sultan had fled from Stamboul, leaving his capital to the violence of the mob, the Americans, to save Constantinople from the fate of Alexandria, would be compelled to occupy the city of Constantine; and, as our experience has long shown, it is much easier to occupy than it is to evacuate Every day that the Stars and Stripes floated over the gates of the Euxine would tend to familiarise Europe with the idea that, of all possible solutions, the indefinite occupation of Constantinople by the Americans might be open to fewer objections than any other conceivable solution Thus, at any moment, owing to what may be regarded as a normal incident in the methods of Ottoman misrule, Cobden's dream might be fulfilled, and the great Republic of the West become the agent for restoring prosperity and peace to the desolated East.

To this vision of things to come I have little to add to-day. But I may remind English readers who know little or nothing concerning the extent to which the Americans have entered the missionary field that there are more communicants in connection with the churches founded by the American missionaries than there are in connection with the churches founded by missionaries sent out by the United Kingdom The Americans are behind us in the total amount of money raised every year, but they have more communicants and more native adherents and more Sunday-schools The figures extracted from the report of the Œcumenical Conference of Missionaries held in New York two or three years ago are very striking. They are as follows :—

STATISTICS OF AMERICAN AND ENGLISH SOCIETIES DIRECTLY ENGAGED IN CONDUCTING FOREIGN MISSIONS

	United States	United Kingdom
Number of Societies .	49	54
Income Total .	$5,403,045	$8,266,374
Ordained Missionaries	1352	1984
Physicians { Men . . .	160	205
{ Women	114	74
Lay Missionaries, not Physicians (Men) . .	109	765
Married Women, not Physicians .	1274	1148
Unmarried Women, not Physicians .	1006	1668
Total of Foreign Missionaries	4110	5937
Ordained Natives .	1575	1729
Unordained Native Workers .	15,013	29,779
Total of Native Helpers . .	16,605	31,740
Stations . . .	7321	15,576
Organised Churches . .	4107	5100
Communicants . .	421,597	326,979
Sunday Schools . .	7231	3817
Sunday School Membership .	344,385	213,935
Native Contributions	$628,717	$797,355
Native Christians, including Non-Communicants .	1,257,425	1,204,033

The missionaries of the English-speaking world exceed in number those of all the other Protestant nations put together. They can only be compared with those who are sent out by the Church of Rome. The parallel and contrast between the English-speaking race and the Church of Rome is of world-wide interest and very suggestive, for, to use Mr Gladstone's phrase, our race "may almost claim to constitute a kind of universal Church in politics."

On the continent of Africa the Americans have as yet hardly laid their hand. They have had their share in punitive expeditions against the Moslem on the north coast. They originated the colony of freed negroes on the west coast which subsequently developed into the Republic of Liberia An American consul in Egypt by sheer bluff secured for the United States a place among the Powers charged with the control of the International Tribunals. The Methodist Episcopalians of the United States have created the whole African continent into one vast bishopric and placed it under Bishop Hartzell Here and there all over the continent American missionaries are to be found labouring for the conversion of the heathen But the Americans are only pecking at Africa yet. Not

until Booker Washington and his like create an educated race of American blacks will the Americanisation of Africa really begin.

Chapter III.—Asia

THE Americans are changing so many of the currently accepted ideas of the other peoples, that an Englishman may be pardoned a certain degree of satisfaction when he finds that in one very important matter the Americans have adopted English ideas Until quite recently the Americans as a whole were under the influence of the ancient fallacy which dominated the mind of Mr Gladstone,—that the sea was still a divider and not a uniter of nations. A State across which you could walk from end to end, without any need of taking ship when passing from province to province, was held by them to be something altogether superior to a State whose highways were the oceans. The very existence of the British Empire was due to the fact that this doctrine was fallacious, but Mr. Gladstone to the end of his life never succeeded in emancipating himself from its influence. The Americans have only just begun to realise that they also may hope to adopt the proud boast of their British forefathers, and declare that the frontiers of the United States extend to the coastline of her enemies and rivals Once having abandoned their old position, they seem to be animated by the proverbial zeal of the new disciple , and from shrinking nervously from wetting their feet in the Gulf of Mexico, they have now boldly plunged across the wide Pacific, and have established themselves off the Asiatic coast.

Their advance across that ocean has been very rapid It began without any notion on the part of the American people of what was going to happen. The missionaries were, as usual the pioneers first of trade and then of political dominion. The process was uniform. The missionaries in the Sandwich Islands and Samoa laboured to teach the native population the blessings of Christianity ; then came the trader, who introduced them to the blessings of commerce, and after the trader came the administrator, who hoisted the Stars and Stripes, and conferred upon the islanders the blessings of being allowed to stand on the threshold of the American Constitution without being permitted to cross the portal.

Hawaii was annexed in 1898 Its first treaty with Samoa was made in 1872, when the port of Pago-Pago was acquired as a coaling-station for steamers trading between San Francisco and Australia. The treaty was not ratified until

1878 At the end of 1899 Great Britain retired from Samoa, which was left to be divided between Germany and the United States, and on the 17th April, 1900, the Stars and Stripes went up over the island of Tutulla. At Pearl Harbour in Hawaii, and Pago-Pago in Samoa, the Americans had planted sea-castles in the mid-Pacific, as bases for their advances upon Asia.

The event which converted the American Republic into an Asiatic Power was an unforeseen consequence of the war undertaken for the liberation of Cuba The necessity for destroying the Spanish fleet at Manila, which otherwise would have been free to prey upon the American shipping, placed the Americans in command of the greatest commercial city in South Eastern Asia at Manila. It is one of the invariable consequences of war that the passions excited by the combat arouse appetites which can only be satisfied by the annexation of conquered territory. Mr Roosevelt may have foreseen the annexation of the Philippines when, in 1897, as Assistant-Secretary of the Navy, he prepared in advance for the attack upon the Spanish fleet, but it is doubtful whether even he realised the avidity with which the]American people, elated by the easy victory of Admiral Dewey, would fling themselves upon their prey

"At any rate we have got the Philippines," exultantly exclaimed an American citizen in London.

"I beg your pardon," I replied, "it is not so"

"Do you mean to say we have not got the Philippines?" he asked

"Certainly," I answered "You have not got the Philippines; it is the Philippines who have got you."

And everything that has happened since then has justified the remark A naval action of a few hours destroyed the Spanish fleet, and laid Manila prostrate at the feet of her conquerors, but three years of intermittent warfare waged by land and sea have not yet induced the Filipinos to recognise the brotherly love and benevolent intentions of the invaders Aguinaldo has been captured, but the Philippines still require the maintenance of an American army almost as large as the number of white soldiers by which Britain maintains her sovereignty over the 300,000,000 natives of India Nor does there as yet seem any prospect of a material diminution of the burden

But American influence in the Philippines seems likely to be less important than the influence of the Philippines in the United States The acquisition of these tropical islands suddenly dazzled a large section of the American public

with visions of civilising sovereignty and beneficent dominion with which, in this country, we have long been familiar Dewey's victory started the United States upon a career of Asiatic conquest Whether she will persist in it or not remains to be seen but there is no doubt but that the annexation inoculated the United States with that feverish spirit of Imperialism which ministers subtly to the national pride, at the very moment that it offers a soothing salve to the national conscience

The discussion of this subject, however, would lead us away from the question of the Americanisation of the world, to that of the Philippinisation of the United States The necessity for justifying the conquest of the Philippines—a task imposed upon them as an unexpected corollary of a naval engagement—led some Americans to grasp greedily at all the arguments by which for many generations past the British Jingo has justified that war for markets which Sir Edward Clarke stigmatised as "murder for profit" At the same time, "The White Man's Burden," that swan song of the expiring genius of Mr Kipling, supplied an anodyne to the uneasy conscience of men who were keen to persuade themselves that, while apparently following in the footsteps of predatory Empires, they were in reality humbly accepting onerous duties imposed upon them as instruments of Divine Providence The boundless possibilities of the dominion of the Pacific, and the opening up of Asia, stimulated American oratory, and the glowing periods of the orator swelled the heads of his audience with radiant visions of a regenerated East resulting from the establishment of the benign sovereignty of the American Republic at the gate of Asia

After the annexation of the Philippines the cutting of the Isthmian Canal seemed to most Americans to be a foregone conclusion While contemplating the possibilities of the future, Senator Beveridge let himself go in opening the Republican campaign in Chicago on the 25th September, 1900, in the following characteristic outburst '—

' When an English ship, laden with English goods, bound for the Orient, sails westward, her first sight of land will be Porto Rico—and Cuba, also, as I hope—with the Stars and Stripes above them As it passes through the wedded waters of the Isthmian sea, still the Stars and Stripes above them. Half-way across that great American ocean, known as the Pacific, the first port of call and exchange will be the Islands of Hawaii, with the Stars and Stripes above them And further west, as the land of sunrise and sunset lifts before the eyes of the crew of that merchantman, they will behold glowing in the heavens of the east still again, and still forever,

A SKETCH MAP SHOWING POSSESSIONS OF GREAT BRITAIN AND THE UNITED STATES.

those Stars and Stripes of glory And if that ship sets sail from Australia for Japan, it must stop and trade in ports of that greatest commercial stronghold in the world, the Philippine Islands, with the Stars and Stripes above each one of them Lay a ruler on the world's map and you will find that the most convenient ocean highways to the markets of the Orient or to the markets of the south are dominated by American possessions—by Porto Rico, by the canal, by Hawaii, by the Philippines, ours now, and ours forever—aye, and, through the choice of her own people, by Cuba too, ours in the future, and when once ours, then ours forever, with the Stars and Stripes above them."

Having thus established themselves in the Philippines, it was necessary for the Americans to discover what immense use could be made of their new possession Senator Beveridge was careful to point out that they were next-door neighbour to all Asia they were nearer to India than St. Louis is to New York, to China than St. Louis is to San Francisco They were the stepping-stone to the most sought-for market in the world. There were 300,000,000 consumers in India, to which the Philippines gave us almost equal access with England herself To China, with her 400,000,000 consumers, the Philippines gave us quicker access than even Japan has to Australia, and all Oceana, to which again the Philippines give us easier access than England herself.

This pocket argument was reinforced by the customary appeal to the sacred obligations of duty to the unfortunate Filipinos. Again to quote Senator Beveridge :—

"When Circumstance has raised our flag above them, we dare not turn these misguided children over to destruction by themselves or spoliation by others, and then make answer when the God of nations requires them at our hands, "Am I my brother's keeper?""

And so it came to pass that the United States within a few months of having recoiled with horror from any suggestion of over-sea dominion, declared in the immortal words of Mr. Croker —

"I am in favour of holding on to all that we have got, and reaching out for more."

To us in the Old World the phenomenon is too familiar to excite more than a passing comment But when we hear the old familiar arguments pronounced with an American accent, it reminds us how much of the old Adam has survived in the New World.

The Americans having thus become, almost against their will at first, but afterwards by their deliberate choice, an Asiatic conquering Power, were compelled to confront and discuss international questions of the first magnitude, and, primarily, the one great question which con-fronts all in the East, namely, what should be their attitude in relation to Russia. The schism which tore the English-speaking world in twain had its advantages as well as its disadvantages, and one of those advantages was that it left the Republican section of the English-speaking world immune to the ravages of Russophobia. The Russians, the only European race equalling in numbers the English-speakers of the world, have always been in as friendly relations with the Americans as they have been at cross-purposes with the British When the American Republic, newly planted on Asiatic soil, had to reconsider its traditional policy in relation to Russia, it was a fateful moment in the history of the race. Tempters were not wanting to tell Mr McKinley and Mr Hay that they should modify their traditional policy in relation to Russia by taking up a position more or less akin to that of Great Britain The old saying about blood being thicker than water, which was first coined in the fight on the Peiho, seemed capable of a new application, and there were not wanting those who believed that an Anglo-American alliance with an anti-Russian objective was close at hand

Fortunately the world was saved from this disaster by the good sense of the Americans Mr. Hay seemed to waver for a moment, but finally he maintained his equilibrium, and the Americans adopted a policy in China which brought them into harmonious relations with all the Powers, without committing them to antagonism to Russia Equally with Great Britain America advocates the policy of the Open Door, demanding only a fair field and no favour in the international competition for the Chinese market But whenever British statesmen talk about "open doors" there is always the suggestion of menace directed against Russia The United States is more likely to keep the door open by adopting a different policy and by being equally ready to co-operate with Russia or with any other Power, so long as the main objects of their policy are identical with her own

The United States were fortunate in having, during the critical period when the fateful decision was taken, a Chinese Minister at Washington who had assimilated American ideas so perfectly that he became for the time being a veritable force in American politics In all America no one was more Americanised than Wu Whether he was driving his automobile about the streets of Washington, or lecturing in Chicago, or contributing to the *North American Review*, he showed himself thoroughly up-to-date and capable of employing all the resources of Western civilisation for the purpose of furthering the interests of the great empire of the East.

G

He assisted in forming a strong public sentiment in favour of the maintenance of the integrity of the Chinese Empire, and made a gallant and unsuccessful struggle against the race prejudice which led the Americans hermetically to seal their doors against Chinese immigration at the very time when they were insisting upon the maintenance of the open door in China. Although the United States adopted the sound policy of co-operating with Russia and the other Powers in maintaining the territorial integrity of the Chinese Empire, on condition that that great market was thrown open to all comers on equal terms, the growth of her trade in China led her to reconsider her refusal to accept a concession of land offered her some time ago by the Chinese Government at Tientsin. Since then the imports of America brought into Tientsin from America have exceeded those from Great Britain, and the imports of American petroleum have exceeded those from Russia. In view of the increase of trade the American minister, Mr Conger, has received instructions to ask the Chinese Government to grant a concession of land at Tientsin, where the American traders may establish an American municipality.

This, however, in no way implies that the United States contemplate any fishing in the troubled waters of "spheres of influence" and the like. They played their part in the defence of the Legations, and the American troops were among the best behaved of those despatched for the relief of the beleaguered residency in Pekin. One of the unfortunate consequences of the war was that it tended somewhat to discredit the American missionaries, who, if the testimony collected by Mark Twain may be accepted, showed tendencies in dealing with the Person Sitting in Darkness that savoured more of the severity of the Mosaic dispensation than of the sweet reasonableness and merciful forgiveness inculcated by the Founder of their creed. In this respect, however, the American missionaries resembled most of their cloth, whether Protestant or Catholic, and they share the responsibility of having contributed to the moral bankruptcy of Christendom in China.

One of the most remarkable instances of the exercise of American influence, the far-reaching consequences of which are absolutely incalculable is that of the awakening of Japan. One of the most striking achievements of the Nineteenth Century was the awakening of Japan. That awakening was largely due to the action of the American Government. Baron Kantero Kaneko, President of the America's Friends Society of Japan, in 1901 unveiled a monument to commemorate the fact on the forty-ninth anniversary of the arrival of Commodore

Perry, of the United States Navy, who was sent to Japan for the purpose of concluding a treaty of commerce and friendly intercourse between the two nations. Until that time Japan had been hermetically sealed to Western civilisation. Dutch and British envoys had in vain attempted to induce the Japanese Government to open the country to foreign trade, but it was not until 1853, when Commodore Perry arrived as the emissary of the Government of President Fillmore, that the Japanese were induced to abandon their policy of exclusion and embark upon that career of revolutionary reform which has carried them so far. Baron Kantero Kaneko, in the circular inviting subscriptions to the monument, said —

"True, Japan has not forgotten—nor will she ever forget—that next to her reigning and most beloved Sovereign whose high virtues and great wisdom are above all praise, she owes in no small degree her present prosperity to the United States of America in that the latter rendered her great and lasting service . After the lapse of these forty-eight years her people have, however, come to entertain but an uncertain memory of Kurihama, and yet it was there that Commodore Perry first trod on the soil of Japan, and for the first time awoke the country from a slumbrous seclusion of centuries—there it was where first gleamed the light that has ever since illumined Japan's way in her new career of progress."

A year after Perry's visit, in spite of the strong opposition of the Barons, and without waiting for the sanction of the Emperor, the Regency concluded a treaty of commerce which opened the ports of Japan to American trade. Similar conventions were afterwards signed with Russia, France, Holland, and England. It was not, however, until fourteen years later that this important step bore its final fruit in the revolution which has placed Japan in the forefront of the most progressive nations of the world.

In the period that intervened between 1854 and 1868 the American Government, together with England, Holland and France, bombarded Shimonoseki. After the town was destroyed, an indemnity of £750,000 was exacted from Japan and divided among the Powers. The United States Congress, many years afterwards, authorised the President to return to Japan the sum of £137,000 which was in excess of the expenditure actually incurred. This is an almost unique instance, possibly quite unique, in which any civilised Government having exacted an indemnity in excess of damage done, made restitution of the surplus. If all the civilised Powers had been equally honest in their dealings with Asiatic races, much bloodshed might have been avoided.

The influence of America upon Japan has not, however, always been an influence for good. The career of Mr. Hoshi Toru, who was assassinated in 1901, showed that the vices as well as the virtues are exportable from the United States. Mr Hoshi Toru was a man of undoubted ability, who, during his sojourn in Washington, where he was attached to the Japanese Legation, was much impressed by the power and wealth which the Boss system of American politics placed at the disposal of the Boss. He went back to Japan, and in no long time had established himself as the Croker of the Japanese capital. His power was so firmly established that the Reformer, Iba Sotaro, despairing of ridding Japan of this American importation in any other way, slew Hoshi Toru in full light of day, and then surrendered himself to the authorities. Whether Bossism will revive in a land where the assassination of the Boss ranks as an act of patriotism, remains to be seen.

The kingdom of Corea is another field which offers promising openings to the American capitalist and the American adventurer. Already the concessionaire is busy, and sooner or later we shall find American influence potent and possibly supreme in the Hermit kingdom. The American trolly has already invaded the capital, and with the trolly come many other American notions which are likely to have considerable influence in deciding the future of the country that has been so long a bone of contention between Japan and Russia.

American influence in the rest of Asia until quite recently has been chiefly confined to the teaching of American missionaries. They have taken an honourable and useful part in the presentation of the doctrines of the Christian religion to the myriads of Burma and India. Every British missionary is regarded more or less as representing the Government which he obeys. The Americans, who do not labour under this disadvantage, often find it easier on this account to win the confidence of the people among whom they labour. In consequence of this detached position, they are able sometimes to affect more directly the action of the Government than the British missionaries.

The most notable illustration of this was afforded by the immense service which was rendered to the cause of morality and humanity by the action of two American ladies, Dr Kate Bushnell and Mrs Elizabeth Andrews, who succeeded in bringing to light the existence of a deliberate attempt on the part of the military authorities of India to set the decisions of the House of Commons at defiance in the matter of the official regulation and patronage of vice. There are few things finer in the recent annals of India than the way in which these two women, alone and single-handed, penetrated into cantonment after cantonment, ascertained the existence

of the terrible facts which officialdom, civil and military, insolently denied, and then, with all their evidence complete, came to London to challenge the authorities, and put them to open and humiliating confusion. Lord Roberts to this day has not forgotten the bitter moment when he had to confess that as Commander-in-Chief he had been in utter ignorance of facts the existence of which he had denied. To have extorted a public apology from Lord Roberts, to have convicted the whole of Anglo-Indian officialdom of deceiving the world in order to evade the deliberate decision of the House of Commons, is an achievement which rarely falls to the lot of mortal men, and still more rarely to that of mortal women.

As to what might be the net effect upon India if America and Britain amalgamated their forces, and bore "The White Man's Burden" in Asia between them, it is as yet premature to speculate. At present, however, it is worth noting that the Viceroy of India, Lord Curzon, who governs the country in the name of the King, has as partner and helpmate an American wife. Love, which laughs at locksmiths, makes also short cuts through political barriers, and it may be that in the marriage which made a Chicago girl Vice-Empress of India we see a foreshadowing of things to come, when Britain and America, happily united in the permanent ties of a Race Alliance, may pool their resources and devote their united energies to the work of the amelioration of the lot of the impoverished myriads of Asia.

CHAPTER IV.—CENTRAL AND SOUTH AMERICA.

It sounds somewhat of a paradox, but it conveys a notable truth, that there are few parts of the world which have been less Americanised than Southern America. As I have already stated, the United States does less business with the entire population of Central and Southern America that it does with the 5,000,000 or 6,000,000 people who occupy the long belt of territory running along the Northern frontier. The influence of New York and Chicago is much more felt in London and in Liverpool than it is in Santiago and Buenos Ayres. The fact is that the whole of our geographical notions of space are very much out of date. If distances were calculated not by miles, but by the number of hours or days it takes to traverse them, we should have a much more correct view of the comparative propinquity of places. According to maps, the United States, lying in the same continent as South America, is geographically a nearer neighbour than the United Kingdom. But, if

G 2

PRESIDENT DIAZ OF MEXICO.

BOLIVAR, THE FOUNDER OF BOLIVIA

CENTRAL AMERICA AND THE RIVAL CANALS

any one in the United States wants to reach South America, he will find it a saving of time to cross the Atlantic and start from London.

While the Americans are Americanising England, the English have been for years past busily engaged in Anglicising South America, the Monroe doctrine notwithstanding. As we need to modify our ideas of distance, so it would be well to rid our minds of a good many delusions that are based upon the old superstition that political considerations dominate everything. Political considerations sometimes dominate very little. Religion, literature, trade, have often much more influence than a mere political tie. Take the case of South America, for instance. We have largely Anglicised it from the point of view of commerce, but the people of that continent are much more subject to the Pope of Rome than to Great Britain. Of the outside influences which affect the daily lives of sixty millions of Central and Southern Americans, the Vatican comes first, the English Stock Exchange second, while the United States of America comes in a very bad third. All this may be changed, and the citizens of the United States have made up their minds that it must be changed, and that right speedily; but at present they have placed too much reliance upon a purely negative influence exerted exclusively in the political sphere.

The Monroe doctrine, for instance, by which Uncle Sam may be said to have cast his shoe over the whole of the territory lying south of the Rio Grande, is purely negative. It simply says to all European States, "Thou shalt not annex any fresh territory in the New World." But there it stops. Now a merely negative interdict such as this, so far from exercising influence on South America, is apt to operate in the exactly opposite direction. It is a guarantee, to all the half-bred Republics lying between the North of Mexico and the Straits of Tierra del Fuego, against all danger of annexation from European Powers —that is to say, it removes the pressure of the fear which might have driven them to put their house in order, to introduce the methods of civilisation, and ingratiate themselves with the United States so as to secure the support of the Government at Washington in case of any meditated conquest by any of the Great Powers. The Monroe doctrine annuls this dread. Each Republic feels that it can do as it pleases, that it need take no heed of the wishes of the United States, and that it is under no necessity to provide itself with the appliances of civilisation. We have had considerable experience in the Old World of the mischief which is wrought by

this kind of guarantee. It is true that there is no such hideous negation of God erected into a system to be found either in Central or Southern America as there is in the Ottoman Empire; but there is no denying that, with the exception of Chile and the Argentine, most of the South American Governments leave much to be desired.

PRESIDENT CASTRO OF VENEZUELA.

President Roosevelt sees this clearly enough, and one of the declared objects of the new administration is to establish a direct commercial alliance, with steamers which will place the American ports in direct communication with the seaports of South America. Until this is done the American commercial invasion of South America can hardly be said to have begun. At present the Argentine Republic, Chili, and Peru are commercial annexes of Great Britain. There is no reason to suppose that the advent of the United States will lead to our banishment from provinces which the enterprise of our merchants have made our own with little help from armies or diplomacy. It is forgotten that at the beginning of the century we seized both Monte Video and Buenos Ayres, and if our generals had been men of ordinary capacity it is possible there might have been a British Empire at the extreme south of the American continent to balance the Canadian Dominion at the extreme north. That time, however, has gone by, and since then we have neither attempted to annex South American territory nor seriously to colonise the vast and fertile territory of South America. What we have done has been to lend them money and to invest money, millions of money, in the construction of their railways and tramways, and in ranche companies and mines.

In the Argentine Republic, as Mr. Shaw-Lefevre has recently reminded us: All the railways in the country are practically owned by British capitalists and managed by English companies. The same is generally true of tramways, telephone, and electric lighting companies. The principal banks, and loan and trust companies, and very many industrial concerns are worked with British capital and managed by Englishmen and Scotchmen. In Buenos Ayres alone there are 160 miles of tramways under ten different companies, all of which are financed from England. The railway companies under British management can raise money at 4 per cent., while the Government of the Argentine has to pay six. There is an English colony of 25,000 persons in Buenos Ayres, and a great many are scattered all over the country. Mr. Shaw-Lefevre says that it is estimated that nearly £250,000,000 of English capital is invested in the country.

Although we have a colony of 25,000 in the Argentine, the French, who are usually said to be not a colonising nation, are credited with twice the number, and they are at least equalled by the German settlers. But although the Russian Stundists and other nationalities have helped to swell the foreign element in the Argentine, the great majority of the European settlers are Italians. They find the climate agreeable, and they are at home in a land whose population is Latin in its origin and Catholic in its religion. In Chili the British capitalist is as much in evidence as in the Argentine. Sir Howard Vincent, who travelled through South America in 1897, reported that the greater enterprises were almost entirely in British hands ; the principal railways, the ports, the large estates, the main factories. In Valparaiso the greatest mercantile houses are

British ; nearly half the shipping is British. The Chilians, he declared, are the British of the Pacific. The British colonists, largely of Scotch origin, have become naturalised Chilians, and take a leading part in the government of the Republic. In Peru half the shipping arriving at Callao is British, and the Chilians come next, whose officers are nearly all British. The Peruvian Corporation, which took over £50,000,000 of the Peruvian foreign debt, and also ten State railways, are all British.

How vast and fertile are the territories which South America offers to the over-crowded populations of Europe is very imperfectly appreciated in the United States. Geographers maintain that there is more good fertile soil available for colonisation in South America than in any other Continent. The proportion of barren wilderness is smaller there than elsewhere, and the population per square mile is infinitesimal. The whole Continent at present has not the population of the German Empire. Yet the whole of the German Empire might be stowed away out of sight in a corner of Brazil.

The following figures concerning South and Central America are quoted from a very useful pamphlet compiled by Mr. Sanson, of the *South American Journal*, entitled "South America as a Field for Emigrants" : —

Name of Country.	Area in Square Miles.	Population Last Census.	Inhabitants per Square Mile.	Latest Trade Returns.		Trade per head of Population.	
				Imports.	Exports.	Imp.	Exp.
	No.	No.		£	£	£	£
SOUTH AMERICA.							
Brazil	3,218,082	16,000,000	5·3	21,567,000	26,752,200	1· 3	1· 6
Argentine Republic	1,125,086	4,090,000	3·6	21,485,780	26,765,891	5· 2	6· 4
Chili . . .	293,970	3,350,000	11·4	11,875,000	11,955,000	3· 6	3· 6
Uruguay . . .	72,150	840,700	11·5	5,576,000	6,728,200	6· 6	8· 0
Paraguay . . .	98,000	600,000	6· 1	72,500	69,400	0·12	0·11
Bolivia . . .	567,200	2,330,330	4· 1	3,670,050	3,012,563	1· 5	1· 3
Peru	503,000	4,000,000	7·9	1,929,727	3,027,477	0· 5	0·70
Ecuador . . .	120,000	1,270,000	10·5	1,394,578	2,250,000	1· 1	1· 8
Columbia . . .	573,900	4,000,000	6·9	2,500,000	2,670,000	6· 0	0·60
Venezuela . . .	593,940	2,323,500	3·9	2,300,400	3,510,519	1·00	1·07
CENTRAL AMERICA.							
Guatemala . . .	46,800	1,535,000	33·1	776,133	1,098,390	0·50	0·60
Costa Rica . . .	37,000	268,000	7·2	917,223	1,012,102	3· 3	3· 8
Salvador . . .	7,225	803,534	114·7	270,000	1,080,000	0·38	1· 4
Honduras . . .	43,000	398,900	9·2	274,661	256,685	0·70	0·60
Nicaragua . . .	49,500	420,000	8·6	573,236	636,710	1· 4	1· 5
Mexico . . .	767,005	12,619,954	16·4	9,121,810	13,571,513	0·72	1· 1
	8,215,858	74,848,964		£84,323,088	£104,741,840		

'From the above it will be seen that the countries of Latin America occupy an area of 8,215,858 square miles, or about 2 3r times the area of the whole of Europe, but have a total population of less than double that of the United Kingdom. A still closer idea of the relative sizes of the countries may be formed when it is known that Brazil alone is nearly equal in area to Europe, or, taking the area of Great Britain at 88,600 square miles and the population at 40,000,000, Brazil has about 361½ times this area, but only two-fifths of the population. The Argentine Republic is 12·6 times the area of Great Britain, but has only about a tenth of the population.

The Americans of the United States have heretofore done little or nothing to develope this vast Continent. They do less trade with South and Central America than they do with the five millions of Canadians on their northern border. They have not established as yet a single line of steamships between the United States and South America. Britain has invested 500 millions sterling in South America. Every week British steamships leave for South American ports. Commercially, we have annexed the Continent. But as Disraeli said there is room in Asia for both Russia and England, so we may say there is room in South America for both John Bull and Uncle Sam.

We have considerable interest in other parts of South America, but it is in these three States, the Argentine, Peru, Chili, that our commercial ascendency has until recently been unchallenged. Of late we have been losing ground. The Germans are pressing us hard, and Mr. Shaw-Lefevre warns us only this year that unless Englishmen are prepared to work more and play less, they will see themselves supplanted by their more industrious competitors. Notwithstanding all the many hundreds of millions of British capital invested in South America, there has been no attempt to base upon these investments a claim to political influence, much less ascendency. The only Briton of eminence who has ever expressed a wish to alter this was Mr. Cecil Rhodes, who told me years ago when the Argentine made default, that if he had been Foreign Minister he would have occupied the Argentine and held it as we hold Egypt, as a guarantee for the payment of interest on Argentine securities. The fact that this would have brought about an immediate collision with the United States being pointed out to him, he at once answered that the right thing to do was for England and America to have done it together, after the fashion of the Anglo-French condominium in Egypt before 1880. Mr. Rhodes at that time was not so conspicuous a personage in British politics as he became after he was

made a Privy Councillor, and he has of late had a good many other things to think of beyond dreaming of South American adventures. Mr. Rhodes, to do him justice, never wavered from the idea of a race alliance, and the promotion in all continents and in both hemispheres of the ascendency of the English-speaking man. However injudicious his suggestion may have been about the Argentine, it could at least be excused on the ground of his race-patriotism.

But this excuse cannot be alleged for another eminent Briton, the King's brother-in-law, the Duke of Argyll to wit, who some years ago actually published in German a fervent appeal to the German Empire to seize, occupy, and administer the Argentine Republic! The Duke of Argyll (he was then the Marquis of Lorne), writing in the *Deutsche Revue* for September, 1891, pointed out to the Germans that the German Empire was quite capable of acquiring fame and advantage by its warlike or diplomatic conquests. He pointed out what they were already painfully conscious of—that Germans ceased to be Germans when they went abroad.

"Now," said he, "there is a country, the one country in which there is nothing but men to despise, where a new throne is to be mounted. There is a country whose welfare depends on a foreign Power preventing them from knocking off each other's heads every few years—a country with a beautiful capital, a splendid harbour, a good soil, in which everything is excellent, except the government. This country, which only requires a European protectorate to bring into it the long desired order and to make it an El Dorado, is Argentina. Here German rule established in the form of a protectorate, or in any other form, would be welcome, because it would be capable of helping the country out of its distress."

And, lest the Germans should not be sufficiently tempted by the glowing picture which he painted of the Empire which they could win with their good swords, in the South of America, he warned them that one day another Power will come and do what must one time be done there, "and then the German at home will be angry, but he will be too late."

And the man who thus writes was at one time Governor-General of Canada, the representative of the British Empire in North America. But the Monroe Doctrine and the certainty that if Germany had responded to his appeal she would have been involved in war with the United States, never seemed to have crossed his mind, so oblivious are even clever men of the governing factors in a situation upon which they venture to proffer glib advice.

The Germans, it must be admitted, have shown little inclination to respond to the suggestions of the tempter. It is not upon Argentina, but further north, that the Germans at present have fastened their eyes. Great efforts have been made for several years past to deflect

German emigration from North America and
Australia to Brazil German Colonists have
settled themselves in communities in which
nothing but German is spoken, and which are
looked upon in Berlin as the possible germ of a
great South American German Empire. It is
easy to see that if they increase and grow
powerful, these German-Brazilian communities
by their superior culture and discipline may be
in a position to intervene effectually in deciding
the destinies of that vast half continent which,
despite all its fertility, is not one quarter
peopled

Colonel C P. Bryan, United States Minister
at Brazil, declared on his return to the United
States in October, 1901, that he had utterly
failed to discover any disposition on the part
of the Germans or Italians to pursue their
nationalist aspirations in Brazil. In Southern
Brazil he estimates the German population at
present at about a quarter of a million in
number. Many of them have become Brazilian
citizens, and are as much Brazilianised as
German emigrants in the United States are
Americanised. Very few Germans of late years
have been settling in Brazil. In 1898 the
Italians sent 33,000, the Portuguese 11,000, the
Spaniards 6000 emigrants to Brazil, while the
Germans sent not 500.

The Americans are well aware of German
aspirations in the direction of Brazil, and plain
and unmistakable warnings have been uttered
from time to time in what may be described as
the semi-official press of the United States that
any attempt on the part of the German Empire
to establish either a German protectorate or a
German colony under the German flag in any
part of the South American Continent will be
regarded as a *casus belli*

In Central America, the only vital interest
for the United States is found in the fact that
across the isthmus lies the shortest road between
the Atlantic and the Pacific.

American public opinion appears to have
decided in favour of severing the Isthmus which
unites the two Americas. The question as to
whether to make the Isthmus through Nicaragua
or through Panama appears to have been
decided in favour of the longer route. Uncle
Sam has got money to burn, and the digging of
a canal 183 miles in length through a difficult
country at a cost of something under
£38,000,000 sterling may not be good business
from the point of view of dividends, but it is a
much more sensible occupation than that in
which nations frequently engage for the expenditure of their surpluses. It is not for us who
have thrown away £200,000,000 sterling in
order to render South Africa permanently more
difficult to hold than it would have been if we

had never fired a shot, to carp at an expenditure of under £40,000,000 which will incidentally
and among other effects have the result of bringing Melbourne nearer to New York than it is
to Liverpool.   .

It is not necessary here to enter into parti-
culars as to the merits of the rival routes. The
Commission appointed to inquire into the
matter reported that as they could not buy out
the French interests in Panama for less than
£20,000,000, the total cost of the Panama
route would be between £12,000,000 and
£13,000,000 more than the Nicaragua route
If the Americans are prepared to sink
£40,000,000 in constructing a 35 feet deep
waterway across 183 miles of Central American
territory, and are further willing to build fifteen
miles of breakwater and dredge out the sea to
that distance, they will make us all their debtors,
but it is extremely improbable that they will ever
reap any adequate financial return, and as for
the advantages of the canal from a naval point
of view, the less said the better British naval
authorities, at any rate, are tolerably unanimous
in believing that any admiral who would venture
in war time to risk any valuable vessel, let alone
a fleet, in the passage of such a canal as that of
Nicaragua would deserve to be court-martialled

The moment the United States decide to cut
the canal, they must first of all negotiate for a ten
mile strip across the territory of Nicaragua and
Costa Rica so as to give them absolute control
of five miles on either side of the waterway.
Then the American naval authorities are insisting that it will be absolutely necessary to
occupy three or four naval stations, from which
their fleet could defend the safety of the canal.
The maintenance of these coaling stations ought
to be debited to the working expenses of the
canal. The existence of the canal would probably
precipitate the conclusion of the negotiations
which are pending for the purchase of the
Danish West Indies, while other stations would
be occupied in Almirante Bay in Colombia, in
the Gulf of Dulce in Costa Rica, and one of the
Galapagos Islands which are off the coast of and
belonging to Ecuador. From a financial point
of view, the investment of £50,000,000, because
such enterprises always cost much more than
the estimates, is endangered first by the possibility that some one may construct the Panama
Canal, and so offer a short route from sea to
sea, less than one-fourth of the distance This
probability is, however, very remote If the
Panama Canal has never been cut when its
constructors could count upon a monopoly no
one is likely to sink money in it when it would
have to compete with the American Canal
through Nicaragua. Much more serious than
the more or less shadowy danger of the Panama

THE UNITED STATES
OF SOUTH AMERICA.

Journal.] *[Minneapolis.*

A UNITED STATES INSTEAD OF A STATE
OF DISCORD.

THE AMERICAN EAGLE.—"What you folks want is to get
together and have an uncle of your own."

North American.] *[Philadelphia.*

JOHN BULL.—"I quit; you dig."

New York Herald.] THE AMERICAN INVASION.

Canal is the prospect that the Tehuantepec Railway will carry the biggest ships from sea to sea considerably cheaper and much more rapidly. The construction of the Tehuantepec railway is in the hands of a British contractor and it is expected that it will be completed at a cost of five millions—years before the Americans get half way through with their Nicaragua Canal. To cut the canal it will require two years' preliminary work, and six years' hard digging. The Americans will be very lucky if the first ship works its way through all the locks on the Nicaragua route ten years from to-day, whereas the Tehuantepec line will be ready in two years. Sir Weetman Pearson has a lease of fifty years, so if this forecast be correct British enterprise has been doing precisely what Canning boasted to have done when he propounded the Monroe Doctrine, and established British interests in Central America without in any way violating American susceptibilities.

The revolutionary disturbances which compelled the United States to land marines for the purpose of securing the Panama Railway from interruption were an unpleasant reminder of the contingencies which must be faced by those who go a-riding and a-sailing through Central American Republics. Once the canal is made there is little doubt that the whole of the ten miles' strip will become part and parcel of the territory of the United States and will form a base from which the authority of Uncle Sam will be extended both east and west and north and south until the control, if not the actual annexation, of Nicaragua and Costa Rica would be complete.

CHAPTER V.—THE MONROE DOCTRINE.

WHAT is the Monroe doctrine? The best answer is to be found in quoting the words which President Monroe used in his message.

"We owe it, therefore, to candour and to the amicable relations existing between the United States and those (European) powers to declare that we should consider any attempt on their part to extend their system to any portion of this hemisphere as dangerous to our peace and safety."

He added that such a procedure would be viewed as "the manifestation of an unfriendly disposition to the United States," and that it would not be looked upon with indifference by them.

The doctrine was first suggested to President Monroe by Mr. Canning. Canning himself would have been considerably astonished had he seen the result of his suggestion. He said that he regarded his recognition of the Republics of Mexico and Columbia as an act which would make a change in the face of the world, almost as great as that of the discovery of the continent now set free. He went on to say —

"The Yankees will shout in triumph, but it is they who lose most by our decision. The great danger of the time, a danger which the policy of the European system would have fostered, was a division of the world into European and American, Republican and Monarchical, a league of wandering Governments on the one hand, and developing and stirring nations with the United States at their head on the other. We slip in between, and plant ourselves in Mexico. The United States have gotten the start of us in vain, and they link once more America to Europe."

This linking of America to Europe was the one thing which the Monroe doctrine is, now invoked in order to render impossible.

The Monroe Doctrine primarily concerned South and Central America. Its original justification was a desire on the part of the Republican Government of the United States to exclude from the New World the despotic system that prevails on the continent of Europe. Hence its avowed motive when it was promulgated was anti-monarchical rather than anti-European. It originated with Canning, and was prompted by a horror of the Holy Alliance, which was regarded both in England and America as a conspiracy of despots against human liberty. If Canning and Monroe, who may be regarded as the joint authors of the doctrine in its first promulgation, had been cross-examined as to their motives, they would have ridiculed the idea that the new policy had any other motive than that of securing the New World for free Governments and of confining despotism to the Eastern hemisphere. But in the formulation of the doctrine they were not careful to distinguish between a despotic and a monarchical Power, and they used the word European as a synonym for monarchical despotism. In that sense the Monroe Doctrine was proclaimed, and in that sense it was always interpreted down to the time of its great revival six years ago, at the time of the Venezuelan dispute. Then the Americans, ignoring the original objective of the doctrine, used it in order to protest against an extension of British dominions in South America. The British Empire was a European Monarchy, and therefore technically came under the ban of the Monroe Doctrine. Yet not even Mr Cleveland nor Mr Olney would have ventured seriously to assert that a British colony was less free or less progressive than the half-breed Republic of Venezuela or the dictatorial Republic of Mexico. What Mr.

W. D. Howells said on the subject would have been admitted by all educated Americans, namely, that the constitutional monarchies of England, Scandinavia and Italy were in essence Republican, although they still retained their monarchical trappings. It was, therefore, a distinct abuse of the spirit of the doctrine by using its letter for the purpose of forbidding an extension of a British colony at the expense of a nominal Republic. This, however, is a purely academical point, because there is no desire on the part of any Englishman to annex any portion of South or Central America. Indeed there is reason to believe that we are at the present moment in negotiation for the transfer of our jurisdiction over the Mosquito Indian to the Republic of Nicaragua. But it is well to raise this point, in order to show the process by which the Monroe Doctrine attained its present development. The original motive has disappeared. It is not in order to secure the Western hemisphere for free institutions that the doctrine is maintained. It is in order to exclude European States as European States, whether they be constitutional or monarchical. The nature of their Governments has nothing to do with it, and a formula originally invented to put limits upon the spread of despotism, is now invoked in the first place as a measure of self-protection for the United States of America, in the second, in order to exclude Europe from America. This may be right, or it may be wrong. It is not the original doctrine.

President Roosevelt's inaugural message supplied the world with a clear, explicit and authoritative exposition of what the Americans mean when they speak of the Monroe doctrine. The passage is so important that it is well to quote it in full.

"This doctrine should be the cardinal feature of the foreign policy of all nations of the two Americas. It is in no wise intended to be hostile to any nation of the Old World, and still less is it intended to give cover to any aggression by one of the New World at the expense of another. It is simply a long step towards assuring the universal peace of the world by securing the possibility of permanent peace in this hemisphere. During the century other influences have established a permanence of independence among the smaller States of Europe, through a doctrine, and we hope to be able to safeguard like independence and secure like permanence for the lesser States among the New World nations. The doctrine has nothing to do with the commercial relations of any American Power, save, in truth, that it allows each to form such as it desires. It is really a guarantee of the commercial independence of the Americans.

We do not ask under the doctrine any exclusive commercial dealings with any other American State, we do not guarantee any State against punishment for misconduct provided the punishment does not take the form of the acquisition of territory by any non-American Power, and we have not the slightest desire to secure any territory from our neighbours. We wish to work with them hand in hand, so that all of us may get lifted up together. We rejoice over the good fortune of any of them, and gladly hail their material prosperity and political stability, and are concerned and alarmed if any fall into industrial or political chaos. We do not wish to see any Old World military Power grow up on this continent, or to be compelled to become a military Power ourselves. The peoples of the Americas can prosper best if left to work out their own salvation in their own way. The work of building up the navy must steadily continue. All we want is peace, and towards this end we wish to be able to secure the same respect for our rights from others which we are eager and anxious to extend to their rights in return. To insure fair treatment of the United States commercially, and to guarantee the safety of the American people, our people intend to insist upon the Monroe Doctrine as the one sure means of securing peace in the Western Hemisphere. The navy offers the only means of making our insistence upon the doctrine anything but a subject of derision to whatever nation chooses to disregard it. We desire the peace which comes as of right to the just man armed, not the peace granted on terms of ignominy to a craven and weakling."

This is definite, both in what it affirms and what it denies. But it is well to note that the President has put his foot down definitely upon the assumption that the Monroe Doctrine has anything to do with commerce beyond allowing each American State to make what commercial treaties it chooses. We do not ask, he says, for any exclusive commercial dealings with any American State. But, only a fortnight before the President laid down the law in this positive fashion, General James H. Wilson, addressing the American Free Trade League, gave the Monroe Doctrine an extension which he put forward as a plea for Free Trade, but which could be used in a very different sense by American Protectionists. General Wilson said --

"Inasmuch as under the Monroe Doctrine we have assumed the burden of protecting the neighbouring states from foreign aggression, the question naturally arises. Why should we not try to get some commercial advantage from them which, while it may make them richer and stronger, would in a measure compensate us for our trouble and expense? They are clearly under the American hegemony, and if the Monroe Doctrine is to be maintained, they are clearly within the American system of public law. That is, our national will must prevail in all cases where we choose to assert it, if we are strong enough to enforce it, and we are pledged to enforce it in all cases where European governments seriously encroach upon the territorial integrity or the sovereignty of any American State.

"Under this aspect of our relations with them, why should the United States not say frankly to all the States of North America, at least, we will agree to absolute and reciprocal free trade in natural and manufactured products, between our country and all its dependencies, wherever situated, on the one hand, and all the immediately neighbouring countries on the other, under a uniform tariff to be agreed upon by the parties to the arrangement, and to be carried into effect as against all other countries ? "

He admitted that it would prejudicially affect European trade, especially the trade of Great Britain with the Dominion of Canada. He further looked forward to an extension of the same principle to all the South American Republics. This, it must be admitted, has nothing to do with the Monroe doctrine pure and simple. I only note it by the way as indicative of a tendency to give that doctrine an expansion which it does not properly possess, and to note that President Roosevelt has rigidly confined it to the political area.

It is also noteworthy that the President expressly repudiates the theory which some of his friends have expressed in very vigorous terms that the United States should undertake the responsibility of exercising general overlordship over the foreign policy of the Central and South American States. The passage in his speech which will be read with most interest in Germany, is that in which he said that the United States do not guarantee any State against punishment for misconduct, provided that the punishment does not take the form of the acquisition of territory by any non-American Power. From this it follows that if any South American State should find itself involved in a quarrel with any European Power, the United States has now repudiated in advance any right under the Monroe doctrine to protect such American State from European attack. If Germany, for instance, had a grievance against Venezuela which she maintained rendered it necessary for her to inflict punishment upon that republic, the American Government could not, in face of President Roosevelt's declaration, raise any objection if the German Fleet escorted a German Army Corps across the Atlantic, if the Army Corps were landed upon Venezuelan territory, occupied the capital, and imposed any terms by the will of the conqueror upon the conquered, so long as the Germans did not stipulate for the acquisition of territory by Germany. But it is not necessary to acquire

territory in order to establish non-American ascendency in the country in which the punitive expeditions of unlimited severity and duration are permitted by the United States. Americans are perfectly well aware of the precedent of Egypt. Germany could not possibly make more emphatic protests as to her intention to evacuate South American territory than Mr. Gladstone made as to our determination to withdraw our garrison from the Nile delta. What is more, Mr. Gladstone made his declarations in perfect good faith, and intended to carry out his pledges. But nearly twenty years have elapsed since, with the battle of Tel-el-Kebir, the control of Egypt passed into the hands of Great Britain. England has not annexed a square yard of territory in Egypt but from that day to this the will of England has been law in Cairo and Alexandria.

What is to hinder the Germans improving upon the English precedents? They can accept with both hands the interdict upon the acquisition of territory. All they would need to do would be to impose upon the offending state a sufficiently heavy financial penalty, and to insist upon occupying certain points of vantage until the money was paid, or at least until a government should be established in the country with sufficient solidity to satisfy them that they would not have their punitive expedition to do over again as soon as the last man of the expeditionary force was embarked upon the German transports. It is not surprising that President Roosevelt should endeavour to repudiate any responsibility to shield the Southern and Central American Republics from punishment for misbehaviour, because any attempt to prevent the European Powers from avenging their own wrongs would have entailed upon the American Government the effective exercise of the duties of Lord Chief Justice of the Western Hemisphere which Mr. Olney claimed, but which no American statesman is prepared to exercise. If the Monroe doctrine is really to be enforced in spirit as well as in letter, and the European Powers are to be forbidden to establish themselves in South America, the United States will have to reconsider its policy and prepare to shoulder the burden of answering for the maintenance of international law throughout the whole of the American Continent. They may hope to evade it, and the occasion may not arise for some time to come. But by leaving the door open for punitive expeditions to be conducted at the discretion of each and all of the European Powers, President Roosevelt has given the Kaiser the opening which he needs if he really cares to take advantage of it.

I have said that President Roosevelt felt that he was compelled to concede to European Powers the right to punish South American Republics as the only alternative to the assumption by the United States of the functions of the Chief Justiceship of the world It is probable, however, that the Americans will discover a *via media*, which will enable them to avoid the obvious dangers resulting from European punitive expeditions directed against South and Central American States, and the assumption of the office of an international sheriff who undertakes the duty of enforcing respect for law throughout the whole of that vast expanse of territory What is there to hinder the United States of America from laying down the law that, whenever any European State has a grievance against any South American Republic, it shall not be free to redress its alleged wrong until it has submitted the whole question to an International Tribunal of Arbitration, whose award the United States' Government will undertake, with the aid of the other American States, to enforce? This would certainly minimise the evils which are inherent in both the courses which are at present regarded as the only alternatives Arbitration would in nine cases out of ten lead to an amicable settlement of a quarrel, and in the tenth case the United States would not stand alone in enforcing respect for the tribunals which the recalcitrant State first invoked, and then rejected

Certainly some such solution is urgently to be desired Italy and Germany regard the vast half-peopled South American Continent as the natural Hinterland for the overflow of their population Disputes are inevitable, and prescient statesmen would do well to provide in advance for their amicable settlement, and the advantages of a system that would forbid all punitive expeditions across the Atlantic which would not entail the assumption of any onerous responsibilities on the part of the United States will naturally commend itself more and more to the sober common sense of the American people.

When Mr Olney, President Cleveland's Secretary of State, claimed for the United States that it was practically sovereign on this Continent, and its fiat is law upon the subjects to which it confines its interposition," he startled the Old World a little, but he scared the New World much more For while none of the European Powers, with the somewhat dubious exception of Germany, have any aspirations after territory in the Western hemisphere, there is not a government in Southern or Central America that does not regard with undisguised alarm the claim of the big brother

with a big stick way up in the North to exercise lordship or dominion over them.

Recognising the existence of this feeling of alarm, Mr Secretary Hay, in his speech to the New York Chamber of Commerce, made the following declaration with a view to allaying the uneasiness which undoubtedly prevails as to the possible consequences of the Monroe doctrine, as interpreted and extended by Mr Olney's declaration " I think I may say that our sister Republics in the South are perfectly convinced of the sincerity of our attitude They know we desire the prosperity of each, and peace and harmony among them We no more want their territory than we covet the mountains of the moon We are grieved and distressed when there are differences among them, but even then we should never think of trying to compose those differences unless by the request of the parties thereto We owe them all the consideration which we claim for ourselves To the critics of various climates who have other views of our purposes, we can only wish fuller information and quieter consciences "

Notwithstanding Mr. Hay's assurance, it seems to outsiders that the instinct of the South American governments is perfectly sound. The Monroe doctrine demands as its necessary logical corollary the assumption by the United States of the right and the power to compel the other American States to refrain from actions which would give European Powers a legitimate *casus belli*. If European Powers are left to their own resources when face to face with Southern or Central American Republics, they will of necessity follow the time-honoured path They will send first a man of war, then a squadron, they will declare war, despatch troops and do their best to seize the enemy's capital Of course they may do all this, and if when they conclude peace they evacuate the occupied territory and make no attempt to annex American soil, the Monroe doctrine will be left intact But the risk is very great, that if a European Power once establishes its troops as conquerors in a position of vantage on the American Continent, it will be very difficult to turn them out without actual menace of war Not only so, but the experience of the United States in Cuba is sufficient to show how easy it is to establish political paramountcy over a territory without annexation The Monroe doctrine says nothing about paramountcy It relates solely to the extension of territorial possessions If, therefore, President Roosevelt is anxious to keep Europe out of America he will be driven either by mediation, friendly offices, or by downright intervention to prevent disputes between

European and American States ever coming to blows That in the long run will practically mean that all the Central and South American Republics while nominally Sovereign International States, are really subject to the suzerainty of Uncle Sam, and all serious diplomatic business will be settled at Washington. It may be very good for the South American States thus to have the most difficult and delicate diplomatic questions taken out of their hands The case of Venezuela offers an excellent illustration of the advantage which such States occasionally reap from the timely intervention of the big brother from the North, but they do not like it, all the same The small powers dread the great State which is so strong that the fear of man is never before its eyes and which is so supremely conscious of its own absolute rectitude that even when it makes war it is calmly confident that it is acting as the Vicegerent of the Almighty So keen is this distrust that a very well informed American assured me this year that England never made a greater mistake in her own interest when she refused to settle the Alaskan difficulty by arbitration, because the American Government had stipulated that the umpire must be an American. "If," said my friend, who was a lawyer, deservedly much esteemed in the highest Governmental circles, " if I were pleading before such a Court I should have addressed myself solely to winning over one of the English judges. It would have been hopeless to make any South or Central American judge admit anything in favour of the United States England would have had the umpire's decision in her pocket before the case opened, and have it every time " The existence of such a sentiment of distrust is more likely than anything else to provoke action on the part of the Washington Government that will precipitate the extension of the authority of the United States over the whole Western hemisphere.

If Mr Olney's claim for his country to be Lord Chief Justice of the Western hemisphere excited some protest, it was nothing to the indignation provoked by his frank intimation that in the opinion of the American nation it is " unnatural " that any European State should possess territory in the Western hemisphere

Mr. Olney said " That distance and three thousand miles of intervening ocean make any permanent political union between a European and an American State unnatural and inexpedient will hardly be denied "

Lord Salisbury denied it at once But since then Spain has been deprived of her American possessions by war, while Denmark is currently reputed to have sold her West Indian Islands to the United States for a little more than three-quarters of a million pounds sterling

The following are the American territories still remaining under European flags.—

	Area, Square miles.	Population, 1890
Denmark		
Greenland .	34,015	10,516
France		
St Pierre .	90	5,983
Miquelon		
Guadaloupe	721	165,154
Martinique	381	175,863
St Bartholomew	8	2,898
French Guiana .	30,000	25,796
Great Britain		
Canada	3,315,647	4,832,679
Newfoundland	40,200	193,121
Labrador	120,000	4,211
Bermuda	19	15,743
British Honduras	8,291	27,668
Jamaica	4,192	639,491
Trinidad	1,754	198,747
Barbados	166	182,206
Bahamas .	4,466	49,500
Eleven other West Indian Islands or groups	1,500	250,000
British Guiana	109,000	287,981
Netherlands		
St Martin .	227	29,729
Curaçao .		
Dutch Guiana . .	46,000	74,132

From this list it appears that, excluding the possessions of Great Britain, the only footholds the European Powers have on the American Continent are in Guiana and in Greenland Greenland does not matter, as it is a wilderness of ice and snow

All that Europe holds on the mainland is limited to Surinam and Cayenne, a stretch of territory covering 76,000 square miles, on which only 100,000 persons can find a living. So far, therefore, as serving notice to quit upon Europeans may be regarded as serious, it concerns England, and England alone.

It is not likely that England, with whom the Monroe doctrine first originated, will do anything calculated to bring down the wrath of President Roosevelt on her head. So long as we do not attempt to extend our territory in the Western hemisphere, we may take it that no objection will be taken—*pace* Mr. Olney—to our maintaining the territorial *status quo Beati possidentes* So far so good, but we can hardly acquiesce without at least a passing protest against the assumption so constantly made by the citizens of the United States, that no one is an American excepting those resident within the frontiers of the Republic Canadians are every whit as much Americans as their neighbours south of the St Lawrence. Nor can

Great Britain agree to the demand that they shall forfeit any of the inherent rights which they possess as Americans because for reasons of their own they prefer to remain in connection with the British Empire

At the same time we are bound to admit that whatever exception we may take to Mr. Olney's doctrine as to the permanent union between Great Britain and her American colonies being unnatural and inexpedient, there is at least considerable probability that our Colonists themselves may come to be of his way of thinking To say this is not in any way to endorse the views of Professor Goldwin Smith, who has this autumn repeated once more his oft-stated conviction that the majority of the Canadians desire to throw in their destinies with the United States It is merely to register the conclusions arrived at after a cool, dispassionate survey of the forces which are in action within and without the Canadian Dominion.

It would seem that the acquisition by any European power of a coaling station would be resisted as strenuously as the conquest of a tract of territory on the mainland. That this is no exaggeration is shown by the hubbub that was raised quite recently by the announcement that a German steamship company wished to acquire a coaling-station off the coast of Venezuela, a hubbub which only subsided on the formal and emphatic disclaimer by the German Ambassador at Washington that no such acquisition was contemplated by the German Government On hearing this declaration we are told that President Roosevelt expressed his great satisfaction The incident is regarded as finally closing the door upon the acquisition of any coaling-station by a foreign Power in any part of the Western Hemisphere.

By a further process of extension, the Monroe doctrine is held to forbid the transfer of any territory now held by a European Power to any other European Power. The Danes, for instance, have three small islands in the West Indies, which are no use to them, and which the United States are believed to be willing to buy. The Danes would be only too delighted to exchange the islands in the West Indies if, instead of selling to the United States, they could do a deal with the German Empire, and hand over their West Indian Islands in exchange for North Schleswig, in which several hundred thousand Danes groan under the domination of Germany Although it has never been officially stated, it is perfectly well understood that the United States would object to any transfer of the Danish possessions to the German Empire There is no probability of the Germans being willing to exchange North Schleswig for the West Indian Islands,

but they would probably be very glad to acquire these islands by outbidding the Americans in the matter of purchase money The Monroe doctrine, however, deprives Denmark of an open market She can only sell to the United States, if she sells at all

Even without any direct effort on the part of the United States effectively to assert the overlordship claimed by Mr Olney, there is no State in South America which does not regard the possible development of American designs with ill-concealed suspicion and alarm It was this motive which prompted the assembly last year at Madrid of a congress of representatives of the Latin States of America for the purpose of endeavouring to re-establish the influence of Spain, which had been badly shaken by the Cuban war If there is one thing which would dispose any of the South American States to accept a German Alliance, it would be for the purpose of rendering absolutely impossible the establishment of a protectorate on the part of the United States. This road, therefore, being closed, North Americans are diligently setting themselves to ward off the danger of European intervention by the other road that is open to them, namely, by the establishment of the system of arbitration which would minimise the dangers of internecine war between the South American Republics themselves, and establish a system by which difficulties with foreign Powers might be settled without an appeal to the last dread arbitrament of war. For this purpose for the last twenty years it has been a fixed object of American policy to promote what may be called a Pan-American system of Arbitration, of which the Congress which assembled in November in the capital of Mexico is the latest and most conspicuous sign

CHAPTER VI — ON INTERNATIONAL ARBITRATION

IN discussing the influence which the Americans have exercised upon the world at large, reference must be made to the one great international question in which they have uniformly been a potent force in favour of the cause of progress and civilisation I refer to the question of international arbitration The principle of settling disputes between Sovereign States by reference to a judicial or arbitral tribunal formed the very foundation of the American Constitution The fact that from the Atlantic to the Pacific, from the St Lawrence to the Gulf of Mexico, there are to be found no frontiers bristling with cannon, no standing armies to defend the millions of the forty-two sovereign

States banded together in federal union, is due to the Fathers of the Republic having created, as the very corner-stone of their union, a Supreme Court of Justice, authorised to adjudicate upon all questions in dispute between any of the federating States.

Accustomed from the very birth of the Republic to the spectacle of State differences being adjudicated upon not by the bloody arbitrament of war, but by the judicial decision of a supreme tribunal, the Americans naturally attempted to create some tribunal competent to settle amicably disputes between other nations. The principles of the Constitution of the United States have become part of the atmosphere of the American citizen. He may try to get outside it, but he seldom succeeds, and consciously or unconsciously he perpetually suggests the application of the principles of that Constitution to the solution of almost all the difficulties which arise in the outside world. Hence it was natural that the movement in favour of international arbitration should have found in the American people intelligent and enthusiastic support. As Great Britain was the power with which the United States came into most immediate contact, and therefore developed most points of friction, it was equally natural that the principle of arbitration should have been first brought into active operation for the settlement of disputes between the United States and Great Britain.

The first arbitration between the two countries took place in 1816, when a dispute arose about the St. Croix River, and the Lake boundaries A few years later a question arising out of the Treaty of Ghent was referred to the arbitration of the Emperor of Russia In 1827 a question about the north-eastern boundary of the United States was referred to the arbitration of the King of the Netherlands. In 1853 a dispute about some liberated slaves was settled by arbitration, and in 1863 a difference that arose between the Hudson's Bay and the Puget Sound Company was also settled in the same way

The great arbitration, however, which constitutes a landmark in the history of the two countries, was that by which the Alabama claims under the Treaty of Washington of 1871 were referred to the Geneva Tribunal. In the same year the disputed San Juan boundary was referred to the arbitration of the German Emperor, and a further dispute about the Nova Scotia fishery was also settled amicably.

In 1891 the question of the seal fisheries in the Behring Sea was referred to a Court of Arbitration in Paris, and the long list of Anglo-American arbitrations was closed by the arbitration which settled the disputed boundary between the British Empire and the Republic of Venezuela in 1899. No other two nations in the world have had so many arbitrations as Great Britain and the United States

The English-speaking States have not been content with endeavouring to influence the world by the force of their example. They committed themselves nearly thirty years ago to an active support of the principle as will be seen by the text of the following resolution which was passed by both Houses of Congress in the year 1874

"Resolved by the House of Representatives, that the President of the United States is hereby authorised and requested to negotiate with all civilised Powers who may be willing to enter into such negotiation for the establishment of an international system, whereby matters in dispute between different Governments agreeing thereto may be adjusted by Arbitration, and if possible without recourse to war"

In 1890, Congress again in both branches of the Legislature passed the following resolution —

"That the President be and is hereby requested to invite, from time to time, as fit occasions may arise, negotiations with any Government with which the United States has, or may have, diplomatic relations, to the end that any differences or disputes arising between the two Governments which cannot be adjusted by diplomatic agency, may be referred to Arbitration, and be peaceably adjusted by such means"

In 1895 Senator Sherman introduced a bill for the purpose of enabling the President to give effect to the resolution of 1890 by authorising him to conduct negotiations through the regular diplomatic agents of the United States, or at his discretion to appoint a commission to visit the Governments of other countries for the purpose of entering into negotiations in order to create an international arbitration tribunal or other means by which disputes may be amicably settled and war averted.

When the Venezuelan dispute arose, President Cleveland evoked a storm of enthusiastic approval by formulating his demand for arbitration Mr Carnegie, the most peaceful of men, declared that arbitration was the one thing in the world for which he was willing to fight. Mr. Olney laid down the law that war was condemnable as a relic of barbarism and a crime in itself, and there was only one possible way of determining the question, namely, by peaceful arbitration The American demand thus enthusiastically supported by the American people compelled Lord Salisbury to abandon his position Then an attempt was made to create a permanent treaty of arbitration between the two States, but unfortunately nothing has yet been done to give effect to the wishes that were thus expressed

In 1890 the official representatives of seventeen American Republics assembled at Washington and passed the following resolution, which was subsequently accepted by sixteen of the Republics, including Brazil :—

"The Republics of North, Central, and South America hereby adopt Arbitration as a principle of American International Law, for the settlement of all differences, disputes, or controversies that may arise between them concerning diplomatic and consular privileges, boundaries, territories, indemnities, right of navigation, and the validity, construction, and enforcement of treaties, and in all other cases, whatever their origin, nature, or occasion, except only those which in the judgment of any of the nations involved in the controversy may imperil its independence."

Three years previously the Central American States made a treaty by which five Governments solemnly promised, in case of disagreement between them, whatever the motives, to submit the same to arbitration.

The first international treaty providing for arbitration in all cases was made between the United States and Honduras.

Up to the year 1895 the Government of the United States had entered into forty-seven agreements for referring matters to arbitration. It was not, however, until the Peace Conference at the Hague that the principles of pacific arbitration had an opportunity of getting into practical effect. There was from the first a kind of friendly rivalry between Lord Paunce-

fote and the American Delegation as to which could most effectually promote the establishment of a Permanent International Tribunal. Honours were divided. At the Hague Lord Pauncefote led, but America scored by the mission of Mr. Holls to Berlin which brought Germany into line. Mr. Holls went to Berlin for the purpose of extricating Germany from a position which would have left her isolated. In interviews with the Imperial Chancellor and the Foreign Minister, he was able to convince the statesmen of Germany that whatever attitude the German delegates chose to take up, the principle of an International Tribunal of Arbitration would be adopted by the Conference, and that Germany had only the alternative of standing in with all the great civilised Powers or of taking up a position with no backer or supporter save the Sultan. The German Government was convinced by his representations that the train was going to start anyhow, and not caring to be left forlorn on the platform, followed the example of the others, and the Convention was unanimously approved by all the Powers.

A record so honourable, lasting over a whole century, and culminating in the greatest International Parliament which met in the capital of Holland, is one of which every American citizen has good reason to be proud.

Capt. Crozier.   Mr. Newall.   Mr. A. D. White.   Dr. Seth Low.   Capt. Mahan.   Mr. F. W. Holls.

THE AMERICAN DELEGATES AT THE HAGUE.

PART III.

HOW AMERICA AMERICANISES.

CHAPTER I.—RELIGION.

THE impulse which drove the earlier dis-
coverers across the Atlantic in search of the
Golden Indies was not entirely mercenary. In
the fifteenth century, as in the nineteenth, there
is visible a curious blend of avarice and religion.
In our times, the missionary has usually preceded the filibuster, but in the Spanish conquest
of America the filibusters took the initiative
And no sooner had the Spanish and Genoese
adventurers discovered the existence of a new
world beyond the seas than the Church of
Rome hastened to exploit the discovery by
the despatch of missionaries of the Cross, who
were accommodated with free passages on board
the barks which bore the freebooters of the
Old World to their destined prey The map
is still shown in Rome in which the Pope
solemnly divided up the New World between
Spain and Portugal, two nations which, both
being devotedly Catholic, accepted the papal
delimitation as the voice of the Oracle of God
Destinies, however, were less obedient, and
to-day when the visitor at the museum of the
College de Propaganda Fide surveys the map,
he indulges in melancholy reflections upon the
vanity of human expectations as he remembers
that not over even one single islet of that new
world now floats the Spanish or Portuguese flag.

If the Old World imposed its faith at the
sword's point on the aboriginal populations
of Central and Southern America, Northern
America has not failed to confer similar benefits
upon the Old World, although by a very different
method of propaganda Prescott has given us
in his story of the conquest of Peru a curious
picture of the methods pursued by the pious
pirates who conquered the kingdom of the
Incas. The unfortunate Peruvians who were
captured by the Spaniards were given the choice
of conversion to Christianity or Death It is
not to be wondered at that multitudes accepted
the faith thus imposed at the point of the sword ;
but, if the early chronicle may be believed, their
conversion was attended with even less than the
usual modicum of intelligent conviction To
expound the Christian mysteries on the stricken
field, while the soil is still fresh with new-spilled
blood, is apt to be a somewhat summary process, but it has seldom been so grotesque a

burlesque as that which was enacted in Peru.
The Spanish conquerors were ignorant of the
language of their captives, and, had perforce,
to depend upon the services of stray interpreters
whose intellects were unfamiliar with the subtle-
ties of the Athanasian Creed. Hence, when
the Peruvian was summoned to profess his faith
in the Christian religion and its fundamental
dogma of the Trinity, he was told by the interpreter that he was required to declare that there
were three Gods and one God, and that made
four Gods ; and on assenting to this arithmetical
proposition he was incontinently baptised and
admitted as a true believer within the pale of
the Christian Church.

Such were the primitive methods of Pizarro
and many a less famous Spaniard who preached
the gospel with the sword only four centuries
ago The unfortunate millions of the peaceful
aborigines whom the Spaniards ground to death
by enforced labour were graciously vouchsafed
the alternative of heaven beyond the grave in
compensation for the very real hell on this earth
into which they were plunged by the Spanish
conquest.

For the time being, no doubt, the triumph
of Spain and of Rome seemed complete. To
this day, from Northern Mexico to Tierra
del Fuego, the Roman faith reigns supreme.
It was in the South American continent that the
Jesuits found an opportunity for realising their
political and religious ideals, and at this moment
it is in the States of Colombia where the dis-
possessed friars from the Philippines are finding
their warmest welcome Southern and Central
America have been, since their conquest, veritable States of the Church But churches, like
individuals, are often cursed with the burden of
a granted prayer The religion of Rome thus
forced upon the southern half of the Western
Hemisphere has been singularly devoid of vitali-
sing power. It would be difficult to specify a
single religious movement originating in Southern
America, or to name a single eminent man or
woman that the Southern or Central American
States have produced who has exerted any influence upon the religious life of the world. To
this day the state of South America is one of the
scandals of the Catholic Church After a period
of dominance, during which priest and Jesuit
reigned with unchallenged sway, the forces of

revolt asserted themselves with violence, the Jesuits were expelled, and South American Freethinkers gave ample proof, by their anti-clerical legislation, that Gambetta's watchword —" *Le cléricalisme—voilà l'ennemi !*"—could be as inspiriting a rallying cry in the New World as in the Old But the fierce passions engendered by the conflict between the forces of orthodoxy and of unbelief failed to purify the Church The morality of many of the priests in South America left so much to be desired that there was a great deal of talk some years ago at the Vatican of the necessity for such an exercise of the Pope's authority as would suspend for a time the enforced celibacy of the clergy, which in South America had produced, not chastity, but almost universal concubinage Instead of being a glory, the South American Church has become the scandal and the reproach of Catholic Christendom

Far otherwise was it with the northern half of the Western Hemisphere. Here the religious impulse was the most potent factor in the colonisation of the country The gold mines of California were happily unknown in the sixteenth and seventeeth centuries The Johannesburg of the New World lay in the South, and thither hastened all the adventurers and gold-seekers, the early prototypes of the Outlanders of the Rand The United States of America and Canada were to the *conquistadores* as unattractive as were the pastoral regions of the high veldt in the Transvaal to Messrs Werner, Beit, and Eckstein. They left these North lands to those who, like the primitive Boer, trekked into the wilderness in search, not of gold, but of liberty Hence, while South America was colonised by the devotees of Mammon, North America was opened up by stern idealists, who fled from the city of destruction of the Old World to the virgin wilderness in which they hoped to rear on eternal foundations the City of their God

It is true that the earliest colonists, those who went out with Raleigh to Virginia, were not of so lofty a type They were more like our colonists of the present day, who were tempted by prospects of carving out estates for themselves and founding a family in the rich tobacco-producing regions that lay south of the Potomac They were first in the field ; in social position they were possibly superior to the men of the *Mayflower*, but after three centuries, during which mankind has had an opportunity of observing the comparative potency of the different elements when distilled in the alembic of history, we see many things which were hidden from the eyes of our forefathers in the seventeenth century. When Byron visited the dungeon of Torquato Tasso, he contrasted in glowing verse the difference between the Duke,

who in his palace signed the decree that flung the poet into gaol, and the captives of his will

Thou ! formed to eat, and be despised and die,
Even as the beasts perish, save that thou
Hadst a more splendid trough and wider sty
He ! with a glory round his furrowed brow,
Which emanated then and dazzles now

There is something of the same contrast between the affluent and luxurious descendants of the Cavaliers who peopled the Southern States and the grim, stern men who settled on " the wild New England shore " The Southerners had the wealth and the ease, the fertile field and the radiant sun, but the shaping of the destinies of the continent lay, not in their hands, but in those of the despised fanatics of the North, proscribed fugitives fleeing in slight cockle-shells across the Atlantic to escape the persecuting zeal of prelate and of King.

The impulse which drove the men of the *Mayflower* across the sea was primarily religious, secondly, political It was to a very slight extent economical or financial. At the time the movement seemed comparatively insignificant To the Sovereigns and statesmen of the Old World what did it matter that a colony or two of pinched fanatics should establish themselves on the western shore of the Atlantic? But to-day every one realises that it was an exodus as fateful in its influence upon the history of mankind as the Exodus of the Chosen People through the Wilderness to the Promised Land The last century also witnessed a somewhat similar exodus, which may yet be as potent in the making and unmaking of empires The trek of the Dutch Boers northward across the Vaal seemed even less significant than the landing of the Puritans at Plymouth Rock, but to-day it seems not impossible that as the one led to the founding of the greatest Republic on earth, so the other may lead to the shattering of militarism throughout the world

But it would be grossly unjust to regard the Puritans of New England as the only element which religious enthusiasm has contributed to the creation of the American Commonwealth The Roman Catholics who colonised Maryland were also to a large extent exiles for conscience' sake The propagandist efforts of the Roman Church in North America differed *toto coelo* from the brutal fashion in which the work of prose-lytism was carried on in the South The Jesuits, who were at once missionaries and explorers of the type of Livingstone, were the pioneers of European colonisation both in Canada and along the Mississippi. On the Pacific coast it was the fathers of the various religious orders who were the only pioneers of Christian civilisation in the Far West, until the Argonauts of 1849 broke

THE LATE DWIGHT L. MOODY.

IRA D. SANKEY.

THE LATE HENRY WARD BEECHER
(Photo by Elliott & Fry.)

THE LATE MISS FRANCES WILLARD.

in rudely upon their pastoral simplicity. As it was in the beginning, so it has remained ever since The two continents of the New World have been divided between the principle of Authority and the principle of Liberty. The American Commonwealth from its very birth asserted with unmistakable emphasis, as inalienable and fundamental rights of mankind, liberty of conscience and liberty of religion.

In matters of religion the indirect influence of America upon the world has probably been more potent than any direct effect produced by American teachers or American preachers, although, as I shall proceed to show, the influence of the latter has been by no means insignificant. It was the citizens of the United States who supplied the world for a century and more with a great object-lesson as to the possibility of the maintenance of religion without the intervention of State churches and without the penal enactments of intolerant legislatures. To a Europe, hide-bound with the old tradition that there could be no religion unless the State established and endowed some form of religious creed, the United States presented the spectacle of a great Christian community, in which the rites of religion were as regularly performed and where the spirit of real religion was at least as visibly potent in the fruitful works of righteousness as in any community where the Church was privileged to strut abroad bedizened in all the gorgeous livery of State. That potent influence is still working in the Old World to-day The example of the United States has been a far more potent dissolvent of the Old World ideas as to the necessity for an inseparable union between Church and State than all the activities of the Liberationist Society. Cavour's formula of a Free Church in a Free State was not uttered till more than two centuries after the same ideal had been formally accepted as the basis of the American Commonwealth In a world in which men can still find themselves in high office bravely confronting the twentieth century with the ecclesiastical conceptions of the Middle Ages, the example of America streams like the radiance of the rising sun across the dark and misty world.

Apart from this all-pervading, subtle, indirect influence of the American ideas as to Church and State, and liberty of conscience, not even the most cursory observer can overlook the direct influence which American religious life and religious thought has had upon large sections of the English-speaking people in Great Britain, and in the Greater Britain beyond the seas It is natural that it should be so, because at least one-half of the English-speaking people is ecclesiastically much more in sympathy with the Americans than with the Anglicans. The

Anglican Church in England is the church of an influential, cultured, richly endowed, socially arrogant sect. It is a thing apart, as distinct from the life of the race as the House of Lords or the monarchy Neither monarchy, House of Lords, nor Established Church reproduce themselves beyond the seas. An Episcopal Church, no doubt, that is ecclesiastically affiliated with the Anglican Church, exists in all the Colonies and in the United States, but it is nowhere established and endowed, its clergy are never inoculated with the virus of social ascendency, and although in some the evil leaven of sacerdotalism works, it is in a very attenuated form The Nonconformists of this country are spiritually and ecclesiastically in much more vital union with the American Churches than they are with the Anglican establishment. This is especially true of the Independents and Baptists, the Unitarians, and, to a less but still to a very real extent, of the Presbyterians As for the Methodists, who had no share in the glorious traditions of the founding of New England, they have increased and multiplied so much in the United States as to outnumber the Methodists in the old country, so that Methodism may be regarded as the most Americanised of all the religious sects On an Œcumenical Council of Methodism, if the representation were adjusted to numbers, the American Methodists would outnumber those of all the rest of the world The Nonconformist and the Methodist, who are conventionally regarded by the Established clergy as aliens to the Commonwealth of Israel, who are reminded at every turn that they are pariahs not worthy to sit at table with the Brahmins of the Establishment, find themselves at home in the wider and freer area of the American Commonwealth The Congregationalists, Baptists, Unitarians, and Presbyterians are *solidaires* with the Puritans and their descendants. The Methodists in all their divisions are equally *solidaires* with the Methodist Episcopal Church They interchange pulpits, they use the same books of devotion, above all they sing the same hymns Whenever a great stone is flung into the lake of American or British religious life, the ripple is never arrested by the Atlantic The ever-enlarging circles extend without a break from continent to continent

To the man in the street, who may be presumed to belong to no religious organisation, these ties, ecclesiastical or denominational, as you may please to call them, may seem of small importance But to most Methodists, and to very many Nonconformists, their denomination appeals much more frequently and more deeply than the national organisation of the country to which they belong Politics which appeal to the patriotic sentiment of an Englishman, make only an occasional demand upon his active service. If he votes at a local election once a year and at a general election once in five, and if he pays his rates and taxes, that often represents the maximum of the service which is claimed by the State from the citizen. His chapel is much more exacting. It is always with him. Twice on Sunday, at least, it summons him to the worship of God in some stated public service. But this is merely a fragment of the demands which it makes upon him. He must attend the prayer-meeting, and class-meeting, teach in the Sunday-school, distribute tracts, take part in cottage-meetings, do his share of local preaching, and, in short, give up no small portion of his leisure to the discharge of his religious duties. While his church or chapel is always with him, demanding voluntary exertion and taking continuous collections, the service demanded by the State is intermittent and comparatively insignificant. Hence solidarity based upon the identity of religious belief is often a far more real and vital thing than the solidarity that springs from the inhabiting of the same country. It is otherwise, of course, in time of war. When the country is invaded, the sentiment of patriotism is supreme. But the English-speaking race at the present time does not know what it is to be invaded. The immense majority of men who speak the English tongue have never heard a shot fired in anger. Hence the idea of the country as a living entity, demanding imperiously the sacrifice of life and fortune in its service, has never dawned upon many minds. But to the religious man and religious woman the warfare with the forces of evil never ceases. The Church is the army of the living God, always mobilised for action. Naturally the thought of her members turns far more upon the chapel or the church than upon the State.

To those who have been brought up in the sectarian seclusion of the Anglican cult, it is difficult to realise the extent to which American books, American preachers, American hymnody, mould the lives of the Free Churchmen of this country. If I may be pardoned an autobiographical reminiscence, I may say that there rises vividly before my mind's eye the bookshelves of my father's study in the days when I was a small boy in a Congregational Manse on Tyne-side. In the post of honour, formidable and forbidding to me, at least, stood the stately volumes which contained the writings of Jonathan Edwards, the stern teacher of New England, who represented Calvinism in all its grim austerity. On another shelf stood the works of Channing, the Unitarian, whose loving spirit hardly condoned for the

offence of his Unitarian heresy. There was Barnes' well-thumbed commentary upon the New Testament, side by side with Baxter and Matthew Henry, and other Puritan Divines. Of Jeremy Taylor and Barrow and South, and the classic writers and preachers of Anglicanism, there was no trace. Chalmers and Guthrie represented Presbyterianism of Scotland, but among modern preachers the works of Henry Ward Beecher were the most conspicuous, although Spurgeon came after him, *cum longo intervallo.* It may be admitted that it was but a meagre theological outfit, although there may be some doubt whether many of my more cultured readers, who sneer superciliously at the narrow range of the Independent minister's book-shelves, have read as many theological works as the few which I have just named. My point, however, is not the dimensions of my father's library, but to show how teachers and preachers of New England of the Puritan Commonwealth stood side by side, and were held in equal honour as supplying the spiritual pabulum for a Nonconformist household. I have some reason to think that my experience was not exceptional, and to this day I am inclined to believe that, if the rank and file of Free Churchmen read theology or sermons at all, it will be found that their reading is chiefly confined to the authors who represent the Puritan Commonwealth, the Wesleyan Revival, and the religious life of the Americans. Hence, it is not surprising that the religious public in the three Kingdoms have been singularly susceptible to the religious influences coming from beyond the Atlantic.

Looking over the religious movements of last century in the English-speaking world there are five distinctly discernible. Of these five only one is of English origin. The Tractarian movement of the Middle Century was distinctively Anglican, but beyond a certain stimulus given to the sensuous exercise of divine worship its influence was strictly confined within the limits of its own sect. The other four movements have been much wider in their sweep. The first and most persistent has been Revivalism. This was distinctly American in its origin. No doubt there have been revivals or, as Catholics would say, missions, in all ages of the Church, but the systematised revival, the deliberate organisation of religious services for the express purpose of rousing the latent moral enthusiasm of mankind, is a distinctly American product of last century. Wesley and Whitfield may have sown its seed but it grew up across the Atlantic. Revivalism flourished in the United States long before it was acclimatised on this side of the water. In Professor Finney, of Oberlin College, Revivalism found its expositor and its mouthpiece, and, as a direct result of his teaching, we have the Salvation Army, which is simply Revivalism organised on a permanent basis and put under quasi-military discipline. It is easy to sneer at Revivalism, but it has been the means by which hundreds and thousands of men and women have found their way to a higher and purer life. The Revivalist may seem often rude, uncultured, even vulgar, but in his untutored eloquence millions of men have heard for the first time the echoes of the Divine voice that spoke on Sinai, while the penitent form and the inquiry-room have been to many a sin-stricken soul the ante-chamber of heaven. In this practical work-a-day world men affect great admiration for those who do things, as opposed to the men who talk about them. Revivalism has done things which the more cultured and refined would not even have ventured to attempt

Nor is it only one form of Revivalism which has come to us from the United States, there has been a long list of Revivalists whose services were greatly welcomed both in England and in the States Of these the best known were Moody and Sankey. Moody in speech, and Sankey in song, exercised a wider influence than any other two men upon the British people in the latter half of last century Sankey's hymns still hold the first place in thousands of places of worship throughout the British Empire. They are sung much more constantly, and by a much greater number of people, than any other songs, with the one exception of the National Anthem.

The second great contribution which America has made to the religious life of the world is one, the full significance of which is appreciated by few. The strange, mysterious phenomena of Spiritualism first began to be noticed at what are known as the Hydesville rappings in about the middle century. But it was not until D. D Home began to develop his mediumship about the time when England was weltering in the bloody morass of the Crimean War, that the outside world recognised the dawning of a new force in the world D D Home, like Mr Carnegie, was born in Scotland, but he crossed the Atlantic when nine years of age, and did not return to his native land until he had been thoroughly Americanised. Of his mediumship and his extraordinary missionary tour through-out the Courts and capitals of Europe, it is not necessary to do more than make mention The majority abused him as a charlatan Robert Browning ridiculed him as ' Sludge the Medium", but his wife, much more spiritually gifted than he, recognised the reality of the phenomena which held out to mankind the

promise of the possibility of communication with those who had passed beyond the veil.

This is not the occasion for discussing the value of the contribution which Spiritualism has made, or rather the promise which it holds out of making, to the solution of the great problem — if a man die, shall he live again? but it is sufficient to mention two facts One was the saying of Lord Brougham, "that even in the most cloudless skies of scepticism, I see a rain-cloud, if it be no bigger than a man's hand It is modern Spiritualism." The other is the fact that many of the most eminent of modern scientists, men of the standing of Sir William Crookes, Professor Alfred Russel Wallace, and Camille Flammarion, have publicly asserted their belief in the reality of the phenomena commonly called spiritistic, and that the late Mr Myers, after devoting a quarter of a century to a painstaking scientific investigation of psychical phenomena, arrived before his death at the firm conviction that the persistence of the personality, after the dissolution of the body, was capable of scientific demonstration. For my own part, I can only say that I entertain no firmer conviction than that this doctrine is as the stone which the builders rejected, which has become the head-stone of the corner. When the persistence of the soul after the dissolution of the body has been found to be as capable of scientific verification as any other fact in nature, it will constitute a political, social, and moral revolution of unspeakable magnitude

The next movement of religious origin which has influenced the world was the combination of temperance enthusiasm with the recognition of the right of women to full citizenship It would be too much to claim that the temperance movement had its origin in the United States, but it undoubtedly has drawn no small portion of its strength from New England The State of Maine has long occupied a prominent position as a Prohibition State, and the Maine Liquor Law has for fifty years been the object of the despairing admiration of prohibitionists in Great Britain and in the Colonies. The movement for the emancipation of women did not originate in the United States. Mary Wollstonecraft may fairly be regarded as the prophetess of her sex. But it was not until the Americans took up the question seriously that the question of the enfranchisement of women came within the pale of practical politics. To this day it is only in some of the States of the American Union, and quite recently in Australia and New Zealand, that the right of women to full citizenship has been fully recognised. The two movements may be said to have been combined in the Women's Christian Temperance

Union,* which had its centre in Chicago, with Miss Willard as its inspiring spirit   The Women s Christian Temperance Union is one of the world-wide organisations which took their rise in America, and have since established branches in every part of the English-speaking world.   Its indirect influence in compelling women at once to realise their responsibility and to recognise their capacity to serve the State in the promotion of all that tends to preserve the purity and sanctity of the home, has been by no means one of the least contributions which America had made to the betterment of the world.

The fourth movement which, beginning in America, has Americanised every English-speaking land, is the Christian Endeavour movement. The Christian Endeavour movement is the latest born but one of the most thriving illustrations of the enthusiasm of humanity organised under Christian auspices.   It was first founded in the State of Maine by the Rev Francis E Clark.   It has since encircled the world with a chain of associated societies, all of which are organised on the same general principles for the attainment of the same beneficent end † The Christian Endeavour movement appeals primarily to the young, which is in itself a distinctively American characteristic ; it asserts the absolute equality of the sexes, the binding obligation of the moral law upon man and woman alike ; it inculcates temperance, and—therein differing from many distinctively Evangelical movements—it asserts in the strongest terms the duty of its ·members to try to purify public life, and to use the power of the State to help on good work   It is quite possible that many of those who read these pages may never have heard of the existence of the Christian Endeavour or the Women's Christian Temperance Union, or if they have heard the titles, have regarded them as sounds without meaning , but none the less for that, are they living and growing organisations, for the like of which we look in vain in any similar societies founded in the same period in the United Kingdom.   In all these four there is no pretension that Americans are being Anglicised.

Apart, however, from these distinct movements, which are not dependent for their existence on any English organisations, there is

* The Women's Christian Union has now half a million members, 300,000 of whom are in the United States, 100,000 in Great Britain   There are fifty-eight countries and colonies represented in the Union.

† The following figures are quoted from the latest returns published by the Christian Endeavour Union   Number of Christian Endeavour Societies in 1901, 61,605, with a total membership of 3,695,280   Of these societies 43,848 are "Young People's," and 16,195 "Juniors "

another very potent spiritual influence profoundly affecting the religious life of millions, which has been exercised by certain notable Americans, whom it is sufficient to mention Among those who have contributed to broaden the religious outlook of the English-speaking world, are Channing, Emerson, and Theodore Parker, and James Russell Lowell, who embodied in verse the transcendental philosophy which Emerson crystallised in his essays   Next to them, although nearer to the pale of the orthodox Church, was the brilliant orator and catholic-minded philanthropist, Henry Ward Beecher. Still farther removed from orthodoxy, but still distinct forces in the religious life of our race, were thinkers like James Fiske, Dr. Draper and Mr. A. D. White.

It would be impossible to close this imperfect and cursory survey of the religious influence which America and the Americans have brought to bear upon the religious life of the world, without at least a parting tribute to the memory of Father Hecker.   The United States of America, being predominantly Protestant, has influenced most directly those parts of the world which have broken loose from the papal dominion.   It is the glory of Father Hecker that he succeeded, to a large extent, in infusing a spirit of healthy Americanism into the life of the Church of Rome.   The forces of reaction, it is true, have triumphed for a time, and the doctrines of Americanism lie under the ban of the Vatican, but the work which Father Hecker did, and the principles which he taught, still continue to bear fruit   The Roman Catholics of America, like loyal sons of the Church, have bowed submissively to their teacher's decree   But the present century will not be much older before Rome will again find its base washed by the rising tide of the American spirit   It is probable that the Pope, whoever he may be, will again pronounce his condemnation. But when the tide rises for a third time, the supreme Pontiff will recognise that the principles of Americanism are part and parcel of the sacred deposit of truth which it is the duty of the Church sedulously to preserve and to disseminate among the nations of the earth.

CHAPTER II —LITERATURE AND JOURNALISM.

TILL comparatively recent years it was the fashion to deny that America had produced any literature.   Not a quarter of a century since supercilious British culture disdained even to know of the existence of such a person as Mark Twain, and this hauteur on our side was encouraged by a humility on the other side which

MARK TWAIN AT HOME

does not entirely accord with our conception of the American character In his "Fable for Critics," Russell Lowell makes one author say —

" His American puffs he will willingly burn all
 To gain but a kick from a transmarine journal "

Down to the middle of the century and later American literature was largely a reflex of English literature The influence of the new environment had not materially affected the character of the transplanted stock.

But all that has now disappeared American literature, like the American Constitution, is a thing which, while it bears ample evidence of the parent from which it sprang, is nevertheless distinct, original, and independent. The old, almost pathetic humility with which American writers listened to the criticisms of Europe, has disappeared. The American is rapidly becoming as self-assertive in literature as he has long been in other departments of human activity, and in proportion as he becomes self-conscious and self-reliant we may expect to find him exercising increasing influence on the literature of the world.

This is no place for a critical estimate of American literature as such I am merely concerned in noting the influence which American writers have had upon the world outside America, and especially the Mother Country Even in the first half of the century Americans were still largely under the influence of English tradition ; they produced many writers whose works constituted no small addition to the common stock of the literature of the English-speaking race. Books which are never read outside the American Union may indirectly have affected human thought by the extent to which they inspired foreign writers, but the direct influence of American books on the non-American world can best be gauged by the American books which the non-Americans read. This reduces the examination of the influence of American literature to an inquiry in the first instance, at least, as to what American authors were read in Europe.

The Americans being pre-eminently politicians, much of their genius for political expression found vent in political oratory ; but the oratory of politicians needs no Chinese wall or prohibition tariff to confine its consumption within the country of origin The fathers of the American Constitution, the statesmen and political thinkers and judges who moulded its early development, are practically unknown to the ordinary European. Educated Englishmen, and some politicians interested in the working of the federal principle, have read the books which form the political Scriptures of the American politicians, but, speaking broadly,

we get their influence second-hand through Tocqueville and Mr. Bryce.

The influence of religion was hardly second to that of politics in the New England States, and the pulpit for many years divided with the forum the articulate genius of America. But I have already touched upon the influence of America on the religious life of the world, and in this chapter I will deal more distinctly with their contributions to literature in the shape of printed books.

The first American whose writings were widely circulated in this country, and who exercised a perceptible although slight influence upon English thought, was Benjamin Franklin He has gone out of vogue in the last thirty years, but in the first half of the century the proverbial wisdom of "Poor Richard's Almanac" was familiar in many English households Franklin was a much greater name to our grandfathers than he is to-day ; it is possible that after a period of comparative obscurity his reputation may revive throughout the English-speaking world.

De Tocqueville did more to make American political thought a potent influence in Europe than any native writers The first Americans to be extensively read in this country were the group of New Englanders who made Boston the literary centre of the New World Foremost among these was Emerson, whose essays are probably read to-day in England more than those of any English writer His "English Traits" figures in the list of almost every popular series of reprints, and his stiletto-like sentences continue to administer subcutaneous injections of transcendental philosophy to the somewhat adipose tissue of John Bull. Emerson may be regarded as the literary and philosophical flower which blossomed on the somewhat thorny stem of seven generations of Puritan preachers from whom he was descended The roots of him were buried deep in the granite of Calvinistic Puritanism, but the growth of two centuries culminated in the evolution of the mystical piety and poetical philosophy of the Sage of Concord. The ethical fruit of centuries of Puritan preachings, and the stern discipline of the New England Christianity, are minted into a kind of universal currency in the winged words and pregnant apothegms of Emerson On our library shelves he stands among the first five essayists who are read everywhere to-day — Montaigne, Bacon, Addison, Lamb, Emerson. Of these five, Emerson, so far as the general reader is concerned, is probably first or second.

After Emerson, Longfellow was the American author most appreciated by the English-speaking world It is probable that to this day by the million he is the best known poet of the nineteenth century, if we exclude the poets who were born at the close of the eighteenth century, and who blossomed into song in the first decade. If we were to attempt to estimate quantitatively the infusion of poetry which has been administered by the poets of England and America to the English-speaking man, it would probably be found that he had absorbed a larger dose of Longfellow than of any poet of the old country. Taking the English-speaking world, even outside the United States of America, it is probable that there are ten persons who are more or less acquainted with Longfellow for one who has read Tennyson, and a hundred have read Longfellow for one who has read Swinburne.

It is the fashion to say that Longfellow was not American. His culture was distinctly European, and the tendency of his verse bears no relation to the American spirit as we understand it to-day. There is in it none of the hustle and the bustle and the intense strain of nervous irritability which distinguish the modern American type; but in estimating the influence of America upon the world it is well to remember that the mild singer of the "Psalm of Life," "The Village Blacksmith," "Excelsior," and a score of similar poems which have passed into the common stock of the poetic thought of the common people, was by birth an American.

The only other American poet, until we come to Whitman—who revolted against the European tradition—whose influence can be named beside that of Longfellow, was James Russell Lowell. Lowell, indeed, may be said to have succeeded Longfellow, and to a certain extent to have superseded him in direct influence upon the English masses. Although three-fourths of his "Biglow Papers" are seldom read, the remaining quarter has passed into the common stock of our thought. For years Lowell was only known by his "Biglow Papers," and it was not until the later sixties that his merit as a serious poet began slowly to gain recognition. It was not until the nineties that the English public woke up to realise the ethical value and political inspiration of his serious verse. When popular feeling is deeply stirred, and in times of strain and of crisis it is rare indeed to attend an English political meeting, or even hear a pulpit utterance in the more advanced churches, in which you do not hear one or more quotations from Russell Lowell. He has been, and is, a subtle power, making always for liberty, for charity, for righteousness. Of all the influences by which America has affected, and is affecting, the English-speaking race, that of Lowell is one of the most valuable. Whittier, John Bright's favourite poet, has gained in popularity of late years. But he

does not attain to the vogue of Longfellow and Lowell.

In the world of fiction America has produced two writers each of whom has written one book that profoundly influenced the non-American world. One was a man, the other a woman. The man was Nathaniel Hawthorne, and his one book was "The Scarlet Letter." The woman was Mrs. Beecher Stowe, and her one book was "Uncle Tom's Cabin." Both Hawthorne and Mrs. Stowe wrote many other novels, which were read with admiration when they appeared, and may be still read with advantage; but although much of Hawthorne's work is still widely read, none of his works, nor all of them put together, have produced so deep an impression as his "Scarlet Letter."

As the years pass, its influence has increased rather than diminished, and it remains at this day one of the first, if not the first, novel of its kind in the English language for its brevity, its pathos, and its force. Against a vast background of dimly remembered novels of passion and of penitence, it stands out as distinct as did the Scarlet Letter upon the bosom of Hester Prynne.

Mrs. Stowe's "Uncle Tom's Cabin" was famous as the first American work which had literally a world-wide audience. Mrs. Stowe was fortunate in her subject, fortunate in the moment when she published her book, and specially fortunate in the spirit with which she handled her story. When you read "Uncle Tom's Cabin" to-day the artlessness about its art makes you sometimes marvel that a book so slight should have produced so immense an effect. But the book came as a revelation, not merely of the realities of slavery in the Southern States, but of the existence of a high and noble humanity under the skin of the coloured man. Englishmen for a couple of generations had been taught to sympathise with the negro. The propaganda of our early abolitionists forms one of the finest chapters in the history of the early years of the nineteenth century; but our grandfathers cared for the negro very much as the anti-vivisectionists care for the dogs and rabbits who are subjected to the torture of the physiological laboratory. If we could imagine some sympathetic genius who could suddenly make the tortured rabbit of the vivisector speak like a human being, and we could see its heart palpitate with all the noble emotions of the parent and the saint, the effect would be somewhat analogous to that which was produced by the sudden apparition of Uncle Tom. The white world had never before realised the essential humanity of the negro. It was admitted as an abstract proposition that he was a human being, but that he was actually a fellow-creature with

HENRY WADSWORTH LONGFELLOW.

JAMES RUSSELL LOWELL.

HENRY GEORGE.

RALPH WALDO EMERSON.

the same passions as ours, that he lived and loved and sorrowed and died even as we, and that in his heart throbbed the same tumultuous eddies of emotion as those which we experience was a truth which it was reserved to Mrs. Stowe to discover and to make the universal possession of mankind   Her book sped like wildfire throughout the whole reading world. The printing-presses toiled in vain to keep up with the demand for copies of " Uncle Tom's Cabin," while translators in every country in Europe exhausted their ingenuity to invent foreign equivalents for the quaint lingo of the southern plantations   Negro slavery in Southern States was swept away by the tremendous besom of the Civil War, but " Uncle Tom's Cabin " continues to be read throughout the world, and dramatised versions still continue to attract audiences in English theatres   To this day, if you take a million white-skinned men, women, and children, you will find a larger percentage who are familiar with Uncle Tom, Legree, Topsy and Eva, than are acquainted with the names of any American Presidents, with the exception of Washington and Lincoln, or any American men of letters without any exception whatever. To the mass of Europeans of the latter half of last century, Mrs. Stowe was the only interpreter of American life whom they knew and in whom they believed. By her book, whatever may be said of its merits or demerits, she undoubtedly contributed not a little to swell the tide of sympathy and compassion, even with the most forlorn and degraded of the human race, a tide which alas, to-day, seems somewhat on the ebb.

Even in the most rapid survey of Americans who have exercised literary influence outside America, due honour must be paid to the weird, fantastic, and somewhat morbid genius of Edgar Allan Poe   His influence may be traced in many directions, and the note which he sounded —original, distinct, and lonesome, has waked many echoes

An American author who had great vogue in the middle of the century, but whose novels are hardly looked at to-day, was Fenimore Cooper, whose " Last of the Mohicans," and other Indian stories, were the delight of our boyhood. His turn may come again, but for the moment he is no longer in demand

Washington Irving, an earlier writer of more varied range, has always commanded a public He did much to familiarise Americans with English life, and his " Rip van Winkle ' has added an imperishable figure to the Elysian fields in which dwell the immortals of modern romance

Of the American historians, Parkman and Bancroft have exercised but little influence outside the United States   Prescott and Motley

rendered yeomen's service in popularising history, and their works at once took the place among the foremost historians of the world Motley to-day is as popular as Macaulay, and is quite as widely read. He may be counted as one of those who contributed to enlighten the more thoughtful Englishmen as to the real significance of the struggle which is raging in South Africa.

Coming down to more recent times, Walt Whitman may be regarded as the first American who, with barbaric yawp, startled the Old World by a message of defiance and revolt. Whitman aspired to be the Washington of literature, to break the fetters of old tradition, to which all American poets before him had tamely submitted, and to found a new school of American poetry, which was to be without form, but gravid with the new message of the New World   Whitman, a born revolutionist, began by revolutionising the laws of metre, and constructed poems, the like of which had never before been printed in English characters   He was not so successful as Washington, but he won for himself a recognised place among the poets of our time, and enlarged the area and the method of poetic expression   Edward Carpenter in this country has followed in his steps, but Whitman's influence has been much wider than that of his actual imitators and disciples   He was a breezy, healthy, virile influence in modern literature

One of the most distinctive contributions which America has made to the literature of the world, is that of humour, a department in which the Americans have left their English kinsmen far behind. He who contributes to the mirth of the world makes humanity his debtor, and the American humorists have put the English-speaking world under heavy obligation. Their export is balanced by no corresponding import, for in the world of letters, unlike that of commerce, there is no necessary reciprocity   From the days of Sam Slick down to those of Mr. Dooley, there has been an unfailing succession of American humorists whose writings have done much to drive dull care away in many millions of homes. Sam Slick, with his " Wise Saws and Modern Instances," is not an American of the United States, for he hailed from the province now included in the Canadian Dominion ; but he was distinctively American, and it was he who made Britain acquainted with the peculiar note of American mirth

After him there have been humorists of all kinds, from the literary humorist, like the genial Autocrat of the Breakfast-table, down to the latest arrival, the Irish American humorist who has familiarised the world with the dialect and the philosophy of the Chicago saloon Artemus Ward, at one time in the ascendant.

has been eclipsed by Mark Twain, who is *facile princeps* among the American writers of to-day. There is no American author whose works to-day are as widely read and translated into so many languages as those of Mr Samuel Clemens Whether grave or gay, he can always command a world-wide public In the colonies, he is as popular as in the Old Country, and such of his humour as is translatable is current in every European country. The Board of Trade statistics take no account of the product of humour, but mankind which loves laughter feels much more grateful to the owners of the rare gift which enables them to tickle the midriff with printed words than to all its philosophers. America has exported, and continues to export in ever increasing quantities, pills and drugs of all kinds, but a merry heart doeth good like a medicine, and Mark Twain has probably done more to make men happy and healthy and wise than all the artificers of patent medicines who contribute so liberally to the advertising revenue of newspapers and magazines

Uncle Remus, with his inimitable Brer Rabbit stories, has contributed a distinct and welcome novelty to the humorous literature of the world. It is an extraordinary instance of the way in which genuine humour can triumph over difficulties of dialect, so that the public will acquire the dialect in order the better to appreciate the humour Mr Harris has achieved such success with his version of the stories which Uncle Remus told to the little boy, that at this moment Brer Rabbit, Brer Fox, Brer Terrapin, to mention only three of his menagerie of favourites, are much better known and much more appreciated outside America than all the American politicians who have won fame and glory for themselves in the annals of the United States

It is too early to estimate the effect of the modern American novelist upon English literature, but W D Howells, F. Marion Crawford, and Henry James are among the authors who appeal to the whole English-speaking world. They are not only read by the million, but their style has influenced and is influencing more and more the new school of British novelists.

In estimating the influence which Americans have exercised by the use of the printed book, it is impossible to overlook the immediate and world-wide influence that was wielded by Henry George. In the portrait gallery of notables of the nineteenth century, which has just been published by the Berlin Photographic Company, Henry George occupies a distinguished place as one of the Americans of international fame His book on "Progress and Poverty" was one

of the late products of the century, it had considerable difficulty in finding a publisher in the land of its birth, but it was no sooner born into the world than it was hailed by multitudes in every part of the British Empire and also on the Continent of Europe as a veritable gospel of these latter days

America, which represents the triumph of individualism pushed to an extreme, has also produced in these latter days some of the books which have most powerfully re-acted against individualism · Bellamy's "Looking Backward" is perhaps the most conspicuous instance of a book without any particular literary merit which, nevertheless, commanded at once universal circulation, owing to the fact that it portrayed in story form a realised dream of the modern Socialist. Sheldon's books, equally devoid of any literary charm, commanded readers literally by the million, owing to the promise which they held out of better things to come. The American Idealist and Socialist who will have the genius to express with literary charm his idealistic visions of a Socialist millenium will sweep in triumph through the world

In closing this very imperfect survey of the influence of American books on the non-American world, one thing is obvious The influence of American literature has been distinctly good What there is of evil in it has been consumed at home. The broad Atlantic has acted as a potent antiseptic, which has killed noxious germs and only left that which is healthy, helpful, and human to reach our shores. American humour has contributed much to the gaiety of the world, and American poetry has been both refining and inspiring in its influence on the masses of our people

The influence of American Socialists, from the days of Brook Farm down to the speculations of Mr. H. D. Lloyd, have all tended in the right direction in widening the somewhat narrow and circumscribed horizon which is indicated by the phrase "the range of practical politics" The influence of Henry George is very marked in New Zealand and in the Australian Colonies, where it has probably produced much more direct results in legislation than in the country which gave it birth.

American journalism is a much more distinctive product than American literature. The American newspaper, thanks to the absence of paper duties and of advertisement taxes, became popular long before the English newspaper. Fifty years ago every American was reading a daily newspaper, whereas in England not one man in ten could afford the luxury. Hence, the popular journalism of the new country is really older than the popular journalism of the old The cheap press with us is only forty years old In America it is at least twice that age The American newspaper from the first was racy of the soil, was close to its constituency, and represented far more faithfully than its English contemporaries the aspirations, the ideas, and the prejudices of the masses of the people These characteristics it has preserved to this day The American newspaper is the mirror of the life of the American people. It partakes of all their characteristics, their virtues, and the vices of their virtues It is as huge as the continent in which it is produced, and it is often as crude as the half-settled territories over which the American people sprawl It is the fashion among English people, especially among those who know nothing about it, to sneer at American newspapers, but take them altogether, the American newspaper is distinctly ahead of its English contemporaries To begin with, there is more of it, more news, more advertisements, more paper, more print Life would be impossible in America to any American if he had to read the whole of his newspaper, but just as the people have wide and varied tastes, and the interests of the whole community have to be catered for, everything goes in and no reader is expected to do more than assimilate just such portion of the mammoth sheet as meets his taste Hence the busiest people in the world, who have less time for deliberate reading than any race, buy regularly morning and evening more printed matter than would fill a New Testament, and on Sundays would consider themselves defrauded if they did not have a bale of printed matter delivered at their doors almost equal in bulk to a family Bible. They do not read it all, any more than a cow eats all the grass of the meadow into which she is turned loose to graze They browse over it, picking here and there such a tasty herbage as may suit their palates. In this way a newspaper comes to be almost like a Gazetteer or an Encyclopædia. No one sits down and reads a dictionary from end to end. He dips into it So Americans dip into their papers for what they want. Unfortunately newspapers, unlike dictionaries, are incapable of alphabetical classification. Hence arises the tendency which offends so many English readers, of exaggerated headings or scare-heads, as they are called in the slang of the profession The readers of the *Times*, which rarely ventures upon a double heading, excepting on the outbreak of a war or the overturning of a dynasty, are unspeakably offended by finding the ordinary news set out with half a-dozen head-lines with staring capitals But these headlines are almost indispensable as a guide to the contents of the paper, and as a corrective of the excessive smallness of the type in which American papers are printed A man hurrying to business in a tramcar or railway can read the scare-heads without straining his eyesight, and by running his eyes along the tops of the columns, obtains not only a very fair idea of the contents of the paper, but also discovers what particular column it is necessary for him to read

The scare-head is like the display in the show window in which the tradesman sets out his wares The art of window-dressing is beginning to be acclimatised among us, and so is the art of scare-heading. Comparatively few English journalists have appreciated the fact that good journalism consists much more in the proper labelling and displaying of your goods than in the writing of leading articles. The intrinsic value of news is a quality which does not depend upon the editor, but the method of display and the setting of the diamond is that which affords scope for the editorial art

American journalism, as compared with that of Great Britain, is more enterprising, more energetic, more extravagant, and more unscrupulous The stander traditions of English newspapers restrain even the most reckless of pressmen within narrower limits than the broad field in which many American journalists are permitted to wander The interview was a distinctively American invention, which has been acclimatised in this country, although with odd limitations The *Times*, for instance will never publish an interview with any person if it takes place on British soil, but if the same person is interviewed by one of its foreign correspondents and the interview is sent over the wires, it appears without question

American newspapers differ endlessly.* There are some that are almost as staid, not to say stodgy, as any paper published in Great Britain. There are others that go to the furthest extreme of vulgar sensationalism, but setting one off against the other, the American newspaper is much more varied in its contents than the journals of the Old World. They have more space, and they take much greater pains to serve up their news in a vivid, interesting

---

* I very much dislike overloading my pages with statistics, and prefer, when possible, to relegate unreadable columns of figures to a foot-note. The following figures, extracted from the United States Treasury Department's Report on the progress of the United States and its material industries, are too suggestive to be omitted

	1870	1900
Population	38,558,371	76,303,387
Salaries paid in Public Schools	$37,832,566	$128,662,880
Newspapers and Periodicals	5,871	21,178
Post-Offices in existence	28,492	76,668
Receipts of Post-Office Department	$19,772,221	$102,354,579
Telegraph messages sent	9,157,646	79,696,227
Railways in operation (miles)	52,922	190,883

manner No doubt, American journalism has the faults of its qualities, and the perpetual straining after immediate effect is often indulged in with disastrous results to what an English journalist would regard as consistency and decorum Whatever ministers most effectively to the mood of the moment is supplied hot and strong from the press, and if the mood of the moment changes, then the subject is dropped incontinently, as if it were a hot potato. There is nothing better in journalism than a good interview conscientiously reported by a capable journalist, but there is nothing worse than many of the abominable perversions and inventions which are often served up under that head To make a story, to secure a " beat " of news, almost any manœuvre is regarded as legitimate, with the result that in some papers the value of an interview is as much depreciated as were the assignats in the critical times of the French Revolution Almost all the best dailies in America devote considerable space to illustrations and caricatures, while some of them in their Sunday editions produce coloured supplements for the amusement of children with which we have nothing to compare.

The British Empire is sadly lacking in capable caricaturists Since Sir John Tenniel retired Mr Gould is first of British caricaturists, and there are some on the staff of *Punch* who are worthy of the Tenniel tradition. Mr. Furniss is still with us, but has fallen far below the level of his best days Mr. Ben Gough is the most capable caricaturist whom Canada has produced, while the artists of the *Sydney Bulletin* and the *Melbourne Punch* produce work which is certainly not deficient in force and point But there are many more American caricaturists of the first rank than the British. *Judge* and *Puck* have the advantage of producing their cartoons in colour, but the men on *Life*, to say nothing of those on the *Journal* and the *World* of New York, and the *North American* of Philadelphia, can be relied upon to turn out good work almost every day One of the most capable cartoonists of the United States, is Mr Bart of the *Minneapolis Journal*, while in Mr P. J Carter the *Minneapolis Times* possesses a very smart craftsman, Minneapolis having much more than its fair share of this particular kind of talent

It is in the newspaper offices that the drive, bustle and intense strain of American life is preeminently centred, and the so-called " yellow " journals are those where the national characteristics find the freest scope and the widest range Among " yellow " papers the Hearst papers stand easily conspicuous. Mr Pulitzer founded this latter day journalism, and for a time reigned supreme in the *New York Herald* His success provoked Mr. W. R Hearst to enter the field, and by

dint of lavish expenditure and great journalistic flaire he succeeded in building up a newspaper which is at once the wonder and the despair of its competitors Mr Hearst is still a young man, with command of unlimited capital, who has spanned the continent with his three papers, the *New York Journal,* the *Chicago American,* and the *San Francisco Examiner* The style of all these journals is loud. There is no limit, save that of the typographer, to the eccentricity which they adopt for the purpose of displaying their news, and of calling attention to their wares. During the Cuban War, the *Journal* would sometimes come out with its front page consisting solely of about four or five lines in huge type, resembling nothing so much as the news bills of the London evening papers. But it is a great mistake to regard the *New York Journal* as a mere catch-penny news-sheet It is a paper which has a very clearly defined creed, which it preaches with consistency and energy It is true that the preaching friars who use it as their rostrum sometimes " ding the pulpit to blads," but when you are addressing the cosmopolitan, polyglot, very busy millions of people to whom the *Journal* appeals, it is impossible to speak with the well-bred whisper of diplomacy. There is a difference, of course, between the diplomatic whisper and the megaphonic roar of the *Journal,* but the wise man looks more to the substance of what is said than the manner of its delivery

Mr Hearst's famous definition of the difference between journalism that does things and the journalism that only chronicles them, is continually receiving fresh illustrations In his own way he has grasped the idea, not perfectly but still resolutely, of government by journalism, and when experience and age have brought a little more steadiness Mr Hearst may become the most powerful journalist in the world He embodies and exaggerates all the distinctively American qualities of the later days. He is self-assertive, pushing, defiant, and determined at whatever cost to " get there " every time It is a popular superstition among the respectable Americans that no one ever reads the *Journal* " Its name, we never mention it ; oh, no, 'tis never heard," and Mr Frederic Harrison, after making a prolonged tour in the United States, was able to assure the readers of the *Nineteenth Century* that during the whole of his travels he had never once met any person who ever saw or spoke of a yellow journal.

" Doth not Wisdom cry ? and understanding put forth her voice ? She standeth in the top of high places, by the way in the places of the paths. She crieth at the gates, at the entry of the city, at the coming in at the doors. Unto you, O men, I call , and my voice is to the sons of man" It is to be feared that a good many cultured people in the olden time, who dwelt in their studies or in their lecture-rooms, were as deaf to the voice of Wisdom thus publicly crying in the highways and byways of the city as Mr Harrison was to the voice of yellow journalism. No one can understand America to-day, with all the sum of its turbulent activities, with its best and its worst, who closes his eyes to the so-called "yellow" journals.*

One of the most recent exploits of the Hearst papers was to assist two young women in Chicago who, on behalf of the Teachers' Federation, took legal action for the purpose of compelling the officials to make a fair assessment of property in Chicago As the result of the support given to the teachers, property valued at £47,000,000 was added to the rateable value of the city of Chicago, which rendered it possible, without raising the rates, to add half a million to the revenue of the city The Judge, in giving his decision on the question, declared that the *Chicago American*, in fighting the tax-dodgers, had been fearless, and there was no question of its devotion to public honesty As the *Journal* pleasantly remarked "This is only one of a hundred instances in which the Hearst newspapers have stepped with spiked boots on the toes of thieving corporations Hence you can begin to appreciate the extent of the animosity against them among the predatory classes"

It maintained, not without reason, that many "respectable" persons, who foamed at the mouth at the mention of "yellow journalism" did so because they feared its fearlessness The virulent fanatic hatred with which yellow journalism is regarded led Mr Hearst to say. "What is the trouble then? It has nothing to do with morals, for the *Journal*, the *American*, and the *Examiner* are more scrupulous in regard to the character of the matter they print than any other papers of general circulation in their respective cities. It has nothing to do with politics, for these

journals have set an example of fair and courteous treatment of political opponents, that has been gratefully recognised by the partisan leaders they have fought" The real secret of the hatred is because they come down with spiked boots upon so many dishonest people's toes. Another delusion is that the Hearst papers have no policy On the contrary, they have maintained a very definite policy both in home and foreign affairs Most of their demands in foreign affairs are now accepted by the nation, and are recognised as part and parcel of the policy of the United States In home affairs they propounded at the beginning of the year 1901 the following seven-headed programme, which is worth while bearing in mind —

(1) Election of senators by the people, (2) destruction of criminal trusts, (3) No protection for oppressive trusts; (4) The public ownership of public franchises, (5) a graduated income tax, (6) currency reform, (7) national, state, and municipal improvement of the public school system

Here are politics, says the *Journal*, which look towards progress, and represent the truest Americanism

There is some talk of Mr Hearst starting a daily paper in London. There is plenty of room here for spiked boots that come down roughly upon the toes of evil-doers, and to-day we should welcome a vigorous, energetic newspaper of the Hearst kind, even if it did overdo the scare-head and the big type.

The periodical magazine is another form of literary activity in which the Americans have outstripped the British, especially in the matter of illustrations The *Century*, *Scribner*, and *Harper* are three periodicals for the like of which we may search in vain through the periodical literature of the world The *Cosmopolitan*, *McClure's*, and *Everybody's Magazine* are also as good as, and often better than the best of our popular sixpennies. The *American Review of Reviews* is much superior both in price and general get-up and advertisements to the English *Review of Reviews*, from which it sprang We have no magazine comparable to the *World's Work*. Neither have we anything comparable to the *Youth's Companion*, the *Ladies' Home Journal*, or *Success*

Of the non-illustrated magazines, the *North American* may challenge comparison with the *Nineteenth Century*, but on the high-priced magazines the old country still has the pull, and the same may be said of Russia and France. The American magazine has an advantage over its English competitors in the postal rates, which enable second-class mail matter to be sent through the post at an almost nominal charge,

* People seem to imagine that "yellow" is an opprobrious epithet Yellow was the colour which the Jews had to wear in the Ghetto The yellow rose is the badge of Zionism to-day but the yellow of American journalism has nothing to do with that It originated in the fact that first one of these journals and then another employed in its colour printed weekly supplements the picture of a child dressed in a yellow frock, who is known as the "yellow kid" The adventures of this small urchin were described week after week, and the continual reappearance of the yellow-frocked youngster gave the name of yellow to the journals in whose pages it figured There was nothing opprobrious in the epithet, and it has been so absurdly misapplied that yellow, in the mouth of some people, is almost a synonym for go-ahead and enterprising

whereas in England the postage often adds 50 per cent to the cost of the magazine *

Discussing the Americanisation of the world, it is necessary to say at least a passing word upon the Americanisation of the English language It is the fashion in some quarters to believe that the Americans are corrupting the language. The Americans, on the other hand, maintain with considerable show of reason, that many words and phrases which we regard as distinctively American are really from the well of English undefiled as it was to be found in the spacious times of Great Elizabeth. They also maintain that London is the great corrupter of English pronunciation, and it is tolerably certain that if there were to be an Academy of the Language formed, many of the greatest purists would come from the other side of the Atlantic. On the other hand, the Americans have taken the lead in eliminating what they regard as superfluous letters from English words, a process which in time may make great change in the outward appearance, although not in the pronunciation of our mother-tongue. Long ago the Americans dropped the superfluous "u" in such words as "honour," and substituted "z" for "s" in words like "organise."

The National Educational Association formally adopted for use in all its official publications a simplified spelling for these twelve words —*program, tho, altho, thoro, thorofare, thru, thruout, catalog, prolog, decalog, demagog, pedagog.*

The United States Government some time ago appointed a Board to decide on a uniform spelling for geographical names They reported in favour of the elimination of the unnecessary letters, so that Behring Straits in the American official publications is spelt without the "h." A committee of the American Association for the Advancement of Science has also drawn up rules for the uniform spelling of chemical terms. Its most important recommendations, which have been adopted in the school-books, eliminate the final "e" from such words as "oxide," "iodide," "chloride," "quinine," "morphine," "aniline," &c

This tendency to eliminate superfluous letters, although much to be lamented from the point of view of the philologist who wishes to trace the origin of words, nevertheless represents a simplicity in spelling and economy in space

* The privilege of sending periodicals through the post as second class mail matter at a nominal postage rate has been much abused Several so called magazines are serial directories, others are mere advertising pamphlets; and at one time almost any book could be sent through the post at magazine rates, if only it were brought out in a series. These abuses are, however, being vigorously dealt with, to the great benefit of the legitimate magazines.

It is not difficult to foresee the coming of a still greater change. Some day the American, with his characteristic directness and genius for going straight to the point, recognising that the one great obstacle in the way of the universal adoption of the English language as a means of communication between man and man is its spelling, will take courage and reduce the language of Shakespeare and Milton to a phonetic system. The literary sense shudders at the thought of the disappearance of the familiar words, which have become indissolubly associated with the ideas which they express, but from a practical point of view, the convenience of the change would be incalculable. Those who live in the period of transition will have a bad time, but all future generations will gain when the spelling of the words is made to correspond to the way in which they are pronounced. Thus possibly the Americans may adopt the change many years before it is accepted in more conservative Britain. In that case there will be a great danger of our losing the one adjective which describes our common race, for their language will be known as the American as distinct from the English. We shall have two tongues pronounced in the same way, but spelt differently It is easy to see how, if the unification of the English-speaking race is not speedily effected, such an alteration would make a very subtle appeal to the instinct of American patriotism. At the present an American must speak English, for he cannot differentiate the language which he speaks from that of the mother-country, but, if the spelling were altered, the Americans would have a language of their own. Let us hope that from so great a disaster the Race may be saved by the Union which will secure that the alteration in spelling shall be effected simultaneously throughout the whole area of the English-speaking world.

———

CHAPTER III.—ART, SCIENCE AND MUSIC.

FIFTY years ago, even thirty years ago, an allusion to American art would have provoked an incredulous smile on the part of our Royal Academicians. The Americans were supposed to have a supreme capacity for producing pork and corn, but as for the fine arts we have only to turn to English newspapers at the time when Mrs. Trollope and Dickens were regarded as the chief authorities upon things American, to realise how absurd must have seemed a suggestion that even in this field Britons would not be able to hold their own That this is the fact in at least some branches of art has been formally attested this year in the most official fashion The Coronation of Edward VII. is the great ceremonial event to which we are all looking forward in 1902. It is more than sixty years since the old Abbey witnessed the coronation of a British Sovereign. All the resources of the Empire will be employed to make the coronation of the King as perfect a picture and symbol of the Empire as the wit or imagination of man can devise. But when the question arose as to the artist to whom should be deputed the duty of making permanent the picture of the great scene upon which the eyes of the world will be centred next June, the King passed over all British artists, and selected for the supreme task a citizen of the Republic It is by the aid of the brush of Mr Edwin Abbey, an American artist, that posterity will picture the crowning of Edward VII

This Royal homage to Republican genius by no means stands alone, nor is Mr Abbey the only American who in the opinion of the British themselves has been worthy of the highest place among British artists. In last year's Academy Mr. Sargent was *facile princeps* It was Sargent's year, said the art critics, with astonishing unanimity, and some did not even hesitate to accompany their tribute to Mr. Sargent with more or less contumelious reflections upon the British-born artists, whose canvases they declared only served as foils to the supreme excellence of the American.

Mr. Whistler is another notable American whose original genius has triumphed over all the prejudice excited by a somewhat eccentric form of expression. Of course it may be said, and justly said, that the British pictures exhibited at the Paris Exhibition were superior, taken as a whole, to those exhibited by American artists, but it is the excellence of the supreme artist rather than the general average of the rank and file which counts in the history of art

The Royal Munich Academy this year has selected for special honour three English-speaking artists, two of whom, Mr. Sargent and Mr Abbey, are American, and one, Mr. Walter Crane, is an Englishman But both of the American artists are acclimatised in the Old World. Mr. Sargent was born in Italy of American parents, and he may be said to be Europeanised from his birth. Mr Abbey, born in Philadelphia, was educated in America, but he quitted the New World two and twenty years ago. Mr. Whistler is a voluntary exile from his native land. It is inevitable that the Old World should attract the artists for a time, but that time is passing American sculptors find a most congenial home in Rome, and American

artists prefer Paris and London to New York or Chicago

But while they go abroad to be Europeanised and to profit by the picture galleries of Europe, they cannot be Europeanised without each of them exercising a more or less Americanising influence upon the society in the midst of which they live For the American, like a lump of sugar or a drop of vinegar—whichever you prefer —in a glass of water, always makes his personality felt. American students troop to Paris in such numbers that they have an association of their own, which every year holds an exhibition The Association is not composed exclusively of Americans, but the citizens of the United States predominate It is said that there are no fewer than two hundred American architects at the Beaux-Arts, while American artists are much more numerous

In England we have recently witnessed the formation of an International Society for sculptors, painters, and gravers, which holds its own exhibitions, at which its members show their best work in such a fashion that it may be seen to the best advantage. Its President, Mr Whistler, is an American Mr. Pennell, who is one of the best black and white artists in London, is also an American. Mr. St. Gaudens, Mr MacMonnies, Mr. Chase, Mr. Alexander, and Mr. Melchers, are among the honorary members; Mr. Humphreys Johnston, Mr. Muhrman, Mr. Mura, among the associates; while this year Mr Lungren and Mr. McLure Hamilton were exhibitors So that the International Society will be largely American That is, indeed, but symbolical of the change which is going on on a larger scale in every department of life The Americans are a great internationalising element Being themselves an amalgam of many nations, they constitute a kind of human flux, which enables the diverse elements of hostile nationalities to form a harmonious whole In our Royal Academy we have at present only two Americans, but they worthily uphold the honour of the United States.

There is a very excellent reason why American artists should prefer to paint in the Old World. Mr J W Alexander, the painter, in a recent lecture before the National Art Club of New York, explained one reason why the artist prefers to paint outside his native land. A prophet has no honour in his own country, and Mr Alexander declares that the price of a picture painted in the United States is scarcely more than one-fifth of what it would bring if it had been painted abroad by the same artist in the same style and with the same merits. Pictures, in the opinion of American collectors, still, it would seem, require the hall-mark of Europe

I 2

A heavy duty imposed upon works of art, a kind of protection for American artists, fails in its purpose, and leads American collectors to keep their collections in London rather than in New York

The American with his brush as yet has probably had less influence upon European art than the American with his dollars, for Mæcenas, who in the old days was patron of all art and letters in Imperial Rome, has been reincarnated nowadays with an American accent In all the great cities in America picture galleries are growing up, to which from time to time the masterpieces of Europe are transported with reverent hands, and displayed as a perennial source of culture before the eyes of the young Democracy A French artist, M. Edmond Aman Jean, who recently visited America, has lately published a rather remarkable appreciation of American art. He said that although he had often served on the Salon juries in Paris, he had never seen so much justice and such a strict honesty as was manifested in the examination of the works which made up the Carnegie Exhibition in 1901. And then, going on to speak of American art as a whole, he declared —

"My conviction is that, like Venice, the United States will have one day the most magnificent school of painting in the world Venice commenced like America, by industry and commerce. She had her sellers before she had her painters. She was obliged to acquire opulence and domination before she could found a school of art. Generations must pass away yet before in the field of art old Europe will be definitely vanquished, but the generations will be born, will live and die, and the new art will come permanently into existence."

American architecture is ill understood by those who imagine that its culminating triumph has been the construction of thirty-story sky-scrapers. No one is likely to fall into such an error who visited the World's Fair in Chicago The Court of Honour, with its palaces surrounding the great fountain, the slender columns of the peristyle, the golden dome of the administration building, formed a picture the like of which the world has not seen before The long stately lines of the great palaces, the glory of the colonnades, and the beauty of the lagoons, in which the great buildings were mirrored when the waters were not disturbed by the gondolas, left an impression of perfect beauty and stately symmetry never equalled in any of the most famous architectural marbles of the Old World. Yet the buildings had none of the associations of history and of tradition which contribute so largely to impress the pilgrims to the great cathedrals of the Middle Ages or the temples of Greece and Rome. The buildings were new from the architect's hands It was a great tribute to the genius of their builders that the buildings which they reared could produce so constant and abiding an effect. The race which could produce the Court of Honour in the World's Fair will cover the Continent with imperishable monuments of its genius.

In sculpture the Americans are as productive as original and as instinct with forceful virility Mr St. Gaudens is probably the greatest living sculptor, if we except M Roden.

Passing from art to science, the first two American naturalists whose names became known to the Old World were Audubon in ornithology, and Professor Agassiz. It is a long time since they passed away, so long that they appear almost to belong to a vanished world. In the Twentieth Century there seems to be ample ground for believing that the Americans will distance us in science more decisively than in almost any other department of human activity The reason for this lies, not only in the genius of the people, but because the provision made for scientific research by the munificence of American millionaires is infinitely in excess of anything that is provided in the British Empire Sir Norman Lockyer recently made a bitter lament as to the scandalous neglect of science by the British Government Recommendations made years ago for the appointment of a Scientific Council have never been carried into effect, and there is hardly any department of scientific research that is provided even with sufficient funds to find itself with its necessary instruments Not only do the Americans equip all their great universities with magnificent apparatus and adequate endowments, but they send their ablest students abroad to study with the best experts in every branch of science. They tap the brains of the world, and keep themselves fully abreast of the latest results of modern research.

Not only is this true of what may be called the Brahmins of science, but American news-papers take much more pains to popularise scientific discoveries than is thought worth while by their English admirers. The yellowest of yellow journals will describe, in page after page, the latest discovery in astronomy or the most recent speculations as to the art and culture of Palæolithic man

Another notable advantage which the Americans have in the scientific field is that they draw both sexes, whereas in England, with very few exceptions, science is a monopoly of the male. One of the most remarkable instances of the advantage of being able to lay the talents of both sexes under contribution in the work of science is afforded by the story of the Klumpke sisters. There are four of them. Miss Dorothea Klumpke, the brilliant San Francisco girl, won for herself a distinguished and unique position in the Paris Observatory, where she has been employed for years at the head of a large staff of girls in making a chart of the heavens. She was one of the astronomers selected by the French Government to observe the recent eclipse of the sun. Not only is she an astronomer, but also she is an intrepid aeronaut, and, if current gossip be well founded, she was in a balloon at the fateful moment when she found her destiny in the stars in another than an astrological sense. The Klumpke girls form a remarkable group, perhaps the most remarkable group of sisters at present on this planet. Dorothea, the astronomer, is the eldest. After her comes her sister Anna, who is an artist, and famous as the intimate friend and legatee of Rosa Bonheur, Augusta, a doctor, was the first woman to obtain an appointment as house-surgeon in a Paris hospital, and she subsequently married a French doctor. Julia Klumpke has already achieved fame as a violinist and a singer. A few more families like the Klumpke girls would Americanise Europe with a vengeance. Unfortunately such groups are rare, even in the United States.

It would be impossible to attempt even the most cursory survey of the contributions that Americans have made to human science, which, being of no country and cosmopolitan in its nature, bears perhaps less trace of Americanisation than many other departments of human activity. It would be presumption on my part to attempt even to summarise in outline the contributions which Americans have made to modern science. All that I wish to do here is to remind the public, and especially my own countrymen, of the achievements of the Americans in this as in other departments of life, in order to combat the prevalent delusion which still lingers in many old-world quarters, that the Americans are nothing more than growers of corn and rearers of pork.

Astronomy is one of the oldest and most sublime of all sciences, and it is precisely in this science that the Americans are leading the world. Sir Robert Ball, Astronomer-Royal, recently declared to Mr G. P. Service, an American astronomer, that—

"America now leads the van of astronomical science." "The greatest advance," he said, "that astronomy has recently made is what the Americans have been doing. It is the work accomplished by Professor Keeler at the great Lick Observatory in California. I do not know of anything in astronomy so important as what he did a little before his death, when he discovered the nebular wonders of the heavens. I do not know of anything that can be compared to this discovery in the recent advance of astronomy for its immense importance and significance, for the light which it throws upon the origin of the solar system, and the suggestion which it makes as to the beginnings of the manner of formation of such systems."

So said Sir Robert Ball at the end of last October, and three weeks had hardly passed before the astronomers in the Lick Observatory reported a new conquest in the unexpected and startling discovery which they made in photographing a star in Nova Persii.

About the same time occurred the publication of a report of Professor Pickering, of Harvard describing the results of his spectroscopic analysis of lightning, which, in his judgment, suggests that hydrogen is not an element, but only a compound. Professor Pickering further reported that "there is a close resemblance between the spectrum of lightning and that of the new star in Perseus." Science may be thus started upon new fields.

One of the early characteristics of the American, noted by all Englishmen who visited the country in the first half of last century, was the intense spirit of curiosity, of Yankee inquisitiveness, as it was called. In those early days the habit of cross-examining a stranger down to the ground upon all the details of his life and business may have been carried to lengths which were hardly consistent with the hospitality due to the stranger within their gates. But the essence of inquisitiveness is the spirit of inquiry which forms the basis of all scientific progress. The Yankee who in the railway car asked you who you were, what your income was, what you had done, and what you hoped to do, was treating you as every man of science treats every unknown phenomenon which presents itself to him. The scientist is a perpetual note of interrogation, and this intense eagerness to know, to find out things, and a certain child-like faculty of constantly renewed wonderment, affords broad and deep foundation for the future pre-eminence of America in scientific pursuits.

With sandwichmen parading the streets of London, announcing two performances daily of De Souza's band, we have one side of American music brought very prominently before the attention of the London public.

The "Washington Post March" has drummed itself into the ears of the whole world. The great American composers, however, have yet to be born, but American prima donnas are arising to charm the Old World with the native wood-notes wild of the New World. For many years American audiences have been thrilled by the notes of European artists. They are beginning to repay their debt. It is rather odd to read that a young Illinois woman, Miss Minnie

Methot, after beginning her career as soprano in the first Congregational Church in Evanston, Illinois, has been chosen to sing one of the leading parts in Paderewski's new opera of " Manru " in Berlin

Not less interesting, but even more significant, is the fact that German jealousy of American competition has shown itself on the operatic stage, and that more than once American singers have been compelled to abandon *rôles* which they were recognised as the fittest to fill, because of the jealousy of their fellow-artists of the old world, who resent American rivalry on the stage as much as German Protectionists resent the import of American goods into the market

Emma Nevada is another of the American cantatrices whose talents have commanded European recognition, and it will be remembered was one of the last singers commanded to sing in private before Queen Victoria. The use of singing as a means of Evangelisation, if not originally an American notion, received its chief recognition from Americans. Mr Philip Phillips, the Singing Pilgrim, began it, but it was Mr. Sankey who made sacred song more important as an instrument of revival than the sermon The latest movement among the churches in Chicago has been the formation of a plan at Chicago Theological Seminary for starting a school of church music where preachers and choirs could study under professors selected for their special knowledge of the best use of music in religious worship.

Few things struck me more when I was in Chicago than the attention which was paid to music, and the popularity of high-class music. Some people say that the Americans owe this to the large infusion of the Germans · · If this be so, Americans have taken to it very kindly A remarkable tribute to American music was recently paid by Dr. Wilhelm Klatte, who, last November, in the course of his series of lectures on the history of music, declared his conviction that the United States would be teaching Europe music within twenty years.

" America," he said, " is undoubtedly on the threshold of a great musical career. Native composition is only emerging from its infancy, and most American musical exponents are fresh from European schooling. But music, like everything else, will become typically American,"

What evidently impressed Dr. Klatte deeply was the presence in Berlin of such large numbers of earnest and devoted students of music from across the Atlantic.

" The records of our Conservatories show that out of an average class of five hundred, one-fifth is composed of Yankees, while the

remainder are Germans. Never fewer than forty-five Americans obtain first honours, while if two hundred Germans manage to secure a like position, the percentage is high "

Some American critics have looked askance at Dr. Klatte's compliments, with a suspicion that he is poking fun at them with his complimentary prophecies But Dr. Klatte is a distinguished musical critic on the most widely circulated Berlin newspaper, and there is no reason to believe that he was not expressing a genuine conviction as to the future triumphs of America in the musical world

---

CHAPTER IV.—THE THEATRE.

" THE Theatre " is a subject upon which I am unable to speak with any personal knowledge, and for this reason I have asked Mr William Archer, the foremost literary critic of the drama, to supply this chapter on the American invasion of the English theatre. Mr. Archer writes —

" The American invasion of the English theatre began about fifteen years ago, with the first visit of Mr. Augustin Daly's company to London. Long before that, indeed, we had seen many American actors in England ; but they came as ' single spies,' not ' in battalions ' The first great American tragedian, Edwin Forrest, met with such scant appreciation on this side that the resentment of his admirers led to the sanguinary Astor Place riot in New York, during William Charles Macready's farewell visit to America Thomas Abthorpe Cooper, too, was scarcely successful in London , and several other American actors, such as Davidge, Hackett, and E. L. Davenport, made no great mark on the English stage. (Here let me say that I am writing at a distance from all books of reference, and must crave indulgence for possible small inaccuracies) Even Edwin Booth on his first visit to England passed almost unperceived It was not till he acted at the Princess's Theatre and (by Sir Henry Irving's invitation) at the Lyceum in 1880 that his genius met with adequate recognition, and even then he was scarcely a popular success. Charlotte Cushman and Joseph Jefferson, on the other hand, were highly appreciated, and (if I mistake not) were almost the first American actors to make considerable profits in England The ' Bateman Children,' an American family, appeared in London as early as the eighteen-fifties, and grew up to take a prominent position on the English stage. It was under the management of their father, H. L. Bateman, at the Lyceum, that Henry Irving rose into fame. One or two American 'variety actors,' such as J. K Emmett and Miss Minnie Palmer, were very popular in the seventies and eighties, while in the same decades comedians such as John T. Raymond, W. J. Florence, and Henry Dixey, tragedians such as John McCullough and Lawrence Barrett, made only a faint impression On the whole, it may be said that down to 1895 Miss Mary Anderson was the only American 'star' of the first magnitude who had taken a very prominent place in the English theatrical firmament

"Meanwhile many English actors had brought back cargoes of dollars from America—George Frederick Cooke, Edmund and Charles Kean, Ellen Tree, Macready, Tyrone Power, E A. Sothern, and others Sir Henry Irving's American tours (with a complete English company) were from the first immensely successful, and so were the visits of Mr and Mrs Kendal at a somewhat later date. The 'balance of trade,' down to the last decade of the nineteenth century, was entirely and obviously in favour of England.

"The tide began to turn, as above suggested, with the first visit of the Daly Company. It was not the first American company to be imported entire I remember at least one predecessor—the 'Salusbury Trouhadours'—who appeared at the Gaiety Theatre about 1880. But the Daly Company was the first to establish itself permanently in the good graces of the English public. Its visits were looked forward to as almost an annual institution, and Miss Ada Rehan and Mr. John Drew, Mrs. Gilbert and Mr James Lewis became as popular in London as in New York. After a few seasons Mr Daly built the handsome theatre in Cranbourne Street, which still bears his name, and 'The Star-Spangled Banner' was played along with 'God Save the Queen' on the opening night Mr. Daly's good fortune, however, did not long abide with him in his own theatre, and the leadership of the American invasion soon passed into other hands

"Mr. Daly had shown us no genuinely American plays The staple of his productions consisted of farces adapted from the German—more rarely from the French—with three or four Shakespearean revivals The first entirely American play of any note presented in London by an entirely American company was Mr William Gillette's 'Secret Service' It was a great success, and encouraged the manager, Mr. Charles Frohman, to make further efforts. He became more or less intermittently interested in several London theatres, and one, the Duke of York's Theatre, he has for some years entirely controlled. In these theatres Mr Frohman has exploited a good many of his New York productions, but they have scarcely ever been American plays Some of them have been plays written by English authors, such as 'The Christian,' by Mr. Hall Caine, which, after making a great success in America, failed conspicuously at the Duke of York's Theatre, others have been English or American adaptations from the French, such as the very low-class farces, 'A Night Off,' and 'Never Again.' On the whole, Mr Frohman's policy has not differed essentially from that of an ordinary English manager. His companies have sometimes been composite, including a considerable proportion of American actors But that is nowadays very generally the case. There are not many English companies which do not include at least one American actor or actress, just as there are not many American companies in which England is wholly unrepresented. It has especially become the fashion of late years for American actresses to seek their fortune on the English stage, and some of them, such as Miss Elizabeth Robins and Miss Fay Davis, have done important and excellent work.

"The third, and not the least notable, battalion of American invaders came on the scene in the year 1898. The form of entertainment known as 'musical comedy' or 'musical farce,' was an English invention, but had been quickly naturalised in America A piece of this nature, 'The Belle of New York,' after having had some success in that city, was transported bodily, with its whole company, scenery and accessories, to the Shaftesbury Theatre, London, where it became immensely popular. The libretto was rather below than above the average of English musical farce, but the music was extremely taking, and the acting and stage management had that nervous briskness or 'snap' which is so much cultivated on the American stage Such a success could not but encourage many imitators, and about a dozen American musical farces have, as a matter of fact, been imported within the last three years by Mr Lederer, the lucky owner of 'The Belle of New York,' and other impresarios Indeed, two new theatres, the Apollo and the Century Theatre (the rebuilt Adelphi), have been opened with this form of entertainment. In no case, however, has the success approached that of the first experiment The pieces have been for the most part even more incoherent than English work of the same order, and greatly inferior from a musical point of view to 'The Belle of New York.' On the other hand, one or two American comic operas (as distinct from musical farces), imported by Mr. De Woolf Hopper and Miss Alice Nielsen, have been fairly successful in London

"Whatever the fate of the individual pieces in which they have been engaged, a good many

American singers and burlesque comedians of both sexes have achieved considerable popularity on the English stage. Were we to extend our survey to the music halls, the case would be still more striking. Here American performers of every description are constantly in demand.

"We see, then, that during the past fifteen years American theatrical enterprise has been steadily widening the area of its activity in England. The invasion has proceeded in three stages, marked by the names of Daly, Frohman, and Lederer. We have sometimes had two or three American musical plays running simultaneously at as many London playhouses; and, as I write, Mr. Charles Frohman has the control of at least three theatres, at one of which, the Lyceum, Mr. Gillette, with his American company, is attracting all London to his American dramatisation of 'Sherlock Holmes.'

"There is, however, another side to the picture. While the importation of American actors, singly or in companies, has been steadily growing, and will soon, probably, balance the exportation of English actors to America, there is very little evidence of a similar increase in the importation of American plays. If we rule out plays by English authors which happened to be first acted in America, and American adaptations of French and German plays,[*] we shall find that for every American play that reaches the English stage, at least ten English plays (at a moderate estimate) find their way across the Atlantic. During the seventies and eighties, about half a dozen clever plays by Mr. Bronson Howard were produced in England (some of them in Anglicised form), and met with considerable success. More recently, Mr. Gillette has given us, besides 'Secret Service,' a stirring military drama entitled 'Held by the Enemy,' and Mr. David Belasco a play of the same type, 'The Heart of Maryland.' Mr. Paul Potter's crude melodrama, 'The Conquerors,' met with deserved condemnation, and Mr. Augustus Thomas's charming comedy 'Alabama' was treated with quite undeserved neglect. Of the numerous works of Mr. Clyde Fitch which have achieved popularity in America, only one, 'The Cowboy and the Lady,' has been seen in London. The same author's 'Pamela's Prodigy' and 'The Last of the Dandies,' both English in scene and both produced in London, can scarcely be regarded as

[*] One can scarcely rank as American plays dramatisations by American authors of English novels, such as "Dr. Jekyll and Mr. Hyde," "Trilby," and "Sherlock Holmes." Nor can America fairly lay claim to plays of European scene and subject, written for the London stage by American authors long resident in Europe, such as Mr. Henry James and Mr. Isaac Henderson.

American plays. A few minor productions, such as Mrs. Madeleine Lucette Ryley's agreeable comedy, 'An American Citizen,' and one or two nondescript pieces of the music-hall type, practically complete the list of America's literary or quasi-literary contributions to the English stage.

"The truth is, that in the absence of a protective import duty on European plays, the native American playwright is fatally hampered by French and English competition. The theatrical season in America comes to an end in the month of April; and the moment it is over, the American play-producers (of whom Mr. Charles Frohman is by a long way the chief) take the first steamer for Europe in order to see and buy up all the French and English novelties that they think at all suitable for the American market. They candidly confess their preference for foreign goods. By observing the effect of a play on an English or French audience, they can estimate with some precision its probable effect on an American audience: whereas it takes a very different quality of imagination and insight to divine the possibilities of an American play, which they have to read in manuscript, and to place on the stage with no help or guidance from an anterior performance. Moreover, a play which has made a great success in Paris or London is thereby 'boomed' in advance, the American public being as yet unpatriotic enough to flock to any play that is thoroughly well advertised, without inquiring whether it be native or foreign. In the face of this discouraging attitude of the managers and the public, it is not surprising that the native American drama makes but slow progress. The two most original and characteristic American dramatists, Mr. James A. Herne and Mr. Augustus Thomas, have found no favour in the eyes of any of the managers who have taken the lead in the invasion of England. Not one of the very remarkable plays of Mr. Herne has been seen on this side of the Atlantic, and Mr. Thomas's *Alabama* (already mentioned) received scant justice at the hands of an English company, which did not appreciate its delicacy. Mr. Clyde Fitch is the only American playwright who is encouraged by the all-powerful Syndicate which holds the American stage in the hollow of its hand. But though Mr. Fitch is an American by birth, and though he has written one or two plays which (in their titles at any rate) appeal to American patriotism, he is certainly the least American of transatlantic playwrights.

"In spite of the hostility of the Syndicate to native effort, it is impossible to believe that America will long be without a national drama. That careful study of all the phases of social, political, and spiritual life, which is so marked a feature of American fiction, must, sooner or later, seek expression on the stage as well. It is greatly to be desired that there should be complete reciprocity between England and America in the matter of plays; but as yet it cannot be questioned that on the whole England is the exporting, America the importing, country.

"Finally, it may be worth while to inquire whether there is any likelihood that a Syndicate or Trust, like that which has captured the American stage, will succeed in possessing itself of the machinery of the English theatrical system? Such a consummation is not, I think, imminent. The strength of the American Syndicate lies in the vast extent of the United States, the great distances between the various centres, and the fact that New York does not hold anything like the metropolitan position with respect to the rest of America which London holds with respect to the rest of Britain. Our leading actors can maintain themselves in London alone, their occasional provincial tours being comparatively unimportant to them. No American 'star,' on the other hand, can subsist in New York alone. He must go " on the road " on pain of sacrificing the greater part of his financial harvest, and the Syndicate, having contrived to get control of all the leading provincial theatres, can impose on him what terms it pleases. For reasons which it would take too long to explain, it would be difficult for any group of monopolists to acquire such absolute control of the English provincial theatres, and even if it did, a popular actor-manager, secure in his London theatre, could easily bid it defiance Therefore I do not think England so promising a field as the United States for the operations of a theatrical Trust.'

CHAPTER V —MARRIAGE AND SOCIETY.

AMONG the influences which are Americanising the world, the American girl is one of the most conspicuous and the most charming,

"Few people have any idea," said Lord Dufferin to me some twenty years ago, in discussing the influence of America upon the world, "of the extent to which the diplomatic service is Americanised by the influence of marriage Nearly all the attachés of the various embassies at Washington are captured, before their term of office expires, by American beauties and American heiresses. The result is that the diplomatic service, the only service which is really

cosmopolitan, is Americanised through and through."

Lord Dufferin was the first to point out what has long since been familiar to every one Count Hatzfeldt, who was for so many years German Ambassador in London, was one of the many German diplomatists who had married an American wife. The most conspicuous features in this romantic marriage were recalled and expatiated upon at length in all the American papers on the occasion of the Count's death.

A still more curious illustration of the extent to which the American woman has married into the very heart of German diplomacy was afforded by the fact that when the German Ambassador at Peking was killed by the Boxers he left an American widow, and that when Count von Waldersee was sent out to avenge his death he had to bid farewell to an American wife before he departed to avenge the wrongs of an American widow.

At the Hague Conference two of the most brilliant representatives of European diplomacy, Baron d'Estournelles, for a long time *charge d'affairs* in London, and Baron de Bildt, Swedish minister at Rome, had both married American wives. These are just passing illustrations of the truth of Lord Dufferin's remark Nothing could be more in the nature of things than that the young naval and other attachés who begin their careers at Washington, having about them the glamour of a distinguished position, and in many cases of titles, should attract the American girl, while on her side she wields the two weapons of beauty and wealth, either one of which would suffice for conquest

English diplomatists succumb quite as frequently as any others. It was noted recently on the marriage of Miss Belle Wilson, of New York, to the Honourable Michael Herbert, now British Minister at the Court of Copenhagen, that a Secretary of Legation had also married an American wife, and therein followed the example of his predecessor in the same post.

It is not only in diplomacy that the American girl achieves her triumphs. Diplomatists are few, whereas men of title and of mark are many. Hence, every year an increasing number of American heiresses marry into European families. This tendency is, of course, most marked in Great Britain, but it is noticeable both in France and Germany In course of time, indeed, it is probable that all European nations will be privileged to contribute bridegrooms who will be offered up as willing sacrifices on the hymeneal altar of America

It is only the more conspicuous heiresses who attract general attention, and in some cases the marriages have been anything but ideal. It has been a case of the bartering of dollars against a

LADY CURZON.
(Photo by Alice Hughes.)

Mrs. GEORGE CORNWALLIS-WEST.
(Photo by Alice Hughes.)

THE DUCHESS OF MARLBOROUGH.
(Photo by Lafayette.)

Mrs. ARTHUR PAGET.
(From a Painting by Edward Hughes.)

title, with a woman thrown in as a kind of arle penny to clinch the bargain. This impression as to the mercenary nature of many of these marriages was curiously illustrated a year or two since by the publication of a correspondence between Queen Natalie and the late King Milan of Servia The ill-mated pair were discussing the best way of rehabilitating the fortunes of the Obrenovitch dynasty by providing for the future of their son, the present king, whose matrimonial adventures with Queen Draga have afforded so many paragraphs to the gossip-mongers of the Continent The suggestion in that correspondence was that the young Alexander had better be married to an American heiress, not because there was any American girl of whose existence they were aware who was likely to be a suitable wife, but solely because the American wife was expected to bring millions as her dower The signing of the marriage contract in this case as in many others was merely to be like the signing of a cheque, which empowered the husband to draw upon the banking account of his wife. " With all my worldly goods I thee endow " is the declaration which in the English marriage service is made by the man It is because the American woman has taken over that privilege that she has come to be regarded as a kind of inexhaustible financial reserve by the spendthrift nobles of the Old World.

Three centuries ago, adventurers who had wrecked their substance at the gaming-table, or had been ruined by the fortune of war, clapped their good swords by their sides and sailed the Spanish main in the confident expectation of being able to return laden with the plunder of the palace of Montezuma or of the gold of the Incas Nowadays the same kind of gentry cross the Atlantic on a similar errand, but their methods are less heroic than those of the olden time. Their objective, however, is the same, and many times they are even more successful Heiress after heiress has been brought back in triumph, bearing with her fortunes which would have dazzled Pizarro, or stayed even the ravenous appetite of the Elizabethan captains who seized the galleons of Spain.

What will be the influence of this continual influx of American heiresses, whose millions replenish the exhausted exchequer of European nobles ? M. Finot, the acute and sagacious editor of *La Revue*, recently expounded to me when I was in Paris a theory of the influence of American work on European development, which was suggestive of much M. Finot maintained that the plutocracy of the New World would give the reactionary party in the Old World a new lease of life. The great landed proprietors, the heirs of historic titles, even

some royal dynasties, were becoming bankrupt. The unchecked operation of economic causes in the Old World, aided by the pressure of American competition, would, in the course of a generation or two, have destroyed feudalism in Europe, and paved the way for the advent of a more or less socialistic republic. But while economic laws with iron teeth are grinding into powder the remains of the feudal system in Europe, hey, presto ! and behold, the American heiress descends like some maleficent fairy to arrest the process of disintegration and decay, and to give a new lease of power to the oligarchy which seemed to be descending into its grave. Old castles are repaired and upholstered with the aid of American dollars Mortgages are paid off, and great estates restored to the possession of their nominal owners. The plutocracy of the New World, reinforcing the aristocracy of the Old, robs democracy of its destined triumph

This diagnosis of the situation is worthy of the shrewd and penetrating mind of my brilliant friend, a man who unites in his single person the genius of three races After all, it may be pleaded in mitigation of the offence of the American heiress, that when she has done her utmost, all her millions can do but little to restore the dilapidation which has been wrought in the feudal ramparts by the steady attrition of American competition. Her fathers and her brothers, from their farms on the prairie and their factories in Chicago, ceaselessly hurl across the Atlantic vast vessels which are like projectiles laden with food-stuffs, whose effect upon the old order in the Old World may be compared to so many dynamite shells Through the breaches thus made in the ramparts of reaction, a whole flood of American ideas are pouring into Europe To stem this the richest of American heiresses is powerless. At best she can only rig up for her husband a temporary shelter amid the ruins.

It was rather a degradation of the idea of American womanhood to regard the American girl as a means of replenishing the exhausted exchequer, a kind of financial resource, like the Income Tax. Indeed, it is not too much to say that when there is no love in the matter, it is only gilded prostitution, infinitely more culpable from the moral point of view than the ordinary vice into which women are often driven by sheer lack of bread.

When I published the " Maiden Tribute " sixteen years ago, Lord Randolph Churchill scoffed at the idea that vice was unpopular. He declared that it was the one bond of sympathy between the aristocracy and the democracy , and this trading with American heiresses for coronets may from this point of view be regarded as the touch of nature which makes the whole world kin. It is at least a proof of the persistency of the spirit of the snob, which not even the free air of the American Republic is able to exorcise. What is bred in the bone comes out in the flesh. Many Americans in this respect bear only too faithful a resemblance to their English ancestors.

It would be a monstrous injustice to suggest that marriage between titled persons in the old country and the heiresses of the New World is never accompanied by affection so sincere that the dollars are mere unconsidered trifles thrown into the bargain. It would also be an absurd misapprehension of facts to assume that the only marriages which take place between men of the Old World and women of the New are accompanied by the transfer of substantial bank balances from America to England. The American girl has no need of dollars to render her attractive to English suitors. She is always bright, vivacious and intelligent, often beautiful, and not seldom a very desirable wife and mother.

The real American girl in her millions never has the opportunity of visiting Europe. We only see in the Old World a very small percentage of American womanhood, that which is drawn exclusively from the wealthier classes. Of the girls of the class represented by Miss Rebecca Hallbom—a Minnesota girl whose fame is trumpeted in the American newspapers as the breaker of all records as the milker of cows—we see very little in Europe. Miss Hallbom at the age of sixteen, every day in the week milks nineteen cows morning and evening, and on an average deprives each cow of its milk in less than five minutes. On occasions she will milk fifty cows in a day.

The attraction which men of the Old World have for the women of the New—for many more American women than English women marry American men—is not difficult to explain. There is a certain glamour about the Old World which appeals to the susceptible feminine imagination. The attraction of ancient lineage, of ivy-clad castles, and the associations of a great historic name, appeal irresistibly to many minds. It is also true that American men are as a rule more immersed in business than men of a similar class in the Old World. There is more leisure here, less rush, and more opportunity for the cultivation of domesticity. And our interests are often more varied, and the Old World life is both picturesque and novel. It is also asserted (although far be it from me to express any opinion on the subject) that the lovers of the Old World are more ardent in their devotion than American men, while others maintain that the sex loves a master, and that

the deeper instinct of the American woman craves for a husband who will be her lord and master. This I take leave to doubt, for the instinct of domination which makes the American woman mistress both of her home and all that it contains, including her husband, is as much in evidence on this side of the Atlantic as on the other.

It is a remarkable fact that four English statesmen of Cabinet rank have married American wives. Mr Chamberlain, after having twice married an Englishwoman, has found his supreme felicity in an American, Miss Endicott. Sir William Harcourt married an American, so did Mr. Bryce, and so also did Lord Randolph Churchill, whose wife, now Mrs. Cornwallis-West, is one of the few American women who have counted for anything in English politics. American women on this side of the water are very seldom politicians, although some of them have married into positions where to exercise a political influence would have been both easy and natural. The Marlboroughs, both the late Duke and the present, are remarkable for having gone to America for their wives. Consuelo Vanderbilt, whose millions have rendered it possible to revive some of the glories of Blenheim—for without the American money it would have been difficult for the Duke even to have kept his windows glazed—will some day probably be the wife of the Viceroy of Ireland; while Miss Leiter has for some years past been Vice-Empress of India.

Manchester is another ducal family which has had two American Duchesses in succession. But in neither case have they contributed much to the social, political, or intellectual life of the Old Country.

On the Continent there are many American women whose names figure considerably in the newspapers. The most remarkable princess was Miss Heine, who married the Prince of Monaco. Another princess of a very different character who figured much more prominently in the papers, not altogether by the superabundance of her virtues, was Miss Clara Ward of Detroit, who, when a girl of eighteen, married the Prince de Chimay and Caraman, a Belgian title, bringing with her a dowry of half a million sterling. The prince brought as his marriage portion a dissolute past. When the corruption of the Old World married the wealth of the New, the result was what might have been anticipated. Since the meteoric and meretricious splendour of Lola Montes, few women have created more scandal in the broad expanse which lies between Cairo and London.

Such careers, however, are a rare exception. The American woman in Europe may be extravagant, but she seldom gives any occasion

CLIVEDEN HOUSE, FROM THE THAMES.

KNEBWORTH HOUSE.

for scandal A writer in an American magazine, who discussed the question of transplanted American beauty, says :—

"One thing is quite certain No American girl who has married into European society wishes to return home to the stay-at-home life of American women Although many difficulties have beset their paths, with few exceptions Anglo-American matches have been most happy ones It seems to be a woman's crown of glory —in England, at least—that she is American-born. Until Mrs. Lewis Hamersley married the Duke of Marlborough, no great fortune had gone from this country into England, and it is safe to say that nine out of ten marriages there were love matches."

The Spanish Princess Eulalie, who visited the United States at the time of the World's Fair, recently contributed an article upon the American girl to an American magazine. She concluded her article by the following cryptic phrase. "When American girls go abroad and marry foreigners, they are affectionate, not only in proportion to the attention they receive, but also by reason of the dowry they give."

It is unnecessary to do more than refer in passing to some of the more famous of the marriages which have introduced an American strain into an Old World family. The Countess Goblet d'Alviella, wife of the well-known Count Goblet d'Alviella, Liberal leader, scholar, and senator of Belgium, is an American. So is the wife of M Henri Monod, the Directeur de l'Assistance Publique in Paris. The Count Bosan de Perigord and Talleyrand, the son of the Princess de Sagan, made one of the most recent of notable American marriages when he married a daughter of ex-Governor Morton.

· The Castellane marriage, which made Jay Gould's daughter Anna a French countess, is not one of those unions which go to the credit account.

· The sisters Woodhall—Mrs. Bradley Martin, who combines her social functions with the editing of the *Humanitarian*, and her sister—Mrs. Blomfield Moore, the friend of Browning and the patroness of Keeley, of Keeley motor fame ; · Mrs. Mackay, Mrs Sherwood, Mrs. Arthur Paget, who is one of the smartest of our smart set—represent, each in her own way, various conductors of American influence upon English and European life

But marriage, is not the only means by which society is being Americanised. The process by which Great Britain is being converted into the family seat of the race is going on steadily. Every year one or another American family hires or buys some ancient country seat or famous mansion. A certain number still remain true to their Paris James Gordon Bennett

appears permanently to have forsaken his native land for the attractions of the Riviera, and here and there in the pleasant land of France may be found Americans who, having made their pile across the Atlantic, find more of the amenities of life and a more congenial atmosphere in country-seats which are not too far from the boulevards.

Apropos of the American absorption of English steamships tobacco companies, and castles, the New York journal *Life* publishes some amusing prophetic pictures of what we may expect to see ere long. The pictures are reproductions of the familiar photographs of well-known London buildings and monuments, with additions. The first of the series is a view of Trafalgar Square, with a view of the Nelson monument surmounted by a gigantic statue of Uncle Sam. The second shows us Parliament House, underneath which we read the inscription "The residence of Mr John B Grabb, of Chicago. This building is historically interesting as having been formerly the seat of the British Parliament." The statue of the Iron Duke from Hyde Park Corner is furnished with the American flag, and labelled · "This statue is now on its way to Pittsburg." There is a view of the Royal Exchange surmounted by a gigantic bust of J. P Morgan, with the legend *E pluribus unum*, and the corners are surmounted by the American eagle and an American coat of arms.

We have not yet come to this, but according to the latest bogus story in the American newspapers, American millionaires are bidding eagerly for the privilege of becoming tenants of Osborne House, where the Queen died. Senator Clarke of Montana is said to have written to the King, asking him how much he will take. Mr Charles G Yerkes, of Chicago fame, is said to be also in the field, having as his dangerous competitor Mr. W. W. Astor, who is credited with a desire to present Osborne to his daughter Pauline on her approaching marriage

We have not, of course, got quite so far as this, but events seem to be going somewhat in that direction. The purchase of Cliveden from the Duke of Westminster gave a certain shock to English society, for while we are accustomed to · the sale, by impecunious nobles, of their hereditary possessions to American millionaires, it was a novelty to find that one of the richest dukes was willing to sell, provided he had his price, to the American tempter. Mr. Carnegie snapped up Skibo Castle in North Britain ; and one of his partners, Mr. Phipps, occupies Knebworth Castle, which is famous for its association with Lord Lytton. These are but illustrations of the way in which the new Plutocracy

JOHN BULL TAKES A STROLL.

JOHN BULL IN HIS BUSINESS OFFICE.

HE SIMPLY PLOUGHS THROUGH THEM.

JOHN BULL TAKES A CAR.

THE AMERICAN INVASION.

Some Cartoons by Mr. F. Opper in the "New York Journal."

is nestling itself in the old haunts of the English aristocracy. The newcomers have plenty of money, but their expenditure, as a rule, is not characterised by a reckless extravagance. It somewhat startled the West End when an American newspaper proprietor rented a palace here, and provided a stud of thirty horses as part of the appurtenances necessary to his existence; but that was exceptional. We have suffered little from the vulgar ostentation of the wealthy parvenu. The Americans who have settled in our midst have been educated gentlemen of means, whose chief ambition has been to merge themselves quietly and unostentatiously in the society in the midst of which they have taken up their abode.

It is estimated that there are about 15,000 Americans more or less constantly resident in London. It is a shifting population, but the majority are permanent. In order to form a social centre for the feminine section of this Colony, Mrs. Hugh Reid Griffin, formerly of Chicago, founded the Society of American Women, which has as a badge the arms of the City of London surmounted by the American eagle, with the Union Jack on one side, and the Stars and Stripes on the other. The society was framed on the lines of the Sorosis Club of New York, and its declared object was the promotion of social intercourse between American women.

Mr. J. Pierpont Morgan in the City is a name to conjure with. But his influence is financial, rather than social. The mention of Mr. Morgan recalls the fact that it was he who undertook to defray the whole cost of installing the electric light in St. Paul's Cathedral. The sum of £9,000 is trivial to a millionaire, but somehow or other the British-born millionaire does not seem to think of it.

And this leads me to a concluding observation as to one beneficent side of American influence on English life. The habit of giving is one of the Americanisms which have not yet been successfully acclimatised in the Old World. The first American to make a distinct impact upon the English conscience by the force of his example was Mr. Peabody, whose effigy in bronze, seated in an armchair in the midst of "streaming London's central roar," is a much less valuable memorial than the continued usefulness of the Peabody Trust, and all the other trusts for rehousing the poorer classes of our great cities, which have sprung into existence as the result of his initiative.

But no one has preached the gospel of wealth so vigorously and has begun to practise it of late years so munificently as Mr. Andrew Carnegie. He is at present engaged in a valiant but wholly unsuccessful effort to escape the malediction which falls upon those who die

rich. At the same time it must be admitted that probably no one has ever given away in a single year as much money as Mr. Carnegie distributed in the last twelve months. According to a list published on his return to New York last November, he succeeded last year in distributing eight millions sterling in various quarters. One-fourth of this sum is represented by the two millions with which he endowed the Scottish universities; one million went to the libraries of New York City; more than one and a half millions went to the Carnegie Institute in Pittsburg; and £800,000 to a pension fund for his workmen in the same city. Miscellaneous gifts in the United States represent £850,000, and the rest of the money appears to have been distributed for the most part in the endowment of libraries in Scotland and in the United States.

The widow's mite which she cast into the Treasury will no doubt outweigh all the benefactions of the millionaires. But although it is not given to Mr. Carnegie to break the record of that widow, we may at least point to his example as one which we should be glad to see British-born millionaires attempt to imitate.

ANDREW CARNEGIE.

CHAPTER VI.—SPORT.

No one who remembers the important part which the Isthmian Games played in ancient Greece will be disposed to deny the political importance of athletics and of sport generally as a means of promoting a sense of unity among the English-speaking peoples of the world. Among the millions of the United Kingdom, cricket did more to make Australia and the Australians living realities than all the geographies and all the political discussions which have taken place over the Federation of the Australian Commonwealth. It is one of the advantages of contests, whether on the turf, the cricket field, or on the water, that defeat is as potent as victory in creating interest and promoting a sense of comradeship. The brotherhood of the Turf may not be the highest of brotherhoods, but it has been for many generations a very real fraternity which has done a good deal in England towards bridging the chasm between the classes and providing a democratic meeting place in which dukes and bookmakers, jockeys and millionaires could meet, if not exactly on an equal footing, at least upon common ground. Sports which twenty years ago were almost exclusively national have now become international, and every year increases the number of events in which the primary interest of sport is reinforced by national rivalry.

The most conspicuous contest of 1901 was the stoutly contested struggle made by Sir Thomas Lipton's yacht *Shamrock II.* to win the America Cup. To the eyes of the philosophic moralist there was a dangerous resemblance between the popular interest in the Cup races off Sandy Hook and the popular interest of the Byzantines in the races between blue and green charioteers in the circus. For a fortnight the progress of the campaign in South Africa upon which, we are told, the very existence of the Empire depends, was completely obscured by the latest telegrams describing the varying fortunes of the competitors for the Cup. In this great international yacht race we have been beaten decisively. Eleven times the British have attempted to lift the America Cup, and eleven times have they failed. We were beaten on our merits. The Americans have built better yachts, and the better yacht has won. Sir Thomas Lipton has apparently not yet made up his mind whether he will make a third attempt in 1903, but if he fails no one else seems disposed to renew the challenge. It is not without significance that but for Sir Thomas Lipton, who is a partially Americanised

SIR THOMAS LIPTON.
(Photo by Elliott & Fry.)

Irishman, no attempt would have been made to dispute the primacy of America. On the two previous occasions the challenger was Lord Dunraven, who is also an Irishman; while all our best yachts are built in Scotland. England, except for sail-making, would appear to have definitely quitted the field.

Possibly if the America Cup is to leave the United States it may be carried off by the Canadians or by the Australians, although the latter have as yet shown no disposition to enter the lists. But whatever be the result, it is admitted that in the designing of yachts the Americans have led the way ever since they carried off the famous Cup in a struggle with rivals around the Isle of Wight. It was they who made the centre-board and the "skimming dish" the potent factors which they are to-day, and though there has been a tendency of late years to modify these extreme types, the American racing machine has permanently modified for good or evil the yacht construction of the whole world.

The only other form of aquatic sport in which the general public take a keen interest is that of pair-oar sculling, leaving on one side the University eight-oar matches. The single sculling championship of the world was wrested from Great Britain when E. H. Ten Eyck, of Worcester, defeated Blackburne, and carried off the

K

DON'T GO HOME MAD.

JOHNNIE BULL.—"Well, it ain't no fun to *play* and *always* be beaten, and you know it, SAMMIE."
SAMMIE.—"Well, say, Johnnie, is there any game you *can* play?"

championship across the Atlantic Difficulties were raised about his rowing at Henley and this year, after having in vain challenged any one to contest his claim at the National Regatta on the Schuylkill, he retired on his laurels. When we come to eight-oar racing, the English Universities have retained the lead, but there is no disposition on the part of Yale or Harvard to acquiesce in their supremacy. Recently there was an ugly moment when it seemed as if the stewards at Henley would bar foreign competitors from the Henley course That proposal. which would have been regarded as a practical admission that we dared not face our international competitors, was fortunately rejected

After aquatics the sport which excites the greatest interest is the Turf. The year 1901 was famous in the annals of the British Turf by the fact that for the first time in our history both the great classic races, the Derby and the Oaks. were won by Americans Volodyovski was bred by Lady Meux, and was only leased by Mr W C Whitney, the American, under whose colours it was run But he was trained by an American, Mr. Huggins, and ridden by the American jockey, Lester Reiff Mr Whitney also established a record by handing over the Derby stakes to charity The Oaks was, however, a more genuine American victory than the Derby, for Cap and Bells II was bred in the United States, owned by Mr Foxhall Keene, and ridden by Martin Henry, the American jockey. The filly was, however, trained by an Englishman

The American invasion of the British Turf is no new thing Nearly fifty years ago, Mr Ten Broeck brought over Lexington and her stable companion Priorus, who won the Cesarewitch after a dead heat. Mr Whitney, who won the Derby this year, and threatened to leave the English turf as the result of the sentence upon Lester Reiff by the Jockey Club, only began racing in England in 1899 The most notable American on the English turf is Mr Richard Croker, who has established himself at Wantage, and finds the English racecourse his most delightful tonic.

Newmarket for 1901 closed in a blaze of triumph for the Americans. Of the five leading events, including the Cambridgeshire, only one was won by a horse in which Americans were not directly interested Two of the five chief winners were bred in America , three of the winners were trained by an American, and four were ridden by American jockeys

The American owner is, however, of less importance to the mass of the public than the American jockey, whose style of riding first startled and then dazzled his English competitors The American jockey sits upon the shoulders of his horse, almost on the neck, a method of horsemanship which in the opinion of Mr. Croker is

equivalent to a reduction of the riding weight to the extent of half a stone Sloan and the two Reiffs found little difficulty in taking a first place among the winning jockeys of the last two or three years Unfortunately the brilliance of their success has been somewhat marred by the censure passed upon Sloan and Lester Reiff by the Jockey Club The verdict upon Reiff was confined solely to one race at Manchester, in which he was accused of not having done his best to win. Sloan in 1899 is said to have received £15,000 as his riding fees, and to have won as much more in wagers Mr. Huggins who came over with Mr. Lorillard, was reputed to have received a salary of £10,000 a year, plus a percentage on the winnings of the stable There has been a good deal of discussion as to the secret of the success of American and American trained horses upon the English turf One theory which finds much favour among American authorities is that the American horse wins for the same reason that the American citizen is more energetic than his English rivals Transatlantic breeders do not breed in and in like those of England, and they have imported steadily for years past the very best blood of England, France, and Australia They hold that the practice of in breeding tends to make the English horse unduly nervous

In leaping the American horse holds the record Heatherbloom, last November at New York. cleared with ease a barrier 7 ft 4 ins high. He was given a sixty yards run In private practice the week before he is said to have jumped 7 ft. 8 ins

Of the success of the American trainer there can be no doubt. Again and again an American trainer has taken a horse which was regarded as altogether out of the running, and has sent him to the post in such a condition that he has won stake after stake For instance, Wishard, who turned out more winners in the racing season of 1900 than any other American, bought Royal Flush for 400 guineas, trained him for an American, Mr. Drake, put an American jockey J Reiff, upon his back, and carried off first the Royal Hunt Cup, and then the Steward s Cup at Goodwood He afterwards won several plates and handicaps, and was sold at the end of the season for 1250 guineas. It is the brains of the man rather than the breeding of the horse which enables him to gain the victory In one department of racing the Americans have the field entirely to themselves No attempt has ever been made in the United Kingdom to rival the fast trotters of the United States At present Cresceus is the champion trotter of the world, having broken all record this year by covering the mile in two minutes and two and a quarter seconds

Polo is also taking its place among international events. In 1900, American and English teams competed at Hurlingham, the Americans being beaten by eight goals to two

In athletic sports, strictly so called, the contests between the two nations is kept up very briskly, although the balance even here inclines to the United States. In most quick races in which everything depends upon the rapidity with which the runner can obtain a maximum speed, the Americans beat the more phlegmatic Englishman. When Oxford and Cambridge sent their best men to the United States this autumn, the English won the half-mile and the mile and the two miles, all these races being carried off by Cambridge men The Americans won the hundred yards and the quarter mile.

They were also victorious in hammer throwing, the high jump, the broad jump, and 120 yards over hurdles In 1900, when the Americans came over to Stamford Bridge, they carried off the prizes for the 100 yards and $\frac{1}{4}$ mile races They were also victorious in putting the weight, the high jump, throwing the hammer, the long jump, and the hurdle race

The Americans have beaten us in cycling In boxing the Americans have had it their own way. The championship of the world in the prize ring has gone to the United States, and is likely to remain there. This, which was at one time the distinctive sport of Great Britain, is now practically abandoned to the Americans In golf, which the Americans have taken up keenly of late years, we may expect to find a keen struggle for the championship Last year Miss Genevieve Hecker of Connecticut won the American Woman's Championship, at the age of nineteen

Hitherto the Americans have not done much in cricket, but encouraged by the success with which they defeated a second rate English eleven they are now preparing to enter the field against us on our own ground.

It is not without significance that the international Olympian games, which were revived at the close of the nineteenth century by a committee, of which Baron de Coubertin is the chairman, should hold their next meeting in Chicago. Their first was held at Athens This international athletic contest will last for a month to six weeks, and will be held in September, 1904. The United States Legations and Consuls throughout Europe will probably act as agents for distributing information and advertising this fixture, so as to give it the importance of a great world-wide *fête*.

CHAPTER VII.—" THE AMERICAN INVASION."

IT was not till the close of last century that the United States could be said to have secured the commercial primacy of the world * But the fact that they would supersede us had long been foreseen by the more prescient amongst us. Conspicuous among these was Mr. Gladstone, who in 1878 and again in 1890 expressed in the clearest terms his conviction both as to the inevitableness of the change, and also, what was more important, his view as to the way in which it should be regarded by this country —

" It is America," he said, " who at a given time and probably will wrest from us that commercial primacy. We have no title I have no inclination to murmur at the prospect If she acquires it, she will make the acquisition by the right of the strongest, but in this instance the strongest means the best. She will probably become what we are now—head servant in the great household of the world, the employer of all employed, because her service will be the most and ablest We have no more title against her than Venice, or Genoa, or Holland has against us."

The moral which he drew from the certainty of our relegation to a secondary position was one to which unfortunately we have given but little heed. Mr. Gladstone in 1878, as previously in 1866, implored his countrymen to recognise the great duty of preparing "by a resolute and sturdy effort to reduce our public burdens in preparation for a day when we shall probably have less capacity than we have now to bear them."

In 1866, when Mr Gladstone first uttered his memorable warning as to our prospective loss of commercial primacy, our national expenditure amounted to £66,000,000. Thirty-four years afterwards the extent of our response to his appeal for " a sturdy and resolute effort " may be gauged by the fact that our expenditure for 1900-1 amounted to £183,592,000 sterling, and we are still engaged in a war which will indefinitely increase the weight of the burdens which we shall have to bear in future

As to the fact that we could not possibly hope to hold our own against the United States,

* The following figures condense into a nutshell the story of the last thirty years' material progress of the United States

Products.	[In millions]			
	1870.	1880.	1890.	1900.
Wheat (bu).	235 8	498 5	399·2	5222 2
Corn (bu)	1094·2	1717·4	1489·0	2105·1
Cotton (bales)	3 0	5·7	7·3	9·4
Wool (lbs.)	162·0	232 5	276·0	288 6
Petroleum (gals., 1877)	383 5	836 3	1476·8	2396 9
Bit coal (tons, 1876)	28 9	38 2	99 3	*172 6

Mr. Gladstone had no doubt whatever. He said —

"While we have been advancing with portentous rapidity, America is passing us by as if in a canter There can hardly be a doubt, as between America and England, of the belief that the daughter at no very distant time (it was written in 1878) will, whether fairer or less fair, be unquestionably yet stronger than the mother

The process, inevitable in any case, would, he thought, be accelerated if the Americans adopted Free Trade.

"If America " he wrote in 1890, "shall frankly adopt and steadily maintain a system of Free Trade, she will by degrees, perhaps not slow degrees, outstrip us in the race, and will probably take the place which at present belongs to us , but she will not injure us by the operation On the contrary, she will do us good Her freedom of trade will add to our present commerce and our present wealth, so that we shall be better than we are now "

A remark which is hardly consistent with his previous warning as to the necessity for our reducing our probable burdens on the ground that our capacity to bear them would be not greater, but less than it is now

Few things are more topsy-turvy than the popular notions concerning trade. Convictions which are most firmly held by millions of people are demonstrably false, but they influence legislation, they dictate politics, and they dominate public opinion. Take, for instance the balance of trade It is admitted that all trade is barter, and that no nation will part with its goods to another nation without receiving a corresponding equivalent. If two persons are doing business with one another, and Mr. Jones sends £1000 worth of wool to Mr Smith, he expects to receive back goods of equal value On the other hand, if instead of receiving say coal to the value of £1000 in exchange for the £1000 worth of wool he receives coal only to the value of £750, every one would admit, and Mr. Jones first of all, that he was £250 to the bad He sent out goods worth £1000, and only received in return commodities to the value of £750 What can be more obvious? But the moment you substitute for Mr Jones and Mr Smith two nations, and you raise the value from a thousand to a hundred millions, people believe and assert that it is an advantage to export a hundred millions' worth of goods and receive only seventy-five millions' worth in exchange If any man went on trading, giving £1000 worth of wool for £750 of coal every one admits that he would go straight to the Bankruptcy Court , but if a nation sends out a hundred millions' worth of exports and only receives in exchange seventy-five millions, the nation whose imports are 25 per cent. less than her exports declares that the balance of trade is in her favour

to the extent of twenty-five millions a year ! Political economists have repeatedly and laboriously explained that the excess of exports is a balance against the exporting nation, but nothing seems to be able to shake the inveterate delusion that a nation which exports more than it imports makes a profit to the extent of the difference.

That is one paradox. Another which is at present even more widely diffused on this side of the Atlantic is that a nation is injured when it is able to buy the goods that it requires more cheaply from another nation than they could be produced at home Take, for instance, this question of the so-called American ' invasion " It is obvious that there would be no foothold for the American invader in this country if he were not welcomed by the inhabitants of this country. The American invasion succeeds because the American invaders are able to give the British purchaser either better or cheaper goods, so that he gets more value for his money than he would get by trading with any one else If the American invasion was a bad thing for us, we could only be compelled to take American goods by compulsion exercised either at the point of the bayonet, or in some other way. The very reverse is the fact The American invasion prospers because Englishmen and Europeans find it more to their personal interest and individual profit to deal with Americans rather than to deal with their own countrymen The presence of the American invaders in our midst is resented as if it were an outrage on international amity, as if the Americans bearing gifts in their hands were bent upon doing us the greatest possible injury. It is, of course, perfectly true that the manufacturer who produces dearer goods finds the presence of the American competitor who supplies cheaper goods or better goods very inconvenient , and, unless he can compete on equal terms, he will go to the wall But if he goes to the wall, he goes there by the very choice of the people of this country, each one of whom, when he has sixpence to spend, is as absolute as any Tsar or Kaiser as to the way in which he will dispose of that particular coin of the realm which he has in his pocket when he goes out to shop

It is the more extraordinary that this doctrine should have obtained so much hold among Englishmen, of all people in the world Although to-day we are all talking of the American invasion for the last hundred years it has been the peculiar glory of Englishmen that they have invaded victoriously all the neutral markets of the world, and that they have supplied cheaper goods and better goods to the inhabitants of every continent It is obvious

THE AMERICAN INVASION OF ENGLAND.

JOHN BULL GOES TO BED, AND THIS IS WHAT HE DREAMS.

that what for a hundred years has been an exploit justifying us in acclaiming ourselves as the benefactors of humanity cannot become a cause of complaint when the people who are conferring this benefit happen not to be domiciled in the United Kingdom, but are English-speaking men who are domiciled in the United States of America. The outcry which has been made against American competition, which may be excused in all protectionist countries, is singularly out of place in the mouths of the great free-trading nation which, for fifty years past, has proclaimed aloud in the hearing of all mankind the supreme duty of buying in the cheapest market and selling in the dearest. The Americans are only doing to-day what we have to the uttermost of our ability been endeavouring to do ever since they came into existence, and unless the recognised principles of political economy upon which we have acted since the days of Peel and Gladstone are exploded heresies, the presence of these invaders in our midst is not an evil but a blessing, however much for the moment it may be disguised

It is therefore in no unfriendly spirit that we direct our attention to what, for convenience' sake, we continue to call the American invasion Let us see, in the first place, with what weapons these invaders from the New World are able to possess themselves of markets which we have hitherto regarded as our own The first and by far the greatest weapon by which the Americans have made the economic conquest of the Old World is in the supply of foodstuffs The old saying that it is ill to look a gift horse in the mouth surely should be borne in mind by those who are fed from day to day by the produce of American wheatfields and the slaughter-yards of Chicago. With the exception of the Russian Empire and Hungary, there is hardly a country in Europe which is capable of feeding its own population with the products of its own fields. Lancashire has boasted and still boasts of its achievement in clothing the naked, but man needs to fill his stomach even before he covers his body, and the feeding of the hungry takes precedence as an act of charity of the clothing of the naked. The ingenuity of American mechanism, and the skill of American engineers, have been employed for a generation past in reducing the bread-bill of the British working man Incidentally this has brought in its wake agricultural depression among a minority of our people, but the immense majority have fed and grown fat upon American harvests and the beef and pork of American farms If it is an evil thing to have cheap bread, then the Americans were undoubtedly doing us an injury If, on the other hand, the very existence of our manufactures and our capacity to command

the markets of the world depends absolutely upon cheap food, then the Americans have been of all people our greatest benefactors Imagine, for instance, if some great speculator were able to effect such a corner in American foodstuffs as to absolutely forbid the importation of a single carcase or a single cargo of grain, where should we be? We should be face to face with famine, and the whole forty millions of us would be alternately filling the air with execrations against the speculator who had cut off our supply of food from the United States, or imploring him for the love of God to relax his interdict, and allow our people once more to profit by drawing supplies from the American store. It may be replied that if American supplies were cut off, there would be a great revival of agricultural prosperity in this country, but if the price of the quartern loaf were doubled and quadrupled, we should not be able to supply sufficient food to feed our population We are absolutely spoon-fed from day to day by the Americans

Possibly in time to come, from India, from Australia, and from Canada, we may hope to render ourselves independent of American produce, but that would be no benefit to the British farmer, and we should have to wait many a year before we could secure from our fellow-subjects the supplies which we need from day to day

After food, the second great article by which the Americans have invaded our markets is raw material, notably cotton It is not yet forty years since Lancashire was reduced to the verge of starvation by the outbreak of the Civil War in America, which deprived it of the raw material of its staple industry There we had actual experience of the stoppage of American supplies, an experience the like of which no one who lived through the Lancashire cotton famine wishes to repeat

If we eliminate all food-products and all raw materials from American exports, we have accounted for a bulk sufficient, and more than sufficient, to pay for all our exports to the United States. The cry of alarm which has been raised has been produced by neither of the two great staples of American exports, but by the appearance among us of American manufactured goods But even here a very large proportion of the American goods are such as we are either unable, or have not yet equipped ourselves sufficiently to provide The Americans have brought to us a host of ingenious inventions and admirably perfected machines which we are incapable of producing for ourselves No one can say that in sending us the typewriter, the sewing-machine, the Linotype, the automobile, the phonograph, the telephone

THIS IS THE REAL GAINSBOROUGH J. P. MORGAN
HAS ACQUIRED.

THE NEW ATLAS.

ATLAS.—"Well, that takes a load off my shoulders, and how easily
he seems to handle it."

HIS HANDS FULL.

THE OTHERS. "Guess I'll have to get out of the way."

ALL THE WORLD'S AWHEEL,
AND J. PIERPONT MORGAN IS THE WHEELMAN.

[From the Minneapolis Journal]

MR. J. P. MORGAN—THE GREAT AMALGAMATOR.

the elevator, and the incandescent electric light, they invaded any British industry These things were their inventions After they were introduced, we imitated some of them or invented others on the same principle, but they first opened up the new fields They were as much benefactors to us in this respect as the missionary who introduces ploughs to a savage tribe which never used anything but the spade and hoe. That each and all these inventions were benefits to us is attested by the fact that we have bought them eagerly and continue to buy them Several of our manufacturers who have been taught by Americans how to make these things, yet cry out that they are being invaded and ruined by American competition; whereas but for the Americans these appliances would never have been in demand in this country

It is not until we come to the fourth category of American imports that we come upon ground in which there is a semblance of justification for the complaint that our manufacturers or our workmen are injured by American competition. This covers the wide field in which our people have failed to produce articles comparable in excellence to those which the Americans have offered us Conspicuous in this category are printing-machines, in which the American firm of Hoe introduced a standard of excellence which immeasurably out-distances the machines with which our fathers did their printing After printing-machines come the whole range of machinery and appliances necessary for the utilisation of electricity In this respect we have lagged so far behind the Americans that our manufacturers simply could not supply the apparatus necessary for harnessing electricity to the service of modern industry The Americans have done with electricity what the British did with steam at the beginning of the last century. We were the first to realise the incalculable development that was latent in the invention of Bolton and of Watt We got in ahead of the rest of the world, and we profited accordingly All the nations came to us for steam-engines, just as we are going to the United States for dynamos and all the elaborate, ingenious and costly apparatus necessary for working electric trolleys, "Twopenny Tubes," etc Here no fair-minded man can say that we have any reason to complain It is the early bird that catches the worm, and if we did not wake up to the immense potentiality of electricity, electric motors, electric power machines, and electric traction, that is our fault, and we have no one to blame but ourselves. We want these things We want them now. We cannot afford to wait until our neighbours in the next street wake up to a consciousness of the fact that fortunes are to be made in the supply of electrical apparatus.

Therefore we go to our kinsmen across the sea That they are willing and ready to supply us is a thing we should be grateful for. As a matter of fact as individuals we are thankful to them. the best proof of which is that we are willing to pay them millions of money for the privilege of being supplied with the machines which we want

As it is with the appliances necessary for the utilisation of electricity, so it is to a greater or less extent with what may be described as tools of precision necessary for turning out the exact work needed in the modern engineering industry Fifteen years ago Sir Hiram Maxim complained bitterly to me of the fact that when he came over to this country to manufacture Maxim guns, he found it impossible to buy in all Britain the tools which he needed The old tools, compared to what he needed, were as the flint tools of our early ancestors to a steel knife The perfect tool represents an advance in civilisation The clumsy and ineffective tool is a mark of barbarism Savages no doubt object to be civilised, but it is not for us to complain that we have been, however reluctantly, forced first to use and then to manufacure the more effective tools, which were first brought into use by our American kinsmen.

A very interesting little book by Mr. Fred Mackenzie has been published recently by Mr H W Bell It consists of a reprint of a series of articles which originally appeared in the columns of the *Daily Mail* Mr. Mackenzie is one of the rising younger pressmen of London, and his little book deserves the attentive perusal of all persons interested in this subject. Mr Mackenzie writes a bright and lively style, but when you examine his book you will find that most of the triumphs of which the American invaders have to boast are in fields which we have left them free to occupy

Typewriters he tells us, are imported from New York at an average value of £200,000 a year. The British Government had to buy their telephones for London from the Western Electric Company of Chicago In electric traction half of the motors on British street cars are American The Central Railway Company was equipped by the New York General Electric Company, and another New York firm boasts that they have supplied eleven of the leading street electric tramlines in Great Britain The new West London lines and two dozen others are supplied with a street car equipment from New York

The Eastman Kodak Company imports £200,000 worth of American photographic apparatus every year A similar amount of money is spent every year in the purchase of

American sewing machines   The sale of American drugs in Great Britain amounts to very nearly a quarter of a million a year   The Americans are importing soda-water fountains, blouses for women carpet-sweepers, darning machines, patching up apparatus, and all manner of similar inventions which we had not even the sense to desire nor the ingenuity to produce upon the market.   Our purchase of American pumps and pumping-machines, American pipes and fittings, represents between £300,000 and £400,000 a year.

The American machine tool, Mr Mackenzie says, is triumphant everywhere.   Fifty American annealing furnaces are in use at Woolwich Arsenal, and in Sheffield the makers are using an American apparatus   The most effective passage in Mr. Mackenzie's book is the following :—

"In the domestic life we have got to this The average man rises in the morning from his New England sheets, he shaves with 'Williams' ' soap and a Yankee safety razor, pulls on his Boston boots over his socks from North Carolina, fastens his Connecticut braces, slips his Waltham or Waterbury watch in his pocket, and sits down to breakfast   There he congratulates his wife on the way her Illinois straight-front corset sets off her Massachusetts blouse, and he tackles his breakfast, where he eats bread made from prairie flour (possibly doctored at the special establishments on the lakes), tinned oysters from Baltimore, and a little Kansas city bacon, while his wife plays with a slice of Chicago ox-tongue   The children are given 'Quaker' oats   At the same time he reads his morning paper printed by American machines, on American paper, with American ink, and, possibly, edited by a smart journalist from New York city.

"He rushes out, catches the electric tram (New York) to Shepherd's Bush, where he gets in a Yankee elevator to take him on to the American-fitted electric railway to the City.

"At his office, of course, everything is American   He sits on a Nebraskan swivel chair, before a Michigan roll-top desk, writes his letters on a Syracuse typewriter, signing them with a New York fountain pen, and drying them with a blotting-sheet from New England   The letter copies are put away in files manufactured in Grand Rapids

"At lunch-time he hastily swallows some cold roast beef that comes from the Mid-West cow, and flavours it with Pittsburg pickles, followed by a few Delaware tinned peaches, and then soothes his mind with a couple of Virginia cigarettes

"To follow his course all day would be wearisome.   But when evening comes he seeks relaxation at the latest American musical comedy, drinks a cocktail or some Californian wine, and finishes up with a couple of 'little liver pills' 'made in America' "

What will be the ultimate destiny of Great Britain from an economic point of view?   It depends upon the Britons   Mr Carnegie is of a different opinion   He thinks it depends upon the mineral resources of the country   Three years ago he laid it down as an axiom that "raw materials have now power to attract capital, and also to attract and develop labour for their manufacture in close proximity, and that skilled labour is losing the power it once had to attract raw materials to it from afar "

If this be an axiom, then our cotton mills will migrate from Lancashire to the Southern States of America.   The iron trade of the world will be localised at Pittsburg   Mr. Carnegie, who is a philosopher in his way, maintains that no nation in future will be able permanently to maintain a greater population than it can feed and support with its own products.

"The destiny of the old country seems to me very plain   You will be the family seat of the race.   Your manufactures will go one after the other, but you will become more and more popular as the garden and pleasure-ground of the race, which will always regard Great Britain as its ancestral home.   Probably you will be able to support 15,000,000, not more "

It is well to cultivate a healthy scepticism concerning all such predictions   So far as we can see from the trend of events at the present moment, the producing power of Great Britain is likely to undergo an immense increase, because Great Britain is beginning to be energised by the electric current of American ideas and American methods.   Lord Rosebery recently said —

"In these days we need to be inoculated with some of the nervous energy of Americans.   That is true of individuals, admittedly true, but is it not also true of the nation ? "

He uttered a truth which is even now being largely acted upon   For the last twelve months there has been a constant pilgrimage across the Atlantic from the old country, in which our manufacturers, our railway managers, our ship builders, our iron-makers, our merchant princes, have been wending their way to the United States for the purpose of learning the secret by which the Americans are beginning to beat us in our own market   The British race is a tough race, and it has long been a national boast that the Englishman never knows when he is beaten

But that is not the only encouraging sign.   Here and there all over the country we can see British firms adopting American methods, and beating the Americans at their own game. In the supply of electrical apparatus, a British firm in the north of England, which has frankly recognised the conditions of modern industry, has imported American managers, American machinery, and American methods, and is already beginning successfully to compete with the American companies for the supply of all manner of electrical appliances

What the Preston Electric Company have done others are doing. The attempt of the Americans to rush the cycle trade proved the British bicycle more than capable of holding its own against the American cycle. The American watch for a time swept everything before it. The English, at any rate, have shown that they are capable of holding their own. They are laying down plant in London for the making and supplying of office furniture which will compete with the best American. Depend upon it that John Bull is not going to take his beating lying down, but the enterprise of English firms will hardly be able to cope with the increasing numbers of Americans who are crossing the Atlantic for the purpose of establishing themselves in business here. The most conspicuous illustration of this moving of American capital back to the old home of the race is the Westinghouse Company's works near Manchester, directed by American managers, and managed on American principles. With these Americans who settle in our midst the old country will become the new home of the American colonists.

One American institution, the New York Mutual Life Insurance, occupies a most palatial pile of buildings in the city of London, and its manager, an American born, is more British than a Britisher.

The American soda-water fountain is now manufactured in the city of London. Before long we shall see established in our midst American hotels, and already at the corner of Wellington Street and the Strand, on the site occupied by the *Morning Post* office and the old Gaiety Theatre, a building is being erected which, according to its promoters, will be the largest building to be used as an office in the world. Before long, Siegel, Cooper & Co and Mr Wanamaker will be setting up their huge stores in our midst. Mr. Yerkes is preparing to electrify the Underground, and revolutionise the whole of our street railways. Mr Milholland and Mr Batchelar are impatiently waiting for permission to lay down pneumatic tubes all over London by which all parcels will be shot underground from one end of London to the other. John Bull will have to smarten up; there will be a difficult quarter of an hour for the old gentleman, but

the results will probably astonish no one so much as those Americans who have been calmly selling the lion's skin before the lion was dead.

CHAPTER VIII.—RAILWAYS, SHIPPING AND TRUSTS.

ALTHOUGH there are 200,000 miles of railway in the United States alone, the railway itself is but a thing of yesterday. A curious reminder of this was afforded us this year by the unearthing in Iowa by some enterprising pressman of the very man who drove Stephenson's "Rocket" on the eventful day when on the opening of the Liverpool and Manchester railway the train knocked down and killed Mr Huskisson. Edward Entwhistle was a Lancashire lad of eighteen when George Stephenson took him out of the engine-shop and put him at the throttle of the "Rocket" on the opening day. He is now a man of eighty-six. After acting as engine-driver on the Liverpool and Manchester for over two years, he emigrated to America in 1837, where he took up the trade of stationary engineer. He is still in good health and sufficiently alert to be capable of giving occasional addresses on his reminiscences of Stephenson, in which, judging from the newspaper reports, Mr Huskisson reappears as Lord Erskinson, so that the span of a single life easily covers the whole of the railway era.

It may be regarded as symbolic that the first engine-driver should so soon have emigrated to the United States, as if divining by some secret unconscious instinct that it was there where the genius of Stephenson would bear its richest fruits. By every test, whether quantitative or qualitative, the American stands out *facile princeps* in all things connected with the railway. To begin with, he has built nearly half the railways in the world. Not only has he spanned his own continent with a perfect gridiron of metalled way, but he is now carrying off contracts for the bridge work, which, with the exception of tunnelling, constitutes the most difficult and delicate of all the operations of railway structure. But it was only yesterday that their pre-eminence as bridge builders dawned upon the British public, which has even yet hardly recovered from the shock of discovering that all the Queen's horses and all the Queen's men were incapable of conquering the Soudan without resorting to the humiliating necessity of accepting an American tender for the building of a bridge across the Atbara. The British could have built it themselves, no doubt, but they could not do the work up to time. Few incidents caused more chagrin, and the most conclusive explanations were speedily forthcoming to prove how easily the British builders could have done the task if they had only had a reasonable notice and been treated with reasonable fairness

These explanations, apparently conclusive, temporarily allayed John Bull's ill-humour, but it was only for a time. Last autumn the American Bridge Company carried off contracts for constructing no fewer than twenty-eight bridges and viaducts required to complete the Uganda Railway. The work is now in active progress, and the bridges are in process of shipment across the Atlantic for Uganda, one of the territories which was occupied for the express purpose of developing British trade in South Africa. Money is being poured out like water in order to secure this market for British manufactured goods, and lo ' the American steps in and carries off the contracts for building these bridges without having incurred a penny of expense or an atom of responsibility in opening up the country

The same thing is occurring in other parts of the world. The Americans have just built the largest bridge in the world over the Goktein in Upper Burma. And as it is with bridges, so it promises to be with rails. Mr. Rhodes experienced a cruel shock when in opening tenders for the construction of the southern end of his Cape to Cairo Railway, he discovered that Mr Carnegie was able to deliver steel rails in South Africa at a lower price than any English manufacturer. The patriotic pride of the South African Colossus prompted him to take advantage of a technical flaw in Mr. Carnegie's contract in order to accept the tender of a British firm , but to this day he feels uneasy at the remembrance of the subterfuge to which he had to resort in order to keep the trade in British hands " It would have been too bad," he said, somewhat pathetically, "to think of my Cape to Cairo line being made with American rails '"

In war, as in peace, it is the same thing. While the Imperial Government was importing American mules by the thousand from New Orleans to give mobility to its flying columns at the seat of war, the Cape Government was placing contracts with American engineers for engines which could not be supplied from British workshops, even although, as the Colonial Government plaintively explained, it gave a ten per cent. preference to British manufactures But it is impossible long to carry on business in which contracts, like kissing, go by favour, and not to the best tender, and such devices as ten per cent. preferences and the like are neither more nor less than a confession of defeat If British engineers can only hold their own with a ten per cent. adverse handicap against their American competitors, the question is ended, and the

superiority of the Yankee is attested by the very terms of the competition insisted upon by his rival.

As it is with bridges and with rails, so it is even more conspicuously with American locomotives They are not artistic toys, the giant engines which do the haulage of a continent, neither do they require one month in the paint-shop, as is said to be the case in our own Midland Railway. But they are the strongest haulers in the world, and they go at the greatest speed America holds the world's record both for speed at all distances and for the weight of the trains hauled by a single locomotive Philadelphia railway expresses are constantly timed to run at sixty-six miles an hour, and it is nothing unusual for trains when under pressure to dash along the metal way at the rate of eighty to eighty-four miles an hour. The tendency is ever towards more and more powerful engines, with heavier haulage capacity. The Americans laugh to scorn what they regard as the toy cars in use in the Old World. At one time their average freight cars weighed ten tons, and only carried their own weight. To-day they weigh fifteen tons and carry thirty A single engine will grapple a quarter of a mile of these cars, loaded to their utmost capacity, and make no complaint if half a dozen extra are hitched on behind. The result of this continual development in the direction of greater haulage capacity is that the freight on American railways is about half what it is in this country.

The United States at one time imported locomotives from this country. They are now exporting locomotives to all parts of the British Empire. Recently the reputation of the American engine has been somewhat prejudiced, first, by the inferior quality of locomotives sent to Australia , secondly, by an adverse report made by the Locomotive Superintendent of the Midland Railway as to the extra working cost of an American engine He reported that as the result of a six months' trial, the American engine cost 20 to 25 per cent. more for fuel, 50 per cent. more for oil, and 60 per cent. more for repairs. This report was received with a chorus of delight in English papers ; but, as was immediately pointed out by an American writer in an interesting paper published in the *World's Work* for November, under the title of "The American Locomotive Abroad," the Midland Report was far from conclusive for several reasons. First, the so-called American engines were not of the pure American type, but were modified to meet English ideas , secondly, the report gives no information as to the amount of coal burned, oil used, or money spent in repairs The American locomotives may have burned 25 per cent. more coal, but, on the other hand, they may have been capable of hauling 50 per cent. more freight , and as for the repairs, 60 per cent. against the Americans looks very formidable, but if the total repairs on either engine did not amount to more than 10s., a difference even of 100 per cent would mean nothing All attempts to draw information from the Midland superintendent on this point have failed to elicit any facts beyond those contained in the report

It is a notable fact, says the writer of the article already quoted, that the first American locomotive ever imported into England was built sixty years ago for the purpose of enabling the English railway manager to prove that it was possible to haul loaded trains up a steep incline in the Birmingham-Gloucester Railway. Four engines were ordered in 1840, and they triumphantly accomplished their task. Thus, says Mr. Cunliff, the author of "The American Locomotive Abroad," the Birmingham and Gloucester line, on which the American engines first made their reputation, is now part of the Midland, whose officers have recently tried to ruin that reputation The engines of 1840 and those of 1900 were both built in the same workshops

The Baldwin locomotive works of Philadelphia alone exported about one locomotive a day, year in, year out In 1899 and 1900 they shipped 701 locomotives to the following countries:—

NORTH AND SOUTH AMERICA

Canada	Nova Scotia	Newfoundland	British Columbia
Alaska	Mexico	Costa Rica	Cuba
Porto Rico	Hawaii	Yucatan	San Domingo
Ecuador	Colombia	Peru	Brazil
Chile			

EUROPE

England	Ireland	France	Spain
Belgium	Holland	Bavaria	Denmark
Norway	Sweden	Finland	Russia

ASIA AND AUSTRALIA

Manchuria	Siberia	India	China
Japan	Burma	Assam	Victoria

AFRICA

Algeria	Tunis	Soudan	Egypt
Uganda	Cape Colony		

This represents the majority of the American trade, for the other firms only brought the total export up to 525 engines for one year. For heavy hauls on steep gradients the American engines appear to leave all their rivals far behind. There is said to be only one English locomotive left in the United States. It is on the Pennsylvanian Railroad, and its driver is said to have reported as follows "It's a good enough engine when it has nothing to do, but when it has a load beyond its drawbar, it sits down and looks at you with tears in its eyes."

Patriotic prejudice, no doubt, impedes for a time the introduction of American locomotives

into many countries, and in Russia it would seem the distribution of orders is often governed more by political than by commercial considerations Another obstacle against which they have to contend, is that their enormous weight requires the rebuilding of bridges and relaying of contracts Mr Cunliff tells a story that an English firm, having received notice that the engines which they supplied to New Zealand were unsuited to the colonial tracks and bridges, replied "Then rebuild your tracks and bridges, and we will furnish you with this sort of locomotive or none" Mr Cunliff maintains that an American builder would have replied, "Expect new designs by the first of the month " This is no doubt true, but as a matter of fact the American locomotive builder is compelling the reconstruction of tracks and bridges, none the less certainly because he is less domineering in relation to individual contractors. The American practice of standardising all parts of the machine, and of continually increasing the weight in order to get a still increased haulage power, necessitates alteration in the permanent way, for the railway in the long run has always to be built to suit the locomotive, not the locomotive to suit the railway. Mr. Cunliff thus lucidly explains the contrast between engine-building in the new world and the old "An American builder builds an engine to wear it out Scrupulous attention is paid to all working parts, as any one can see who visits a great locomotive plant. The mechanism of each machine is made easily accessible. Parts are interchangeable, so that repairs can be made with speed. No unnecessary paint is wasted. As soon as the machine is finished, it is put in commission and driven day and night with the heaviest loads it can stagger under. It goes into the repair shop only when it requires overhauling. Men are hired to run it at good wages, men of ability and intelligence, with a typically American personal interest in their charge Under such methods the engine is banged through a quarter century of strenuous activity, and then antiquated, worn out, superseded by advanced types, it goes to the scrap heap. The result is profit

" In England—and in France, for that matter —an engine is built to last Twenty years after it has been superseded by newer and better types, a locomotive is as tenderly cared for as ever. The result is decreasing dividends."

Of course if, as Mr Cunliff asserts, Americans can deliver engines in Japan at £2000, which do better work than English engines which cost £3000, it is out of the question to talk about competition, except such competition as is said to prevail between Lombard Street

and a China orange   The moral of it all is
in this as in everything else, that the American
success has been obtained by skilled workmanship and businesslike methods

Mr Chauncey M Depew in his address to
railway men at Buffalo Exhibition gave some
very interesting figures as to the growth of the
American railroad   Railway freight rates in
the United States were, he said, almost exactly
one-third of what they were when he entered
the service in 1866   At the same time the
wages of the railway men have nearly doubled,
the precise increase being 87½ per cent   As
there are more than a million of them, the gain
in the weekly wage bill of America from this
source alone is enormous   Their annual pay
bill for wages is £125,000,000, or 60 per cent
of the cost of operating the lines.   The United
States with only 6 per cent of the land surface
of the world has 40 per cent of the railroad
track   Its 193,000 mileage is six times that
of any other nation, and Mr Depew declares
that they haul more freight every year than is
moved by all the railways and all the ships of
Great Britain, France, and Germany combined

An American engine recently hauled a train
three-fourths of a mile in length at the rate of
20 miles an hour.   The gross-weight behind
the engine was over 3000 tons   Another
engine on a New York railway developed 1142
horse power   The average load of an American
freight train is 2000 tons, that of the English
only 600   The General Superintendent of the
London and South Western Railway, who has
just returned from an inspection of American
lines, reported that in passenger traffic we have
little to learn, but that we ought to revolutionize
our goods traffic   He said ' Our freight system
is wasteful.   American goods engines can haul
two or three times as much weight by one train
as we can   We must have heavier goods
locomotives.   We must also have air brakes
on goods trains   At present the only brakes on
our trains are the engine brakes and the brakes
at the end of the train.   In consequence of
improved appliances the American railways not
only haul heavier freights, but run much faster
than ours   I shall urge the extension of the
American system of pneumatic signalling for
interlocking, which gives such excellent results
on American lines."

In ship-building we are holding our own
It is true that the Americans have begun to
build a few ships, but as yet they have been
badly beaten in any attempt to produce ships
at the prices at which they can be turned out
on the Tyne, the Clyde, or at Belfast

Whether we shall be able permanently to
maintain our position in ship-building, or
victoriously to repel any further attacks upon

our iron and steel manufactures, are questions
for the answers to which we have to wait   But
there is certainly no reason to despair.   Our
manufacturers have as much work as they can
get through, and so far we have not seen any
great branch of British industry disorganised
and its workmen thrown out of employment
owing to the advent of the American invaders

In the building of swift ocean greyhounds we
are beaten by Germany as in the building of
racing yachts we are beaten by America.   And
although we still can plume ourselves upon our
ability to build more cheaply than any other
nation, this may not last   Dr von Halle, who
was sent out by the German Admiralty to
make an investigation of the shipyards of
Europe and America, reported that the new
Camden works in New Jersey were destined to
be one of the model establishments of the
world   Dr von Halle reported that "the
shipyards of the United States are incomparably
equipped for thorough, economical and rapid
production   This is due primarily to the
splendid transportation arrangements of the
yard areas, the employment of the most improved type of hoisting machinery, and the
widespread use of pneumatic tools."   They
would, he thought, distance in the near future
those of Great Britain, because they were free
from the "tyranny of the workmen"

The Americans, who have been carrying all
before them on the land, would have been false
to their ancestry if they did not hanker after
dominion on the sea.   Captain Mahan, whose
book on Sea Power has done more to promote
the increase of the Navy both in Great Britain
and in Germany than any book that has ever
been written, preached his doctrine primarily
for his own people   President Roosevelt is an
enthusiast for a strong Navy.   He does not say
in the Kaiser's phrase that America's future lies
upon the sea, because he would scorn to confine America's future to any element, even to
that which covers three-fourths of the world's
surface.   But although the Americans have a
Navy very nearly equal to that of Germany they
are not satisfied.   They have few over-sea possessions to protect, and despite various fantastic
schemes published by German officers as to '
a possible descent of a German expeditionary
force on the Atlantic seaboard, they know perfectly well that they are safe from European
attack   Nothing will satisfy them but that they
must have ships of commerce and ships of war
As to ships of war this is merely a matter of
expenditure, and as the embarrassment of the
Secretary of the Treasury is to get rid of the
surplus which is unnecessarily taken from the
taxpayers in excess of the needs of the Republic,
there is nothing to hinder the United States

MR. J. PIERPONT MORGAN

building up as big a Navy as that of Great Britain. When a nation has a large mercantile marine the existence of so many tons of shipping is regarded as an unanswerable argument in favour of building ironclads to protect its shipping. In the United States they have no shipping to protect, so they build a fleet first, and then say they must create a mercantile marine in order to keep the building-yards busy, and in order to rear sailors to man their fighting Navy.

It was this aspiration after ships which led Mr J. P. Morgan to make the famous purchase of the Leyland line of steamers, which may be regarded as the first note of the tocsin which has been ringing in our ears ever since. It is not twelve months since Britain was startled by the news that Mr. Morgan, on behalf of an American combination, had bought up the entire fleet of Leyland steamers on terms which were much better than the shareholders could have obtained from any other purchaser. The suddenness with which the deal was effected, and the fact that Mr Morgan was not an Englishman, and that the Leyland ships were bought on an American account, struck the imagination of the whole English-speaking race. British shipowners took the matter more coolly than the British public, for British shipowners in dealing with their ships are very much like the American engineers in handling their engines. Just as an American is always anxious to work his engine out so that he may get a new one with the latest improvements, so the British shipbuilder has never any objection to sell an old ship in order to raise funds with which to build a new one. The Chairman of the Peninsular and Oriental Shipping Company was far from holding up his hands in holy horror at the Leyland deal, but declared that he would be very glad to sell the whole fleet of the P and O. if terms equally good were offered him by the Americans or any one else. To get new ships for old has never been regarded as bad policy by our shipowners. It is possible that they may carry things a little too far, as, for instance, when two British lines of steamers trading in the Far East were sold to the Germans with the result that the British flag practically disappeared from Bangkok, Borneo, and other regions.

The significance of the incident arose from the fact that it indicated a determination on the part of the Americans to acquire a ready-made fleet, from which we may draw the conclusion that they were so eager to create a mercantile marine that they were willing to take second-hand goods rather than wait until new ships could be bought.

Mr. Gage, in the Report which he presented to Congress at the beginning of last Session, pointed out that only 8 2 per cent. of American exports and imports were carried in American ships This percentage, says Mr. Gage, "is the smallest in our history. Our position on the sea, except as a naval power, is insignificant The Americans have only one line of steamers crossing the Atlantic to Europe, two lines of seven steamers crossing the Pacific to Asia, and one line of three steamers to Australia South of the Caribbean Sea and the Isthmus there is no regular communication by American steamers with either coast of South America. This state of things appears deplorable to the nation which produces more materials for ship-building than any other, and whose artisans are quite competent to construct the best ships that have ever crossed the waves. We build few ships for foreign trade," says Mr. Gage. "It is desirable that we should build many We have very few ships under the flag in foreign trade It is desirable that we should have many." Therefore he recommends as a temporary expedient that navigation bounties should be established in order to overcome the obstacle created by the fact that Great Britain can build her ships cheaper and man them more economically than Americans.

As the Republican party is split upon the question of ship-building bounties, it is difficult for outsiders to estimate what chance there is of the acceptance of Mr. Gage's proposal

The thorny and much debated question of trusts was raised in this country in an active shape by the action of Mr. Morgan. At first the spectacle of the Billion Dollar Trust disturbed the equanimity of the British public. But after a time people began to remember that the two most conspicuous figures in British Imperialism both acquired the fortunes which rendered it possible for them to become politically influential by means of trusts. The De Beers Company is one of the most gigantic amalgamations in the world One by one the competing interests of the diamond-mine owners in South Africa were bought up or acquired, until at last Mr Rhodes and his fellow directors had an absolute monopoly of the diamond industry of South Africa Mr Rhodes was the precursor of Mr Morgan. For the Rockefeller of Britain we look nearer home No one has made any complaint of the legitimacy of the methods adopted by Mr. Morgan or Mr Rhodes in the buying up of the competing interests It is far otherwise with the methods adopted by Mr Rockefeller, when he built up the gigantic monopoly which is known as the Standard Oil Trust of the United States. No small portion of the odium which exists in this country against the American trusts in any shape or form is due ne influence of Mr. Lloyd's book, "Wealth anst Commonwealth," in which the whole of e process of building up a gigantic monopoly described with merciless lucidity. The spectacle is not a pleasing one We have fortunately nothing in the annals of our trade that can be compared to this extraordinary conspiracy of capital to crush out competition by the use of every method, fair or unfair, which did not land the conspirators within the grip of the criminal law. But the art of building up a great property by crushing out competition, without departing one hair's-breadth from the line of strict legality, was one in which Mr Chamberlain was a past master who had no need to go to school beyond the Atlantic

Upon trusts, as upon every other economic question, there is a great difference of opinion The late Governor Pingree of Michigan saw in the trust a kind of anti-Christ whose advent in these latter times darkened the horizon of the Republic. On the other hand, there is a tendency in many quarters to regard the trust as a practical and by no means illegitimate application of the principle of the elimination of wasteful expense and the cheapening of goods for the general consumer After considerable dubitation, President Roosevelt seems to have come to the conclusion that it is better to take the optimist view of the trust, and in his inaugural address he confines himself to a suggestion that it would be well to turn the bull's-eye of publicity upon the trust, and to insist upon due investigation of all its financial methods. This is probably as far as any President of the United States could go at present.

Of the future of Trusts there is much speculation Some, among whom is Sir Christopher Furness, M.P. who has just returned from a long tour of inspection in the United States, think that they will pass with the impending adoption of Free Trade. It is, however, by no means a self-evident proposition that the American Trust system will not survive Free Trade It may even be the instrument for bringing in Free Trade. To the ordinary observer it seems much more probable that the Trust will spread to the United Kingdom than that it will disappear from the United States.

There is no doubt, of course, that the Tariff and the Trusts play into each other's hands for the purpose of picking the pocket of the American consumer. The Industrial Commission, which has just concluded its inquiry into the whole question, found from the replies received from over one hundred manufacturers that American manufactures are often sold at lower prices abroad than in the United States. The home market being secured by the exclusion of foreign goods, the unfortunate American con-

sumer pays through the nose in order that the American producer may supply the foreigner at cut rates. To sell the foreigner the best American goods 25 per cent. below the prices charged to Americans may be very good for the foreigner, but it can hardly be regarded as good Americanism. Perhaps it may be accepted as an illegitimate kind of compensation awarded to the foreigner for the penalties inflicted upon his goods by the Tariff

How to cope with the abuses of Trusts * is a subject which President Roosevelt has frequently discussed His message to the New York Legislature in January, 1900, when he was Governor of New York, should be read in connection with his reference to the subject in his inaugural already quoted Speaking as Governor of New York, he said —

The chief abuses alleged to arise from Trusts are probably the following Misrepresentation or concealment regarding material facts connected with the organisation of an enterprise the evils connected with unscrupulous promotion; overcapitalisation; unfair competition resulting in crushing out of competitors who themselves do not act improperly, raising of prices above fair competitive rates, the wielding of increased power over the wage earners

We should know authoritatively whether stock represents the actual value of plants, or whether it represents brands of good will, or, if not, what it does represent if anything It is desirable to know how much was actually bought, how much was issued free, and to whom, and, if possible, for what reason

But supposing that the result of turning the bull's-eye of publicity upon the Trust and subjecting its method to the microscope of governmental quasi-judicial investigation were to reveal a clotted mass of force and fraud, upon which some of the greater Trusts are said to have been founded, what then? There are those who imagine that in such circumstances, or in the case of any exceptionally high-handed abuse of power by the Trusts, the Federal Government would step in and exercise the reserved right of every community to save itself from the loss of its liberties, by nationalising the Trust This is easier said than done, but the hope is so strong among many who are most opposed to the methods of American Capitalism, that they refuse to make any protest, or to interfere in any way with the legitimate evolution of economic forces which underlie American civilisation. It is better, they say, that their enemies should have one neck, for decapitation will be much easier than if they had a thousand.

* See on this subject a book, "The Control of Trusts," by Professor J B Clark, of Columbia University

L

If Mr. Morgan's foray for the purpose of buying the Leyland steamers was our first warning as to the new factor in international competitive trade, the invasion of the Tobacco Trust was the second, and one which excited much more interest among the mass of the people. For comparatively few were affected by the transfer of the Leyland line. Nearly every other man in the United Kingdom was affected by the entry of the American Tobacco Trust into the British field. They began, as usual, by attempting to purchase the biggest firms in the British tobacco trade. Failing with the biggest, as Mr. Astor failed with the *Times*, they descended upon the second best, and as he bought the *Pall Mall Gazette*, so they bought Ogden's. The alternative offer to the shareholders was very simple. Their property was worth at market quotations £638,000. The trust offered to buy them out, paying for the property £818,000 or £180,000 above the market price. That was the offer to accept or to refuse. If they accepted it, every shareholder would enjoy a sudden and immediate increase of his capital, which he was perfectly free, if so minded, to invest in establishing a new tobacco business, and take advantage of the latest improvements, mechanical or otherwise. If, on the other hand, they elected to fight, the immediate result would have been tumble in the value of their shares and diminution in their dividend, while they would probably be forced to sell in the end for half the price that the trust offered. Under these circumstances it is not surprising that they decided to sell, and the American Trust, masquerading under the specious title of the British Tobacco Co., got the necessary foothold, and began at once the operations necessary to secure control of the market.

For the consumer, the immediate result was a reduction in the price of tobacco, especially of cigarettes, all round. The advent of the American competitor compelled the British firms to form a combination, although they did not call it a trust, of their own, under the title of the Imperial Tobacco Co., for the purpose of defending their own interests by common action. The battle has as yet hardly begun, but it has already yielded handsome first fruits of profit to the newspapers, in which the competing forces are advertising very liberally. How long they will keep it up remains to be seen. But what seems probable is that they will not succeed in establishing a monopoly, but that they will materially reduce the profits of the British companies.

THE H. A. LINE TWIN SCREW EXPRESS STEAMER *DEUTSCHLAND*, HOLDING THE SPEED RECORDS FOR THE ATLANTIC PASSAGE, 1901.

PART IV

THE SUMMING-UP.

Chapter I.—What is the Secret of American Success?

There is no one secret of American success It is due to many causes co-operating to convert the modern American into a dynamo of energy, and make him the supreme type of a strenuous life.

American success may be explained in many ways A young and vigorous race has been let loose among the incalculable treasures of a virgin continent. Into that race there has been poured in lavish profusion the vital energies of many other races chosen by a process of natural selection which eliminated the weaker, the more timid, the less adventurous spirits This great amalgam of heterogeneous energies constitutes a new composite race, which found itself free to face all the problems of the universe without any of the restraints of prejudices, traditions or old-established institutions which encumber the nations of the Old World Americans had no swaddling clothes to cast They sprang into life like Minerva from the brain of Jove, without any need to rid themselves of the garments of infancy They had also the immense advantage of an atmosphere which in many parts of the continent was a perpetual exhilaration. All these causes contribute to American success They belong to the Americans as an inalienable possession, nor can we by any possibility hope to share them. They are as inseparable from the Continent of America as the Falls of Niagara or the Mississippi Valley

But there are other causes which contribute in no small degree to American success, of which the Americans have no natural monopoly "The success of the Americans," said a cultivated Jew, who, born in the Old World, had lived for some time in the New, "may be said to spring from two causes The first is that of the concentration of the whole genius of the race upon industrial pursuits. In Germany" he said, "the maintenance, the equipment, and the organisation of the army diverts to the study of military questions an immense proportion of the genius of Germans In Italy and France the genius of the people finds its natural vent in the study of art, or, in the case of the Roman Church, in theological specula-

tion or in the management of an immense ecclesiastical organisation In England there is a great scattering of energy. The genius of your people expends itself not in one, but in half a-dozen directions You are pre-occupied with your commerce, with your colonies, and with your navy. You have built up a great literature, and you have made a positive cultus of sport. But in the United States the whole undivided genius of the people is concentrated upon the pursuit of wealth. Hence this one thing they do and do with all their might, and therefore easily distance all competitors whose energies are dissipated upon other channels"

"That is one secret of American success," he continued "But there is another to which I attach even more importance. All power arises from restraint. Indulgence is the dissipation of energy. For two hundred years in the New England States, the stern discipline of Puritan morality, repressed with iron hand the animal instincts which lead to a self-indulgent life Each generation which lived and died under that yoke lived and died voluntarily subjecting itself to a sterner restraint than that imposed on any nation before or since. But it accumulated energy which it transmitted to its descendants. Now in our day we see that tremendous spring uncoiling with results at which all the world wonders. The stock of energy which the New Englanders accumulated in two centuries could only have been acquired, as great fortunes are built up, by long years of self-denial, patiently persisted in despite all temptations How long it will last is another question, but at the present moment we can see no sign of that pent-up reservoir of energy being exhausted"

This, however, does not help us much for no one can improvise ancestors of the Puritan type We must, therefore, look further afield if we would discover any American secret by which we may profit

Within this narrowed range a very little observation will lead us to discover three of the American secrets which are capable of export The first is Education the second is increased incentives to Production ; and the third is Democracy It may be well to examine each of these in turn. Nearly seventy years ago when Cobden visited the United States, he laid an unerring finger upon the superior education of the American common people as the secret of their growing ascendency. He said —

"The universality of education in the United States is probably more calculated than all others to accelerate their progress towards a superior rank of civilisation and power. One thirty-sixth portion of all public lands, of which there are hundreds of thousands of square miles un-appropriated, is laid apart for the purposes of instruction If knowledge be power, and if education gives knowledge, then must the Americans inevitably become the most power-ful people in the world The very genius of American legislation is opposed to ignorance in the people, as the most deadly enemy of good government. .   . There is now more than six times as much advertising and reading on the other side of the Atlantic as in Great Britain. There are those who are fond of decrying news-paper-reading, but we regard every scheme that is calculated to make mankind think, everything that by detaching the mind from the present moment, and leading it to reflect upon the past or future, rescues it from the dominion of mere sense, as calculated to exalt us in the scale of being, and, whether it be a newspaper or a volume that serves this end, the instrument is worthy of honour at the hands of enlightened philanthropists."

There is a saying of Confucius, which was often quoted when the French legions went down before the educated Germans—that he who leads an uneducated people to war throws them away. The victories registered on French battlefields were won by the German school-masters ; and so it is to the little red school-house in which the school-marm taught boys and girls together for more than a hundred years, that we must go to find the sceptre of the American dominion. It is little more than thirty years since education became compulsory in the United Kingdom ; and it was in still more recent times that the school-fees were abolished. But education has been universal, free, and compulsory in the United States of America from the very foundation of the New England Colonies. The first object of the Pilgrim Fathers was to found a conventicle in which they could worship God as they thought fit , but after the founding of the Church their first care was to open a school. Hence the average level of intelligence in the United States, despite the immense influx of 19 millions of the unedu-cated European horde, is much higher than it is with us In that vast Republic every one can at least read and write, and upon that basis Americans have reared a superstructure of edu-cational appliance which causes Englishmen to despair. Mr Frederic Harrison, when he visited

the United States last in 1900, was lost in amaze-ment and admiration at the immense energy and lavish magnificence of the apparatus of education. "The whole educational machinery of America," he said, "must be at least tenfold that of the United Kingdom That open to women must be at least twentyfold greater than with us, and it is rapidly advancing to meet that of men both in numbers and quality"

According to some statistics published this autumn by the *Scientific American*, there are 629 universities and colleges in the United States, the total value of whose property is estimated at £68,000,000. The total income was over 5½ millions sterling. In a single year, 1898–99, the value of gifts to these institutions amounted to £4,400,000 The number of students pursuing undergraduate and graduate courses in universi-ties, colleges, and schools of technology was 147,164. Of these only 43,913 were enrolled as students of the three professions—law, medi-cine, and theology The number of students per million, which stood at 573 in 1872, rose to 770 in 1880, to 850 in 1890, whereas in 1899 it had gone up to 1196—more than double in twenty-eight years.

A whole volume might be written in com-paring and contrasting the educational systems of Great Britain and the United States But it is unnecessary to burden the reader with statistics American superiority, as attested by statistics, has its root in one fundamental difference between the two nations In America everybody, from the richest to the poorest, considers that education is a boon, a necessity of life, and the more education they get the better it is for the whole country In Great Britain, Sir John Gorst himself being witness, the educated classes regard education as unnecessary for the labouring classes. The country squire and, broadly speaking, the class which dresses for dinner, are of opinion that those who do not dress for dinner are better without education. Sir John Gorst, the Minister officially responsible for British education, has affirmed this in terms which leave no room for mistake It is this which differentiates the Briton from the American Our men of light and leading, those who have enjoyed all the advantages of superior education, who monopolise the immense endowments of the ancient universities of Oxford and Cambridge, resent the demand that the children of the agricultural labourer or the costermonger should receive the best education that the State can give them Education in this country is not regarded as a good investment. Hence it is that, while American millionaires find pleasure in lavishing millions in the endowment of universities and technical schools and the provision of educational apparatus, the bequests to education in this country amount to a beggarly sum. Mr Carnegie, born a Scotchman, but a naturalised citizen of the States, has given more money for the endowment of university education in a single cheque than all our millionaires have given to our universities for the last quarter of a century. Until a change comes over the spirit of our country, and Society with a big S recognises that unless our people are educated the game is up, we shall not see any material improvement. The future belongs not to brawn but to brain, and the nation which ignores both, as we unfortunately are doing at this moment, will inevitably go to the wall. It may be said that it is no use looking for the conversion of our governing classes. Until our working people who have a vote determine to use it to compel Parliament to give every English workman's child as good an education and as fair a chance of making his way to a university career (if he is bright enough) as he would have if he emigrated to the United States, nothing will be done.

Secondly, Incentives to increased productive power. The second cause of American success, which we could appropriate if we pleased, is that of improved methods of production. We want more machinery, better machinery, and we must not stint its output. The old spirit which led to the machine riots in the West Riding of Yorkshire at the beginning of the century is still latent in the British workman. There is no need to go into old sores or to enter upon disputed ground, but it is unfortunately no longer disputable that our industrial progress is hampered in two directions, first, by the reluctance of the employer to invest in new machinery, and, secondly, by a belief on the part of many workmen that the less work each man does the more work there is for somebody else.

The difficulty about machinery arises largely from the English prejudice in favour of good, solid machines which, if once built, will last for a long time. The American deliberately puts in flimsy machinery which will wear out, as he calculates that by the time he has got all the work out of his machine that it will stand, new improvements will have been invented which will necessitate in any case the purchase of new machinery. Hence he buys a cheaper article, uses it up quickly, and then gets a new one with the latest improvements. The Briton finds that he has a machine almost as good as new when the American machine is worn out, and is loth to cast it on one side.

There is a certain objection to labour-saving machines on the part of many workmen, who regard all such machines as the owners of

stage-coaches regarded locomotives. It is calculated that every locomotive that is turned out of an engine-shop makes work for as many horses as the horse-power which it represents, and there has never been so much demand for labour as since the introduction of labour-saving machinery became universal. The popular fallacy that contrivances which economise labour make less work for the labourer was never so aptly illustrated as in the story of the Tsar and the Dutch Ambassador, who met in the Seventeenth Century on the banks of the Volga. Great barges were being towed up the stream by gangs of 200 moujiks, who were harnessed to the tow-rope, and so, with infinite expenditure of sweat and sinew, they hauled their clumsy craft at the rate of about two miles an hour. The Dutchman addressed the Tsar and respectfully ventured to point out to him that with his permission he (the Dutchman) could rig up a mast and a sail which would enable the wind to drive the boat much more swiftly through the water without any need for this costly human haulage. The Tsar listened for a moment and then sternly reproved the adventurous Dutchman. "How dare you," he said, "propose to me to adopt a contrivance which would take the bread out of the mouths of these poor fellows?"

And so the moujiks went on with their hauling. Every one sees the absurdity of such a reply, but at bottom it is exactly the same spirit which inspires the objection to machines which economise labour.

This, however, is a less danger than the spirit, to which a good deal of attention has been called of late by articles in the *Times* and elsewhere, which leads workmen deliberately to dawdle over their work with the idea that the less work each man does the more work there will be for his mate. The same spirit shows itself in the extreme punctiliousness with which workmen will insist upon never doing anything but their own particular job, under no matter what stress of emergency. In some industries we have almost arrived at the extreme division of labour that prevails in India, which necessitates the employment of twenty servants to do the work of three. The folly of this deliberate limitation of output is recognised by the more intelligent leaders of the working classes, and the experience of the Westinghouse Company at their new Manchester works is full of hope. By the introduction of American foremen, and by a frank and candid explanation to the workmen of what was wanted, the Americans declared that they found no difficulty in getting as much good work out of Englishmen in England as they are always able to get out of Englishmen when they emigrate to America.

But we cannot man all our works with American foremen, nor is it desirable that the English in their own country should be reduced to the level of Gibeonites, to be hewers of wood and drawers of water for the superior race. By far the best way of overcoming this difficulty is by the introduction of some method of co-partnership, or of profit-sharing, which would make every workman feel that he had a personal interest in the prosperity of the concern. At present he feels too often that he has nothing personally to gain by putting his back into his work. The shareholder and not the workman reaps the benefit of increased efficiency To get round that difficulty is not impossible, as the experience of Mr. George Livesey in the South Metropolitan Gas Company shows Profit-sharing is the first, co-partnership the second, and co-operative production the third step which will lead us out of the morass in which we are at present floundering. The experience of Co-operative Works at Leicester, and the neighbourhood justifies confident expectations as to the excellent results which would follow if the consciousness of mutual interest were the rule instead of the exception in British industry.

Neither here nor in the United States can we hope to put the tremendous premium upon individual effort which was offered in the early days of American industry The trade union is likely to become more rather than less powerful in the days that are to come. It appeals very strongly to the Socialist aspirations which seem likely, in America, as well as in this country, to be an increasing factor in the organisation of industry, but that is no reason why the trade unions should not provide for the encouragement of individual capacity among their own members It would be a great mistake, however, to think that trade unions are the only obstacle. We have to face the reluctance on the part of employers to recognise that their workmen have brains which could be utilised. The American workman who suggests an improvement in the machinery which he is working, is encouraged and rewarded. In England he is too often told to mind his own business.

And as it is with the employers, so it is with the law of the land. Our patent laws, instead of encouraging invention on the part of those who have brains but no money, absolutely handicap the poor man, and leave him helpless to profit by his own inventions. Sir John Leng, in a recent address at Dundee, brought out very clearly this contrast between the American and British systems. The American patent law secures a patentee protection for seventeen years for a total cost of £8 To secure a patent for fourteen years in this country requires an expenditure of £99. The American Patent

Office makes a fairly thorough examination of a patent, and, if required, the applicant is assisted to put his application into proper shape. With this stimulus to invention, it is not surprising that the inventive genius of the American has outstripped that of the Old World Fortunately this can be remedied, for our Patent Office is one of those institutions which can be Americanised with the greatest ease.

The third cause of American success which we can also appropriate is that which comes from the frank adoption and consistent application of the principle of democracy. Mr. Choate, the American Ambassador at the Court of St James's, recently declared in a public speech at New York :—

" After all that I have seen of other countries, it seems to me absolutely clear that the cardinal principle upon which American institutions rest, the absolute political equality of all citizens with universal suffrage, is the secret of American success. Aided by that comprehensive system of education, which enables every citizen to pursue his calling and exercise the franchise, it puts the country on that plane of success which it has reached "

" I have no doubt," said De Tocqueville more than sixty years ago, " that the democratic institutions of the United States, joined to the physical constitution of the country, are the cause (not the direct, as is so often asserted, but the indirect cause) of the prodigious commercial activity of the inhabitants." He adds, further on . " Democracy does not give the people the most skilful government, but it produces what the ablest governments are frequently unable to create namely, a superabundant force, and an energy which is inseparable from it, and which may, however unfavourable circumstances may be, produce wonders."

As to the influence of democratic institutions upon the inventive ingenuity and energy of a people, Mr. Wideneos of Philadelphia, discussing the connection between democracy and business, recently said to Mr. W E. Curtis —

" Our greatest success in industry and commerce has been due to the higher intelligence and better education of the American working man. The United States is a democracy where everybody has a chance, and that inspires ambition Look at the list of men who control business affairs in that country. Nine of every ten of them began at the bottom and in a small way, but the road was open to everybody and the best man got there first.

" In England the opportunities are comparatively limited, and the lower classes have no inspiration , no inducement to save their money and improve themselves. There is no use in a boy educating himself for better things when he cannot get them The very best of us are from the bottom. Some of our biggest swells had fathers who worked for days' wages. Yet that was no handicap. They gave them good constitutions, good educations and opportunities. Such men now command the financial, commercial and political world "

We have democratised our institutions piecemeal, but we are still far short of applying the principle thoroughly in such fashion as to make every man feel the stimulus of equality of responsibility, equality of opportunity.

It is not necessary to pursue this in detail, but it is worthy of note that at the present moment the only governing institutions in this country in which we can pretend to be ahead of the United States are our municipalities, where the principle of democracy has been carried out much more thoroughly than in the Imperial Parliament. Imagine the London County Council saddled with a Second Chamber, three-fourths of whom were the ground landlords of London, with a right of veto upon every measure passed by the County Council ' Could anything be suggested more certain to choke the civic spirit which has given new life to London in the last ten years? Aristocratic institutions, no doubt, have their advantages, but they do not tend to develop in the mass of the people a keen sense of citizenship They effectively paralyse that consciousness of individual power which gives so great and constant a stimulus to the energy and self-respect of the citizens of the Republic.

CHAPTER II.—A LOOK AHEAD.

WHAT is the conclusion of the whole matter? It may be stated in a sentence There lies before the people of Great Britain a choice of two alternatives If they decide to merge the existence of the British Empire in the United States of the English-speaking World, they may continue for all time to be an integral part of the greatest of all World-Powers, supreme on sea and unassailable on land, permanently delivered from all fear of hostile attack and capable of wielding irresistible influence in all parts of this planet That is one alternative The other is the acceptance of our supersession by the United States as the centre of gravity in the English-speaking world, the loss one by one of our great colonies, and our ultimate reduction to the status of an English-speaking Belgium One or the other it must be What shall it be ? Seldom has a more momentous choice been presented to the citizens of any country

It is natural that British pride should revolt at the conclusion which is thus presented as the result of a rapid survey of the forces governing

the present political and financial and industrial situation But pride and prejudice are evil counsellors The question is not what we would best like to do, but what is the best course possible in the circumstances ? If it is admitted that the whole trend of our time is towards the unification of races of a common stock and common language, if it is further admitted that such unification would carry with it incalculable advantages in securing the English-speaking nations from all danger either of a fratricidal conflict or of foreign attack, while enormously improving both their prosperity at home and the influence which they can exercise abroad, it is difficult to resist the conclusion that the object is one well worthy of being made the ultimate goal of the statesmen both of the United States and of the United Kingdom That it is possible to constitute as one vast federated unity the English-speaking United States of the world, can hardly be disputed That there are difficulties, immense difficulties, is equally true , but it is well to remember that these difficulties did not appear insuperable to Adam Smith, who wrote nearly a hundred years before the Atlantic had been bridged by steam It is worth while recalling his profound and luminous observations in the first edition of his " Wealth of Nations," which was published in 1776, on the very eve of the revolt of the American Colonies At that time, the great schism had not occurred which has for more than a century banished the idea from the minds of man, but the recent and welcome rapprochement which has taken place between the British and American peoples renders it possible for us to get back to the standpoint of Adam Smith, He contemplated the union of Great Britain with her American Colonies by admitting representatives from those Colonies to the Imperial Parliament. For, as he says in words which are as true to-day as they were then .—

" The assembly which deliberates and decides concerning the affairs of every part of the Empire, in order to be properly informed, ought certainly to have representatives from every part of it."

He admitted that there were difficulties, but denied that they were insurmountable

" The principal difficulty," he said, "arises, not from the nature of things, but from the prejudices and opinions of the people both on this side and on the other side of the Atlantic "

He then dealt briefly with some of the objections that were urged, objections which the lapse of time has answered so effectually that we need not even refer to them here. But in combating one of these objections that might be raised by the Americans—that their distance from the seat of Government might expose them to many oppressions—he used the following remarkable words :—

" The distance of America from the seat of Government the natives of that country might flatter themselves, with some appearance of reason, too, would not be of a very long continuance Such has hitherto been the rapid progress of that country in wealth, population, and improvement that, in the course of little more than a century, perhaps, the produce of American might exceed that of British taxation. The seat of the Empire would then naturally remove itself to that part of the Empire which contributes most to the general defence and support of the whole."

The Imperial idea, therefore, before the disruption of the Empire, contemplated that if the empire held together, its capital in the course of time would be transferred from the Old World to the New. •

The same idea was expressed the other day with much greater eloquence by Lord Rosebery in his address as Lord Rector to the students of Glasgow University. Going back to the time when Adam Smith wrote, Lord Rosebery allowed his imagination to dwell upon what might have been the results to the English-speaking race if the elder Pitt had prevented or suppressed the reckless budget of Charles Townshend, induced George III. to listen to reason, and by introducing representatives from the American Colonies into the Imperial Parliament, preserved America to the British Crown. Had such a measure been passed, he said,

" It would have provided for some self-adjusting system of representation, such as now prevails in the United States, by which increasing population is proportionally represented."

He then proceeded —

" At last, when the Americans became the majority, the seat of Empire would, perhaps, have been moved solemnly across the Atlantic, Great Britain have become the historical shrine and the European outpost of the World-empire. What an extraordinary revolution it would have been had it been accomplished ' The greatest known without bloodshed, the most sublime transference of power in the history of mankind. Our conceptions can hardly picture the procession across the Atlantic The greatest Sovereign in the greatest fleet in the universe, Ministers, Government, Parliament, departing solemnly for the other hemisphere, not as in the case of the Portuguese sovereign emigrating to Brazil under the spur of necessity, but under the vigorous embrace of the younger world."

He admitted that the result was one to which we could scarcely acclimatise ourselves even in idea, but he went on to speculate upon some

of the consequences that would have happened from so blessed a consummation —

" America would have hung on the skirts of Britain, and pulled her back out of European complications She would have profoundly affected the foreign policy of the mother-country in the direction of peace Her influence in our domestic policy would have been scarcely less potent It might probably have appeased and even contented Ireland. The ancient constitution of Great Britain would have been rendered more comprehensive and more elastic. On the other hand, the American yearning for liberty would have taken a different form It would have blended with other traditions and flowed into other moulds ; and above all, had there been no suppression there would have been no war of Independence, no war of 1812, with all the bitter memories that these have left on American soil To secure that priceless boon I should have been satisfied to see the British Federal Parliament sitting in Columbian territory. It is indeed difficult to dam the flow of ideas in dealing with so pregnant a possibility "

The question which it is my purpose to raise in the present treatise is whether the realisation of Lord Rosebery's dream is even now outside the pale of practical politics Would not the gain of the establishment of a Federal Parliament of the English-speaking race on American soil more than compensate us for any loss of what may be described as the parochial prestige of the insular Briton ? Ireland still has to be contented ; the British Constitution, for lack of elasticity, has become practically unworkable ; the Imperial Parliament shows no sign of being able to admit representatives from the distant Colonies ; and danger of collision between the Empire and the Republic, although masked by present appearance, automatically increases as the over-sea ambitions of the United States develop and expand. In its original shape, of course, Lord Rosebery's vision can never be realised. The possibility of uniting the whole English-speaking world under the ægis of the sceptre of a British sovereign, perished for ever when George III. made war upon the American Colonies

But because our forefathers by their prejudice and passion wrecked the possibility of realising the great ideal, that is no reason why we, their sons, should not endeavour to undo the evil results of their folly by attempting to secure the unification of the race by the only means which are still available Unification under the Union Jack having become impossible by our own mistakes, why should we not seek unification under the Stars and Stripes ? We could, of course, keep the Union Jack as a local flag, as in a Federated South Africa we could permit the burghers of the Transvaal to keep the Vierkleur It possesses a historical interest, and is instinct with too many heroic memories for it to be allowed to pass for ever from sea or shore. But the day has passed when the meteor flag of England could stand any chance of being accepted by the majority of English-speaking men In such matters the majority must decide Not only are we already in a minority of nearly one to two, but the majority tends every year to increase Are we as a nation incapable of facing the inevitable and of governing our course in accordance therewith ?

Many years ago when the late Earl of Derby was Colonial Minister in Mr. Gladstone's Cabinet, he discussed this question with Dr E. J Dillon, now well known as correspondent of the *Daily Telegraph.* Dr Dillon asked him as a former foreign Minister of Great Britain, what he thought should be the foreign policy of the Empire. Lord Derby replied that he thought it would be best for the country to have no foreign policy at all, which led Dr Dillon to ask what then did he contemplate as the goal of British policy in the future Lord Derby replied —

"The highest ideal that I can look forward to in the future of my country is that the time may come when we may be admitted into the American Union as States in one great Federation '

It may be said that Lord Derby was a Little Englander, and therefore out of court But this objection cannot be brought against Mr. Rhodes, who is a Big Englander if ever there was one, and who more than any man in our time incarnates the spirit of British Imperialism. But Mr Rhodes, although he would not adopt the terms of Lord Derby's declaration, is absolutely at one with him on the main point Mr Rhodes would undoubtedly much prefer to see the English-speaking race unified under the Union Jack, for his devotion to the old flag approaches to a passion. But Mr Rhodes's pole star has ever been the unity of the English-speaking race. No one can talk to him for long without coming upon the sentiment which is ever present in his mind, of a deep and almost angry regret over the fatal folly which rent the race in twain in the eighteenth century. How often have I not heard him deplore the insensate folly which robbed the world of its one great hope of universal peace. Only this year he inveighed, as is his wont, against the madness of the monarch which had wrecked the fairest prospect of international peace which had ever dawned upon the world.

"If only we had held together," he remarked, "there would have been no need for another cannon to be cast in the whole world. The

Federation of the English-speaking world would be strong enough in its command of all the material resources of the planet to compel the decision of all international quarrels by a more rational method than that of war."

Nor has he abandoned the hope that even yet that great Federation may be brought about He would, no doubt, shrink from boldly adopting the formula that, if it could not be secured in any other way than by the admission of the various parts of the British Empire as States of the American Union, it had better be brought about in that way than not at all He has so intense a longing to realise the unity of the race that, being a practical man, and resolute to attain his end by some road, if that which he has chosen is absolutely impassable, he can be counted upon as one of the great personal forces which would co-operate in the attainment of our ideal

The subject is not one upon which politicians are likely to talk Any utterance in favour of coming together under the American flag could so easily be misrepresented by a political opponent as an act of treason to the Union Jack, that men whose horizon is limited to the next General Election naturally refrain from expressing any opinion on the subject But, privately, no one who moves in political and journalistic circles can ignore the fact that many of the strongest Imperialists are heart and soul in favour of seeing the British Empire and the American Republic merged in the English-speaking United States of the World. This is an ideal splendid enough to fascinate the imagination of all men, especially of those who have proved most susceptible to the fascination of Imperial Federation.

But here it is necessary to observe that, while on this side of the Atlantic there may be a great latent but powerful sentiment in favour of such reunion, it will come to nothing unless it is reciprocated by similar sentiments on the other side of the water. We may be willing to make great sacrifices of national prejudice and Imperial pride in order to attain this greater ideal, but will the Americans be equally fascinated by the ideal of race unity? The United States, it is said by some, is quite big enough to take care of itself It has no longer any need of a British alliance, which might entail considerable complications and involve the Republic in entanglements from which the Americans might not unnaturally recoil

The subject is not one upon which the Americans can very well take the initiative The suggestion has even offended some Americans, as indicating possibilities altogether beyond their reach There is very little evidence, on one side or the other, as to what would be the probable attitude of the masses of the American people should this question be raised in a practical shape. I had, however, an opportunity of discussing the matter quite recently with two typical Americans, who were singularly well placed for forming a judgment upon the matter. One, born in Scotland, had become a naturalised American citizen. The other, born in America, had become a naturalised British subject. The former had been all his life devoted to the cause of peace The other has made his fortune by the success with which he has manufactured arms of war. But upon this question they are absolutely at one. Sir Hiram Maxim and Mr. Andrew Carnegie are both men whose maturity of judgment and wide experience of men entitle them to be heard with respect upon any subject to which they have given serious attention. Sir Hiram Maxim wrote me as recently as the 8th November last after we had discussed the subject for some time —

"I have thought much of the long and interesting conversation I had with you yesterday, and although I do not hope to live to see the consummation of what was foreshadowed by you, still I should not wonder if the baby was already born who will witness the whole English-speaking race consolidated in some great federation forming the greatest, richest, and the most powerful nation that the world has ever known. I think it is true that it is sure to come ; it is only a question of time and civilisation "

I saw Mr. Carnegie on the 25th October, just before he left London for New York. Mr. Carnegie is a remarkable man in many ways, but he is absolutely unique in being at once a prophet and a millionaire. It is the first time in the history of the world in which the two *rôles* have been played by a single man. Mr. Carnegie said to me :—

"Turn up my 'Look Ahead' which I published in the *North American Review* eight years ago, and you will find every forecast which I made then is coming true You remember, I told you that when you sat down to your desk to write that chapter, I was inclined to believe that the whole scheme was somewhat visionary, but that when I sent the manuscript I was convinced that there was nothing more practical or more important pressing upon the attention of statesmen Well, eight years have passed since then, and now when I take a look backwards, at my old article, 'Look Ahead,' I am more than ever impressed with the soundness of the views which I there set out We are heading straight to the Re-united States Everything is telling that way Your people are only beginning to wake up to the irresistible drift of forces which dominate the situation

"It is coming, coming faster than you people in the Old World realise. Mr Frank Stockton was down at Skibo this year, and he told rather a good story bearing upon this question When he was coming down in the train, he foregathered with an Englishman, whom he met in the train, and they got talking about various things, and the Englishman expressed what is now a very common

sentiment among your people—great regret at the folly of George III. 'Just think what he cost us,' said the Englishman 'Why, he cost us America.' 'But,' said Mr. Stockton, 'you must not forget what he cost us ' 'Cost you,' said the Englishman 'What did he cost you ?' 'He cost us Britain,' said Mr. Stockton And there is the whole truth in a nutshell. If we had all continued together, Britain would have belonged to America much more than America would have belonged to Britain, and it will come to that yet."

The theme is a favourite one with Mr. Carnegie. He may indeed be regarded as the leading exponent of the idea. In his "Triumphant Democracy," he maintained that the American Constitution offered a much better, freer, and at the same time more supple system of government than that which prevailed in the old country. He summarised under seventeen separate heads the reasons why he thought the leadership of the English-speaking world must belong to America. Some of these relating to things political and constitutional may be quoted here —

(7) The nation whose flag, wherever it floats over sea and land, is the symbol and guarantor of the equality of the citizen

(8) The nation in whose Constitution no man suggests improvement : whose laws as they stand are satisfactory to all citizens.

(9) The nation which has the ideal Second Chamber, the most august assembly in the world —the American Senate

(10) The nation whose Supreme Court is the envy of the ex-Prime Minister of the parent land. (Lord Salisbury)

(11) The nation whose Constitution is "the most perfect piece of work ever struck off at one time by the mind and purpose of man," according to the present Prime Minister of the parent land. (Mr Gladstone)

(12) The nation most profoundly conservative of what is good, yet based upon the political equality of the citizen.

Since the publication of "Triumphant Democracy," Mr, Carnegie has discussed the question in articles contributed to the English and American magazines, notably to the *Nineteenth Century* for September 1891, in an article entitled ' An American View of Imperial Federation," and in June, 1892, in the *North American Review*, in a paper entitled "A Look Ahead." There are others, but these are the chief. He concluded his articles on "A Look Ahead" by the following declaration of faith—a declaration which might be regarded in other men as a mere fantasy, but which in a hard-headed man like Mr Carnegie, who has shown an equal ability in amassing and giving away millions, will command respect.

"Let men say what they will, but I say that as surely as the sun in the heavens once shone upon Britain and-America united, so surely is it one morning to rise and shine upon and greet again the Re-united States of the British-American Union."

This confidence was based in the first case upon the fact that it was only in their political ideas that there was any dissimilarity, "for no rupture whatever between the separated parts has ever taken place in language, literature, religion, or law. In these uniformity has always existed. Although separated politically, the unity of the parts has never been disturbed in these strong, cohesive and cementing links"

There was a perpetual process of assimilation going on between the political institutions of the two countries. That such a reunion was desirable seemed to Mr Carnegie an almost self-evident proposition. If England and America were one they would be able to maintain the peace of the world and general disarmament An Anglo-American reunion would admit of bringing British goods into the United States duty free The richest market in the world would be open to Great Britain, free of all duty by a stroke of the pen There would not be an idle mine, furnace or factory in the United Kingdom.

Apart from material interests, Mr Carnegie holds very strongly to the idea subsequently adopted by Mr. Chamberlain that the mind of the individual citizen expands in response to the magnitude of the State to which he belongs. Dealing with great affairs broadens and elevates the character—a thesis which it would be somewhat difficult to maintain in face of the fact that the great ideas which have shaken the world have in almost every case been conceived by the citizens of States so small that they could be stowed away out of sight in a corner of a single State like Texas. Men's minds do not always expand in proportion to the geographical area of the Kingdom, Empire or Republic in which they happen to be born. Nevertheless there is a certain truth in Mr Carnegie's remark, although it must be balanced by remembering Burke's famous phrase about statesmen who have the minds of pedlars and merchants who act like princes In this expansion of the political horizon the citizens of both countries would equally share, but Mr. Carnegie does not discuss the fact that the balance of advantage would lie with the British, for the leadership of the United States is secure. Whether reunion is effected or abandoned as an impossible dream, it will not affect the headship of the United States The American will easily be the first Power in the world. But for the Motherland it is otherwise. Mr. Carnegie wrote —

"The only course for Britain seems to be re-union with her giant child or sure decline to a secondary place, and then to comparative insignificance in the future annals of the English-speaking race What great difference would it make to Wales, Ireland, and Scotland if their representatives to the Supreme Council should proceed to Washington instead of to London? Yet this is all the change that would be required, and for this they would have ensured to them all the rights of independence."

Nevertheless, he thinks the idea would be received with even more enthusiasm in the United States than in the United Kingdom. "The reunion idea," said he, "would be hailed with enthusiasm in the United States. No idea yet promulgated since the formation of the Union would create such unalloyed satisfaction It would sweep the country. No party would oppose, each would try to excel the other in approval."

Surveying the whole situation, Mr Carnegie came to the conclusion eight years ago that the causes of continued disunion which admittedly exist in England are rapidly vanishing and are melting away like snow in the sunshine. Canada, the United States, and Ireland were even then ready for reunion, and no serious difficulty existed either in Scotland or in Wales He thought that in England, Ireland, Scotland and Wales a proposition to make all officials elected by the people after the Queen had passed away would command a heavy vote.

In 1898, when I had an opportunity of discussing the matter with him, he was so confident that the reunion was practicable, that he had modified his views in many directions. When he had first launched the idea he regarded it as necessary for the British people to abjure their monarchy, their hereditary peerage, their Established Church, and to do away with their Indian Empire, and as a preliminary to reunion he had contemplated a declaration of independence on the part of Canada, Australia, and South Africa In 1898 he recognised that such a drastic process of demolition and disintegration was not the necessary preliminary to reunion. He thought it was quite possible that special provision might be made for the admission of monarchical States into the British-American Union. He still clung to his idea of the admission of Great Britain and Ireland into the Union They would, he said, cut up into eight States, with an average of five millions each in population This is considerably more than the average of the American States, but it is less than the population of Pennsylvania and New York. It is well that Mr Carnegie should have modified his views so far as to admit that the British race might assent to a reunion without being compelled as a preliminary to abjure their distinctive peculiarities.

Upon this point Cobden, in his well-known pamphlet "England, Ireland, and America," which was published in the spring of 1835, said some words which are worth while remembering and quoting in this connection. Writing immediately after his return from his first visit to the United States, he declared that he fervently believed "that our only chance of national prosperity lies in the timely remodelling of our system, so as to put it as nearly as possible upon an equality with the improved management of the Americans." But, he went on, "let us not be misconstrued. We do not advocate Republican institutions for this country, we believe the Government of the United States to be at this moment the best in the world, but then the Americans are the best people, individually and nationally As individuals because in our opinion the people that are the best educated must, morally and religiously speaking, be the best As a nation, because it is the only great community that has never waged war except in absolute self-defence, the only one which has never made a conquest of territory by force of arms, because it is the only nation whose government has never had occasion to employ the army to defend it against the people the only one which has never had one of its citizens convicted of treason, and because it is the only country that has honourably discharged its public debt Those who argue in favour of a Republic in lieu of a mixed Monarchy for Britain are, we suspect, ignorant of the genius of their countrymen. Democracy forms no element in the material of English character An Englishman is from his mother's womb an aristocrat The insatiable love of caste that in England, as in Hindustan, devours all hearts, is confined to no walks of society, but pervades every degree from the highest to the lowest. No, whatever changes in the course of time education may and will effect, we do not believe that England at this moment contains even the germs of genuine Republicanism We do not, then, advocate the adoption of democratic institutions for such a people "

Nearly seventy years have passed since then, and we have had nearly thirty years of popular education, but there is so much truth in Mr Cobden's somewhat pessimistic observations, that any scheme which necessitated the repudiation of aristocratic distinctions or monarchial *bric-à-brac* would be fatal to the scheme of reunion John Bull would have to experience a new birth before he could qualify as an entirely regenerated citizen of the American Republic. He must be allowed to retain his plush-breeched and powdered footmen, his Lord Mayor's coach, and all the paraphernalia

and trappings of monarchy and peerage, if only to enable him to feel at home in a cold, cold world, and cultivate that spirit of condescension towards Americans which is his sole remaining consolation.

At the same time, it is well to remember that notwithstanding Cobden's estimate of the anti-republican character of his own countrymen, the natives of these islands, when once they leave their native land, never establish anything but what is to all intents and purposes a Republican system of government Sir Walter Besant, when discussing the future of the race, dwelt much upon the significance of the fact that, while all the States that have come out of Great Britain have had to create their own form of government, everyone has become practically a Republic, yet while all the Colonies are virtually Republican, the Mother Country is less Republican than she was twenty years ago In the Colonies, with every generation, the Republican idea becomes intensified, and this, he thought would, as there was no corresponding trend of opinion in the Mother Country towards Republicanism, inevitably result in separation. For, as he said, if the English Government remains what it is, and the English Colonies become more and more obstinately Republican, there will most certainly exist a permanent cleavage between them growing every year wider and wider.

He was so much convinced of this that in his forecast of the future he calmly counted upon the disruption of the Empire as a preliminary to the federation of the race.

But in that case we could separate only in order to reunite, and the basis would be wide enough to afford space for the United States in the centre of the group. It is probable that Canada and Australia and South Africa would find it easier to coalesce with the United States than with the United Kingdom. But the political institutions of the United Kingdom itself are likely to undergo considerable changes in the direction of Americanisation.

Few subjects afford more interesting matter for discussion and speculation than the steps which would be taken by the Americans if they were placed in charge of the administration of the British Empire, with a contract to reorganise it upon American principles. Dr. Albert Shaw nine years ago addressed himself to the consideration of this question in the pages of *Contemporary Review*, with characteristic intrepidity and plain-spokenness. Home Rule seemed to him, as it does to all Americans, the very first step towards clearing the situation for entrance upon a large and worthy Imperial policy; and he did not mince his words as to the silly sophistries and general stupidities which did service as arguments against allowing the Irish people to manage purely Irish affairs in Ireland.

"If," said he, "Americans were to take the contract for reorganising the British Empire, they would lose no time in telegraphing for the strong men of both Canadian parties, for Mr Rhodes, Mr Hofmeyer, and the other empire-builders of South Africa, for the experienced and staunch politicians of the Australian States, and for Englishmen everywhere who were actually engaged in maintaining British supremacy After a Conference, they would draw up certain tentative proposals, and call an Imperial Convention to draft a final scheme of Federation This scheme should provide for a true Imperial Parliament, to take over from the existing local parliaments of the United Kingdom all Imperial business. It would place the Navy, the army, and the postal service upon an Imperial basis. It would establish absolute free trade between all parts of the Empire, although it might allow certain parts to maintain differential tariffs against non-British tariffs. It would allow Ireland Home Rule, as a matter of course, subject not to the United Kingdom but to the British Empire With such an Empire the Americans would have no occasion for controversy. The frictions that have endangered the relations of Great Britain and America in recent years have grown out of the mischievously anomalous political situation of Canada. A unified Imperial economic system might soon lead to a Reciprocity Treaty between the two English-speaking Federations that would hasten the advent of the Universal Free Trade that all intelligent Protectionists anticipate and desire."

Whatever the British reader may think of Dr. Shaw's outline of the reconstruction of our Constitution, there are an increasing number of people in this country who would be very glad indeed to see some very radical changes introduced with a view of restoring efficiency to Parliament and securing the Federation of the Empire But we must not stray further in these speculative regions

---

Chapter III —Steps towards Reunion

It may be admitted by all, even those who are least favourable to the idea of complete reunion, that it would be well to keep the ideal of reunion before our eyes, if only in order to minimise points of friction and to promote co-operation in the broad field in which our interests are identical. Even if we cannot have the reunion, we might have the race alliance. This being the case, we may devote the concluding chapter

in this book to a discussion of some of the suggestions which have been made for the promotion of a sense of race unity, whether or not we regard the ultimate goal as one that is within the reach of ourselves or of our descendants

As a starting-point in this inquiry, it is well to quote the familiar passage from Washington's farewell address to the American people " The great rule of conduct for us in regard to foreign nations, is in extending our commercial relations, to have with them as little political connections as possible" The advice is sound, but it must not be read as equivalent to an interdict upon all political connection whatever All that Washington said was, " as little political connection as possible" Now the irreducible minimum of the eighteenth century is quite impossible in the twentieth century, when politics and commerce are inextricably intermingled. A policy of isolation is denied to China, and is even unthinkable in relation to the United States of America At the same time the general principle is sound The fewer points there are of political contact the less risk is there of political collision Whatever federation, alliance, or reunion may ultimately be effected, it is a condition *sine qua non* that each member of the federation shall retain freedom of national self-government, and unrestricted sovereignty to do exactly as he pleases in every department excepting those which are specifically surrendered to the central authority As Mr. Carnegie says " Each member must be free to manage his own home as he thinks proper, without incurring hostile criticism or parental interference. All must be equal, allies, not dependents."

A good deal may be done, and a good deal is being done already, though a good deal more might be done towards the cultivation of the sentiment of race unity One of the most simple and obvious suggestions which to some extent has been acted upon of late years, has been the celebration of the Fourth of July outside the area of the United States of America The practice of hoisting flags on the birthday of the American Republic has been gaining ground in Great Britain, and here and there Britons have begun to set apart the sacred Fourth of July as a *fête* day of the race. But the proposal to adopt the Fourth as the common *fête* day of the race would be more than the ordinary British subject could tolerate, at least just yet. As year after year passes, he will come to celebrate the Fourth heartily and ungrudgingly , but if there is to be a common *fête* day of the race, it should commemorate the day of reunion rather than the day of separation It would be easy to lose ourselves in premature discussion as to the *fête* day which would meet with the most general acceptance both in the Empire and in the Republic. Shakespeare's birthday is one suggestion ; the day of the signature of Magna Charta is another, but no suggestion that has yet been made seems likely to command so much support as the proposal to set apart the Third of September as Reunion Day On the 3rd September, 1783, the King and Government of Great Britain, in the midst of acclamations and rejoicings of the peoples on both sides of the Atlantic, acknowledged the independence which had been claimed on the Fourth of July, and made peace with all the countries that had been involved in the great controversy On that day Great Britain publicly acknowledged that her first-born son had reached a man's estate, and was fully entitled to rank as a nation among the nations. It was the first day that the divided race celebrated together the pact of peace The 3rd September is also a famous day in British annals It was Cromwell's great day, the day of Dunbar and of Worcester, the day on which he opened his Parliaments, the day on which he passed into the presence of his Maker. Cromwell, the common hero of both sections of the race, summoned his first Parliament on the 4th July, and his inaugural address was the first Fourth of July oration that was ever delivered. It was instinct with the conviction of the reality of the providential mission of the English-speaking race In his own words : "We have our desire to seek healing and looking forward than to rake into sores and look backwards"

Many suggestions have been made as to the outward and visible sign by which the approximation of the two races could be symbolised to mankind When Earl Grey, in 1896, was going out to the Cape to take up the Government of Rhodesia, he noticed on the arm of a steward in the *Dunottar Castle* a somewhat curious tattooed device, with the description of "Hands all round." On asking to look at it more closely, he found that there was a ship in full sail in the centre, with a device of flags, one the Union Jack, the other that of New South Wales The motto seemed so apposite that he copied the design from the sailor's arm, and sent it on to me with the suggestion that "this might serve as an outward and visible sign of the unity of the race." By substituting a mail steamer for the full-rigged sailing-ship, and replacing the flag of New South Wales by the Stars and Stripes, the resulting escutcheon may be commended for consideration to the citizens of both countries.

One thing that might be done and that at once would be the publication of more American news in the English papers. I do not refer so much to telegrams, inadequate as our service is from the other side, but I refer rather to the publication of special articles dealing with the immense multiplicity of matters of interest with which the American newspapers are crowded The Americans are much better informed concerning English affairs than we are concerning the social, industrial and scientific movements of the United States. The news that reaches us from America is almost entirely confined to market quotations and political elections The electoral struggles between parties in either country are as a rule the most uninteresting items of news that could be chronicled in the other

When I was in Chicago, seven years ago, I was much impressed by the immense superiority of the European news service of the Chicago papers to the American news service of the London papers. The Chicago citizen on Sunday morning would find as a rule three special correspondents' letters from London, one from Paris, and one from Berlin, telegraphed the previous night, each of the length of a column or more, giving a very intelligent, brightly written sketch of the history of the week We have nothing approaching to that from the other side in any of our English papers. I remember taking note, for six months after I came from Chicago, of all the items of Chicago news that appeared in the English papers. I think in the six months there was only one telegram, which gave a brief and misleading account of a regulation said to have been adopted by the City Fathers against the use of bloomers by lady cyclists in the city parks That was literally the only item of information which reached this country concerning the life of the second greatest city in the United States There is no disinclination on the part of the British public to read American news. The fault lies solely with those who purvey it.

Passing from matters which lie within the scope of private enterprise and individual initiative, we come to the proposal made some time ago by Mr Dicey and strongly supported in other quarters for the adoption of a mutual agreement between the Governments of the two countries for the proclamation of a common citizenship, so that every subject of the King should become a citizen of the United States and every citizen of the United States should become entitled to all the privileges enjoyed by a British subject in whatever part of the world he may happen to live Mr. Dicey put his suggestion in a very concrete shape He said :—

"My proposal is summarily this · That England and the United States should, by concurrent and appropriate legislation, create such a common citizenship, or, to put the matter in a more concrete and therefore in a more intelligible form, that an Act of the Imperial Parliament should make every citizen of the United States, during the continuance of peace between England and America, a British subject, and that simultaneously an Act of Congress should make every British subject, during the continuance of such peace, a citizen of the United States. The coming into force of the one Act would be dependent upon the passing and coming into force of the other. Should war at any time break out between the two countries, each Act would ipso facto cease to have effect.

"My proposal is not designed to limit the complete national independence either of England or of the United States There would, for the foundation of a common citizenship, be no need for any revolution, even of a legal kind, in the Constitution either of England or of the United States. Community of citizenship would affect not civil, but political rights If the Acts creating isopolity were passed, a citizen of the United States would, on the necessary conditions being fulfilled, be able to vote for a member of Parliament, to sit in Parliament, and, if fortune favoured, become a Cabinet Minister or a Premier He might aspire, did his ambition lead in that direction, to the House of Lords So, on the other hand, a British subject, to whom American citizenship has been extended, might, on the necessary conditions being fulfilled, vote for a member of Congress, become a member of the House of Representatives, or even a Senator .

"The immediate results, indeed, of a common citizenship would be small, but, as far as they went, they would all be good It would, further, be an unspeakable advantage that this sense of unity should be proclaimed to the whole world The declaration of isopolity would be an announcement which no foreign State could legitimately blame or wisely overlook—that men of English descent in England and America alike were determined to safeguard the future prosperity of the whole English people."

This would obviate the necessity of any abjuring of nationality when Americans came to Great Britain or when British subjects settled in the United States A form of declaration could easily be drawn up, which would be equivalent to an oath of allegiance to either the Republic or to the Crown, and which would not in the least impair the original allegiance due to the country in which any one was born. As Americans are likely to settle in increasing numbers in this country, they are more likely to appreciate the advantage of such an arrangement than they would have been at a time when the migration was all the other way. They are also likely to appreciate the advantage of such an arrangement more keenly the more widely they scatter in foreign lands. The more America expands, the more handy will it be for the American citizen to avail himself of the services of the British Consul or British Ambassador wherever he may be After a time, indeed, it might be possible largely to avoid the duplication of diplomatic and consular staffs. But that is a long way off, and need not be considered now. Every American or British citizen could avail himself of the help of two officials, instead of one, and in like manner he could rely upon the support of the fleets of both nations for the punishment of any high-handed wrong inflicted upon him in any part of the world In the Cuban War the protection of American interests in Spain was entrusted to British diplomacy, and in the South African Republics to the American Consul at Pretoria This arrangement worked excellently, and there is no reason why it should not be carried a step farther.

We now come to consider whether anything can be done to assimilate the laws of the two countries so far as they relate to those subjects which are of international interest, such as copyright, trade-mark, marriage and divorce, patents, &c The first practical step towards bringing the Empire and the Republic into organic relations with each other would be, according to Mr. Carnegie's idea —

"The appointment by the various nations of our race of International Commissions charged with creating a system of weights, measures, and coins, of port dues, patents, and other matters of similar character, which are of common interest If there be a question upon which all authorities are agreed, it is the desirability of introducing the decimal system of weights, measures, and coins but an International Commission seems the only agency capable of bringing it about "

After this was done, Mr Carnegie thinks that a "General Council should be evolved by the English-speaking nations, to which may at first only be referred all questions of dispute between them.

"Building upon the Supreme Court of the United States, may we not expect that a still higher Supreme Court is one day to come, which shall judge between the nations of the entire English speaking race as the Supreme Court at Washington already judges between States which contain the majority of the race? The powers and duties of such a Council once established may be safely trusted to increase To its final influence over the race, and through the race over the world, no limit can be set In the dim future it might even come that the pride of the citizen in the race as a whole would exceed that which he had in any part thereof, as the citizen of the Republic to-day is prouder of being an American than he is of being a native of any State in the Union "

Once establish a Court competent to give judgment upon specified questions, they would be settled without any necessity for passing them through diplomatic channels Appeal would be made to the Court direct Questions coming before the Court should be divided into categories The first would include all questions dealing with inventions, treaties, &c , which would be decided upon strictly legal lines. The foreign offices of the two countries would no more think of interfering with the settlement of such questions than the Secretary of State at Washington would think of preventing an appeal to the Supreme Court. The second category would cover ordinary disputes now dealt with by diplomacy If diplomacy failed, a special arbitrator might be appointed to deal with special cases. Supposing that we succeed in establishing the principle of common citizenship, and international conventions governing our international relations on the lines suggested by Mr. Carnegie, it might be well to stop there, and not carry the principle further at present But if we ever get so far, we shall go further.

Few things are more certain than that there will be a great slump in the principle of Protection. The country which can produce more cheaply than its neighbour will not be long in recognising the necessity of the principle of free trade Already the most absolute free trade prevails between all the States and territories composing the American Union It is not inconceivable that the area of free trade may in time be extended, not only to the United States, but to all the countries inhabited by an English-speaking race

There remains the question of whether there should be an alliance, offensive or defensive, between the two States. When the United States was engaged in the war with Spain, the Americans relied very confidently upon the support of Great Britain, and to this day the belief is firmly fixed in the minds of the majority of the American people that the British Government went a great deal further than was actually the case in threatening to ally its fleet with that of the United States if the European Powers ventured to intervene on behalf of Spain. The Americans rightly shrink from any entangling alliances with Great Britain which would involve them in an obligation to sacrifice the benefits of peace whenever a hot-headed English minister chose to quarrel with Russia, or any other European Power But alliances between nations are capable of infinite degrees of intimacy For instance, the Franco-Russian alliance, leaves each Power absolutely free to conduct its own foreign policy and to make its own wars without involving the other in any obligation to depart from the policy of neutrality. The Franco Russian arrangement provided that if either France or Russia is attacked by two Powers, the other party to the alliance is bound to assist its ally ; but if Germany attacked Russia, France would be under no obligation to draw the sword, unless Germany were backed up by Austria. In that case, France would have to enter the field. In like manner, if Germany attacked France, Russia would be under no obligation to interfere unless another Power joined Germany. This represents a form of alliance which secures both parties against an

attack by a coalition without entailing any obligation upon either to assist the other in case of a single handed war or a war of aggression

Mr. Arthur White, writing in the *North American Review* for April, 1894, suggested the following draft of the terms of an Anglo-American Alliance :—

" Great Britain shall become an ally of the United States in the event of any European Power or Powers declaring war against the latter. On the other hand, the United States shall guarantee friendly neutrality in the event of Great Britain becoming involved in war with one or more of the European Powers, concerning issues that in no way concern the Pacific interests of the United States, and in that case the United States shall render to Great Britain every assistance, positive and negative, allowed to neutrals."

The Triple Alliance is closer than that between France and Russia, but still it is an alliance with limited liability

The question as to whether it is possible for a race alliance to be formed between the various members of the English-speaking federation, which would leave each member free to pursue its own foreign policy, while securing each against an attack from a coalition, has been the subject of very thoughtful discussion by Mr Stevenson, who, however, was thinking not so much of an alliance between the Republic and the Empire as of the familiar idea of an alliance between Great Britain and her self-governing colonies Mr Stevenson, foreseeing a time when the Commonwealth of Australia will wish to pursue its own foreign policy in the Pacific, asks Is it possible to gratify the desire of an independent colony to pursue a foreign policy without at the same time compelling the mother country to support such foreign policy by the armies and navies of Great Britain ? He maintained that it was quite possible He expressed his approval of such an alliance between Great Britain and the self governing colonies, whereby they could make peace or war of their own accord, without endangering the mother country or the colonies. His suggestion, was very ingenious He proposed that when the great self-governing colonies should arrive at man's estate, they should be allowed each in its own zone to act as independent and sovereign States in making peace or war, and in concluding treaties, commercial or otherwise, with their neighbours. In place of the Empire, he would substitute a Solemn League and Covenant, by which each member of the Imperial Union would be free either to make common cause with any of the other members of the Union, should they embark upon war, or should be not less free to declare their neutrality. The bond between the English-speaking nations would be reduced to an obligation to guarantee the home lands of the race against foreign conquest, and a joint guarantee by each and all of the right to neutrality. This would work in practice somewhat as follows:—If the Solemn League and Covenant had been substituted for the Imperial tie, Canada would be free to attack France, if she refused to settle the French shore difficulty in a manner satisfactory to Newfoundland. No other State in the League would be under any obligation to help Canada, which could make war or peace with France on her own account. But if France, refusing to recognise this neutrality, were to attack Australia or the United Kingdom, every other member of the League would be bound to make common cause against France in order to vindicate the right of neutrality. Supposing France, recognising the declaration of neutrality, nevertheless defeated Canada and attempted to annex Canadian territory, by right of conquest, then all the other members of the League would be bound to make war on France to compel her to confine her compensation to financial indemnity. The two great basic principles of the League would be the mutually guaranteed right of neutrality and the mutual guarantee of the inviolability of all the territory occupied by the English-speaking peoples.

Twenty years ago Senator Lamar said "Whenever America is in need of allies, I will tell you what will happen. Some wise British statesman will suggest an Anglo-Saxon League, something akin to the League in Europe when Henry IV ruled France. This will not be an alliance offensive and defensive."

Mr Secretary Hay declared in 1897 that "It is a sanction like that of religion which binds us to a sort of partnership in the beneficent work of the world. Whether we will it or not, we are associated in that work by the very nature of things, and no man and no group of men can prevent it. We are bound by a tie which we did not forge, and which we cannot break. We are joint ministers of the same sacred mission of liberty and progress, charged with duties which we cannot evade by the imposition of irresistible hands."

If the reunion of the race is written in the book of Destiny, then in vain do we strive against it. The benefits likely to accrue to the world from such a reunion are naturally more obvious to the English-speaking communities than to those which live outside the pale. But one of the strongest expressions of sympathy with the aspiration of the race for a higher unity came from a foreign observer, who, under the name of Nauticus, contributed a notable article on the subject to the *Fortnightly Review* in

1894. He deplored the schism between the United States and Great Britain on the ground that it divided and weakened the expression of the Anglo-Saxon will, for he declared himself persuaded that this Anglo-Saxon will ought to have upon the world in future an even greater influence than it had in the past. The world, he said, could well afford "to place its confidence in the integrity and fairness of the Anglo-Saxon race. For the sake of peace and disarmament it seems necessary that some superior power should be created. Such a re-united Anglo-Saxondom would be a supreme sea-Power of the world," and as such could give an extension to the rights of neutrals which, in his opinion, would render war impracticable. He said, 'It is not merely that the combined navies would be strong. Far more weighty are the considerations that the British Empire and the United States share between them nearly all the work of providing other countries with the food, raw material and manufactures which those countries cannot provide at home, and of carrying the ocean-borne trade of the world. Why should not your combined navies declare war, refuse henceforth to acknowledge the right of any civilised Power to close her ports or the ports of another Power by blockading or otherwise? Surely that would sound the knell of war.'

Mr A. W. Tourgee, writing in the *Contemporary Review* two years ago, said:—

"An alliance between the great branches of the Anglo-Saxon family means the creation of a world-power against which it is not only impossible that any European combination should make headway, but it will have such control of the commercial and economic resources of the world as to enable them to put an end to war between the Continental Powers themselves without mustering an army or firing a gun. Whether they desire it or not, the necessities of the world's life, the preservation of their own political ideals, and the commercial and economic conditions which they confront, must soon compel a closer entente between these two great peoples. They are the peacemakers of the Twentieth Century, the protectors of the world's development, the protectors of free independence and of the weak nationalities of the earth."

Writing his book on the "Rise of the Empire," Sir Walter Besant thus defined his conception of the great reconciliation which he believed would some day take place between the United States and the British Empire.

"The one thing needful is so to legislate, so to speak and write to each other that this bond may be strengthened and not loosened. We want, should a time opportune arrive, to separate only in form. We want an overlasting alliance, offensive and defensive, such an alliance as may make us absolutely free from the fear of any other alliance which could crush us."

Sam Slick in his homely fashion, hit the nail

M

on the head long ago, when, in his " Wise Saws,"
he said :—

> " We are two great nations, the greatest by a long
> chalk of any in the world, speak the same language,
> have the same religion, and our Constitution don't differ
> no great odds. We ought to draw closer than we do.
> We are big enough, ugly enough, and strong enough,
> not to be jealous of each other United we are more
> nor a match for all the other nations put together
> single we could not stand against all, and if one was to
> fall, where would the other be? Mournin' over the
> grave that covers a relative whose place can never be
> filled Its authors of silly books, writers of silly papers,
> and demagogues of silly parties, that help to estrange us.
> I wish there was a gibbet high enough and strong enough
> to hang up all those enemies of mankind "

A cool observer, who for a long time was a
Nestor among Colonial statesmen, Sir George
Grey of New Zealand, in his closing years loved
to dwell upon the future of the English-speaking
race " Here sat the people of one language,"
was a sentence which he used on one occasion
when, addressing the Federal Convention at
Sydney in 1891, he indicated in one pregnant
phrase the territories occupied by our race
No man was more free from Chauvinistic passion
than Sir George Grey, among few men were more
unsparing critics of the shortcomings of their
countrymen. But in his latest writings he
placed his conviction on record that, if the
reunion were but attained, " it would mean the
triumph of Christianity, the highest moral system
man in all his history has known , and it would
imply the dominance of probably the richest
language that has ever existed The adoption
of a universal code of morals and a universal
tongue would pave the way for the last great
federation—the brotherhood of man "

In fine, we had reached an epoch of federation which was the new form of human
economy —

> " As its result war would by degrees die out from the
> face of the earth If you had the Anglo-Saxon race
> acting on a common ground, they could determine the
> balance of power for a fully peopled earth Such a
> moral force would be irresistible and argument would
> take the place of war in the settlement of international
> disputes As the second great result of the cohesion of
> the race we should have life quickened and developed,
> and unemployed energies called into action in many
> places where they now lie stagnant "

For the attainment of the greater unity, Sir
George Grey suggested that the Governments at
Washington and Westminster should come to a
standing agreement " that whenever any subject
affecting us both arises, or when there is any
question affecting the well-being of the world
generally, we shall meet in Conference and
decide upon common action An Anglo-American Council coming quietly into action when
there was cause, disappearing for the time when

it had done its work, would be a mighty instrument for good."

There is no necessity for constituting an
Anglo-American Council for that purpose If
once the principle were accepted, no important
question of foreign policy would be discussed
either at Washington or Westminster, without
previous consultation between the Foreign
Secretary or Secretary of State through the
ordinary channels of diplomatic intercourse
The American Ambassador at St James's or the
British Ambassador at Washington, would always
be called into Council whenever any decision
was taken involving the possibility of foreign
complications Such an arrangement would be
much preferable to that of the constitution of
an Anglo-American Council as suggested by
Sir George Grey.

Mr. Carnegie shared the opinion of Sir
George Grey as to the beneficent influence
which would be exercised on the world by our
reunited race Such reunion, he declared,
would give us the future dominion of the
world, " and that for the good of the world,
for the English-speaking race has always stood
first among races for peace, plenty, liberty,
justice and law, and first, also, it will be found,
for the government of the people, for the people,
and by the people It is well that the last
word in the affairs of the world is to be ours,
and is to be spoken in plain English "

Mr. Carnegie's idea, which he expounded a
little more at length in 1899, maintained that
patriotism of race involved a mutual alliance
limited for the purposes of self-defence. " The
present era of good feeling," he said, " means
that the home of Shakespeare and Burns will
never be invaded without other than native-
born Britons being found in its pavements
This means that the giant child, the Republic,
is not to be sat upon by a combination of other
races, and pushed to its destruction without a
growl coming from the old lion, which will
shake the earth, but it will not mean that either
the old land or the new binds itself to support
the other in all its designs, either at home or
abroad, but that the Republic shall remain the
friend of all nations and the ally of none, that
being free to-day of all foreign entanglements,
she shall not undertake to support Britain who
has these to deal with. '

Sir Walter Besant was not less sanguine as
to the good results which would follow when
the six great nations—Britain, the United States,
Canada, Australia, New Zealand and South
Africa, were united in a federation, in which a
Board of Arbitration would be the outward and
visible sign of union. He said —

" They would be an immense Federation,
free, law-abiding, peaceful, yet ready to fight,

tenacious of all customs, dwelling continually with the same ideas, keeping each family as the unit, every home the centre of the earth, every township of a dozen men the centre of the Government."

The swelling phrase "dominion of the World" is one at which long experience teaches us to look askance. It should be no ambition of ours to dominate the world save by the influence of ideas and the force of our example. The temptation to believe that we are the Vice-gerent of the Almighty, charged with the thunder-bolt of Heaven, for the punishment of evil-doers, is one of the subtle temptations by which the Evil One lures well-meaning people to embark upon a course of policy which soon becomes indistinguishable from bucaneering pure and simple. But when all due allowance has been made for the danger of exposing the English-speaking man to the temptation of almost irresistible power, the advantages to be gained by the Reunion of the Race are so great as to justify our incurring the risk. Such reunion, to say the least of it, affords the world not merely the shortest but the only road by which we can attain to a realization of the ideal so nobly described by Sir John Harrington, when writing in his ' Oceana," he asked —

" What can you think but, if the world should see the Roman Eagle again, she would renew her age and her flight ? If you add to the propagation of civil liberty the propagation of the liberty of conscience this empire, this patronage of the world, is the Kingdom of Christ. The Commonwealth of this race is a minister of God upon earth, for which cause the orders last rehearsed are buds of empire, such as that the blessing of God may spread the arms of your Commonwealth like a holy asylum to the distressed world, and give the earth her Sabbath of years or rest from her labours under the shadow of your wings."

CHAPTER IV —THE END THEREOF ?

I HAVE now concluded a very rapid and most imperfect survey of some of the more potent forces which are Americanising the world. There remains the great question whether the processes now visible in operation around us will make for the progress and the betterment of the world.

When Mr Gladstone contemplated what he called " the paramount question of the American future ' he expressed himself with the same sense of awe which filled the Hebrew prophet when he had a vision of the glory of the Lord and His train filled the Temple

" There is a vision," said Mr Gladstone, " of terri tory, population, power, passing beyond all experience The exhibition to mankind for the first time in history of free institutions on a gigantic scale is momentous '

With his inveterate optimism, he declared that he had enough faith in freedom to believe that it would work powerfully for good .—

" But together with and behind these vast develop ments there will come a corresponding opportunity of social and moral influence to be exercised over the rest of the world, and the question of questions for us as trustees for our posterity is, what will be the nature of this influence ' Will it make us, the children of the senior race, living together under its action, better or worse ' Not what manner of produce, but what manner of man is the American of the future to be ' How is the majestic figure, who is to become the largest and most powerful on the stage of the world's history, to make use of his power ? "

And then Mr Gladstone went on in his accustomed style to ask various questions as to how the influence which the American would inevitably exercise in the world would be used

" Will it," he asked, " be instinct with moral life in proportion to its material strength ' One thing is certain, his temptations will multiply with his power, his responsibilities with his opportunities Will the seed be sown among the thorns ' will worthlessness overrun the ground and blight its flowers and its fruit ? On the answers to these questions, and to such as these, it will depend whether this new revelation of power on the earth is also to be a revelation of virtue, whether it shall prove a blessing or a curse May Heaven avert every darker omen, and grant that the latest and largest growth of the great Christian civilisation shall also be the brightest and best ? "

To Mr. Gladstone all this pompous detail of material triumphs was worse than idle, unless they were regarded simply as tools and materials for the attainment of the highest purposes of our being. To use his own striking phrase —

" We must ascend from the ground floor of material industry to the higher regions in which these nobler purposes are to be wrought out "

Those who believe in progress, and those who see in the trend of the centuries one endless march of what Mazzini described as the " infinitely ascending spiral which leads from matter up to God," must perforce accept the transformation as part of the great law which presides over the evolution of human society ; but it is impossible not to recognise that this process, while fraught with great and palpable advantages, is not without its drawbacks. Life's fitful fever will become more feverish than ever " The world is too much with us Getting and spending we lay waste our powers," said Wordsworth, and the American tendency is to consume the whole of our powers in the process, leaving none for the cultivation of the higher soul. An English journalist who had spent long years in an American newspaper office summed up the difference between the two branches of the English-speaking race in a sentence. "In England," he said, "you work in order to live; in America, they live only in order to work." Each section of the race carries its natural tendency to too great an extreme. Both would be better were each to contribute of its best to the common stock. The rush and bustle of modern life, the eager whirl of competitive business, the passionate rush to outstrip a neighbour or a rival—all these things have their uses; they tend to eliminate the unfit, and to give the survivor superior efficiency, just as the speed of the deer depends upon the fact that from day to day it is hunted for its life.

But this struggle for existence may easily be carried to such a point as to make existence itself hardly worth having. The universal experience of the wisest and best of mankind speaks with no uncertain voice in condemnation of a life that has no leisure. As one wise writer said, "if you are always catching trains, you have no time to think of your soul." A contented mind is a continual feast. But content is scorned by the go-ahead American. I have learned, said the Apostle, in whatsoever state I am, therewith to be content. But, says the eager exponent of Americanism, the Americans succeed because they are never contented. Divine discontent is very well, but there is such a thing as undivine discontent, and there is a good deal of the latter in the United States to-day. Possibly, when the country is a little older, this tempestuous eagerness natural to youth may give way to a more sedate and tranquil spirit, but at present there is very little evidence of that in the United States. It not only does not exist, but the American journalists glory in its absence. The following quotation from an editorial in the New York *Evening Journal* of this year expresses this point of view with an uncompromising vigour which leaves nothing to be desired —

"The nations of Europe, and especially the English, wonder at the success of the American people.

"If any Englishman wants to know why the American race can beat the English race in the struggle for industrial precedence, let him stand at the Delaware-Lackawanna station, in Hoboken, from seven until nine in the morning as the suburban trains come in.

"Far outside of the big railroad station the train appears, puffing and panting, and while it is still going at dangerous speed, men, young and old, are seen leaning far out from every platform.

"As the train rushes in the men leap from the cars on both sides, and a wild rush follows for the ferryboat. Not a man is walking slowly or deliberately.

"It is one rush to business; it is one rush all day; it is one rush home again.

"The gauge on the engine tells the pressure of steam and the work that the engine can do.

"The gauge on the American human being stands at high pressure all the time. His brain is constantly excited, his machinery is working with a full head of steam.

"Tissues are burned up rapidly, and the machine often burns up sooner than it should. The man bald and gray in his youth, the man a victim of dyspepsia, of nervousness, of narcotics and stimulants, is a distinct American institution. He is an engine burned out before his time, but his work has been done, and that great locomotive works, THE AMERICAN MOTHER, is for ever supplying the demand for new engines to be run at dangerously high speed.

"The American succeeds because he is under high pressure always, because he is determined to make speed even at the risk of bursting the boiler and wrecking the machine."

This is an unlovely spectacle, which seems to those of us who are not without sympathy with the strenuous life, very much like a vision of hell. How great a contrast to the calm, philosophic life of thought, which is the ideal of the Eastern Sage!

> "The East bowed low in solemn thought
> In silent deep disdain,
> She heard the legions thunder past,
> Then plunged in thought again,"

In Asia whole populations have learned the lesson that life is better spent in the contented possession of a few things than in the mad rush after many. There is a wealth which arises from the fewness of our wants, as well as a wealth that is measured by the amplitude of our resources.

> "'Tis not all of life to live,
> Nor all of death to die."

and the solemn inquiry still holds—"What shall it profit a man, if he shall gain the whole world, and lose his own soul?'

INDEX.

AMERICA AND THE HAMBURG-AMERICAN LINE.

THE FLEET AND ITS STORY.

WHEN towards the middle period of the nineteenth century the merchant princes of conservative Europe woke up to the enormous potentialities of the vast territories, stretching from the storm-swept rocks of Cape Horn northwards across the Equatorial Tropics to the golden semi-arctic regions of Alaska and Labrador, they suddenly realised, that this great new land, which combined within her ocean-fringed boundaries the scenic beauties, natural wealth, and endless resources of any other zone known, was only waiting for the practical development of its many as yet untapped riches.

It was thus that the International Commerce of the Old World knocked hesitatingly at young Columbia's portals, and found them to open readily to enter a gigantic new field which, for the safe employment of capital, the establishment of epoch-making industries, and as a satisfactory new home for Europe's overflow of humanity, was rapidly to astonish the civilised world.

Thenceforth America's abnormally quick and prosperous advance and her closer ties of mutually profitable commerce with Europe were assured. Presently other influences for the successful initiation and development of numberless great enterprises were felt far and wide, far even across those seas which after all but unite the nations they divide. Nothing could illustrate the above better than the history of one of the most successful undertakings launched into existence at the time referred to above, viz., that of the enormous corporation, known to every one to-day as the *Hamburg-American Line.*

On May 27, 1847, a few of the most prominent Hamburg merchants met in private conclave and combined their ideas in a scheme of navigation enterprise. Though it was at that period not an easy task to convince every one of the necessity to organise a regular service between the Hanseatic port and New York, the foundation of the Hamburg-American Packet Company was finally decided upon on that date.

Not only in its name, but also in many other

Twin-screw Express Steamer "Deutschland," 1901.

ways, has this company been at all times in closest connection with America, and mainly, thanks to its popularity and the encouragement which from the very start it also found in this hospitable country, it was enabled to develop its capabilities on an ever-increasing scale. The funds with which it was started amounted actually to only *one-third per cent.* of the present capital; and whilst the company's flag is nowadays flying over all the seas of the globe, the total tonnage of its fleet is likewise to-day *unequalled by that of any other existing steamship company.*

The "America," of the Hamburg-American Line, 1848.

The first boats on this Line were sailing-ships, bearing the names of the countries they were destined to connect, viz., *Deutschland* and *America*. They made their first appearance in the ports of the States in October, 1848, and at once won universal appreciation.

The voyages were executed with great regularity, requiring about thirty days east and about forty days westward, and although these results were up to all expectations of the period, the company availed itself of the very first opportunity which arose, and decided, after an existence of only five years, to order the building of two *steamers*. These two steamboats, and two others which were acquired soon afterwards, proved to be very advantageous, and were extremely well patronised both at home as also in America. Passenger services at that period were of course not to be compared with present dimensions; but the company's boats were always much favoured by travellers to Europe from America, whilst American products, mails, etc., provided good return freights. To maintain its premier position the Hamburg-American Line increased the tonnage of its fleet continuously, and did its utmost to be in constant touch with Americans and affairs in their country. Thus in 1850 only 1,420 persons were forwarded on their boats; yet the number in 1865 had already increased to 30,000 passengers, and the freight traffic developed steadily in a similar proportion. In 1867 regular

Hamburg-American Liner "Deutschland" at Hoboken Pier, New York.

lines were established to New Orleans and Cuba, and soon after an additional service to the West Indies was initiated.

The following years brought forth very strong rivals for the company in the ocean trade with America, but the Hamburg-American Line proved itself victorious by absorbing, in 1875, its chief competitor—the corporation known as the "*Eagle*" Line; and with its total tonnage again increased by this combination and by newly-constructed steamers, the various services were kept up with conspicuous regularity for many years. The most far-reaching event in the history of the Hamburg - American Line, however, was the decision arrived at in 1887, shortly after the present Director - General, Mr. A. Ballin, had taken over the management of the company— viz., to adopt the twin-screw system, and to forthwith build *four twin-screw Express steamers*. This progressive resolve startled the shipping world and aroused the keenest interest everywhere. A passenger cabin service was soon established by this new fleet, which, for numbers carried and comforts of accommodation, surpassed any other in existence, and further new lines were rapidly opened to cope with the ever-increasing freight traffic.

Twin-screw Steamer "Pennsylvania," 1895.

In 1891 every important port between the St. Lawrence river and tropical Venezuela was connected with Europe by the steamers of the Hamburg-American Line. The enormous quantities of cargo which had to be forwarded by their fleet to and from New York, Baltimore, Boston, Philadelphia, etc., necessitated a considerable increase in the size of the boats, and it was in 1895 that the directors of the line ordered the *Pennsylvania*, the first of the renowned steam leviathans with a displacement of 20,000 tons, of which particular class no less than eight boats will soon be running.

Besides these and numerous other new steamers, the whole fleets of several other companies, such as the *Hansa*, the *Calcutta*, the *Kingsin*, the *De Freitas*, and *Atlas*, etc., lines were acquired by the Hamburg-American Line, which once more in 1900 attracted the world's attention by putting forth the record-breaking *Deutschland*. The feats accomplished by this new Atlantic greyhound were beyond all expectations; her average speed of 23½ knots across the ocean had been considered an utter impossibility but a very short time ago, securing as it did the "blue ribbon" of rapid ocean passages for the proprietary company.

After an existence of little more than fifty years this company's services to-day embrace the whole globe. It now maintains no less than *thirty-nine different lines, and owns a fleet of 134 large ocean-going steamers registering 668,000 tons,* which in its total exceeds that of any other company up-to-date.

To-day there is no port of any material importance in the domains of the great American Republic, which has not been touched by a Hamburg-American Liner; there is no town of any consequence in its immense territories where this company is not properly represented. More than 40,000 Americans travel yearly on its boats for business and pleasure, even towards the most remote places of the earth; and if the popular patronage it enjoys at present so freely in America, as well as at home, is maintained, there can be no doubt that its prosperous records will in the dim future but tend to draw the natural bonds of brotherhood between the Old and the New World closer than ever.

"Princessin Victoria Louise," 1901.

THE "DEUTSCHLAND," 1901.

THE famous twin-screw express steamer *Deutschland*, the record breaker of rapid ocean trips of the Hamburg-American Line, is 686 feet in length, having a beam of 67½ feet, with a depth of 44½ feet. Her registered tonnage is 16,502 tons, and notwithstanding her enormous size, her lines of design as afloat are the most graceful that can be imagined.

She is fitted with the most powerful quadruple expansion engines, developing up to 35,000 horse-power, driving her across the Atlantic seas on either route at an evenly maintained average speed of 23½ knots; a performance which has aroused the enthusiastic admiration of international civilisation.

It is by the continuous employment of a magnificent floating palace, such as the *Deutschland* is in every sense of the word, that the Hamburg-American Line has succeeded so conspicuously in giving the travelling public the convenience of reaching America in the shortest possible time, coupled contemporarily with absolute safety and unexcelled personal comforts whilst *en route*.

THE "PRINCESSIN VICTORIA LOUISE."

THE luxurious pleasure yacht of the Hamburg-American Line's Fleet, named after His Imperial Majesty's only daughter, is rapidly becoming world-famed by her numerous romantic and picturesque tours to the most beautiful parts of the globe. Already most successful and delightful visits have been chronicled by her to the ever-verdant and historical coasts of the Riviera and the Mediterranean, the mysterious Orient, the Crimea; not to speak of those to Algiers, Morocco, Scandinavia, and the numerous island pearls of the Antilles in the distant West Indies.

The *Princessin Victoria Louise* is built as a powerful twin-screw steamer; she is 450 feet in length, 47 feet in beam, and draws 30 feet, ploughing the summer seas at an average speed of sixteen knots. She is constructed on the best principles of modern naval architecture, and in her external appearance is a "thing of beauty," whilst her magnificent internal fittings defy description in the small space available here. Enough to say that, from the most comfortable state-rooms to the very exquisite *cuisine*, her attractions are almost innumerable, covering such unusual luxuries at sea as gymnasia, baths, photographic dark rooms, etc.; the whole under the charge of most experienced officers, whose courteous solicitude for the comfort of passengers is not the least by far of the many pleasant features of this veritable ocean swan.

THE MISSION OF THE CINEMATOGRAPH.

MANY years ago I wrote an article entitled "The Mission of the Magic Lantern" The article had some considerable success at the time, and succeeded in turning the attention of many people, educationists and others, to the immense importance of utilising Eye-gate as well as Ear-gate for the purpose of education Since then so much progress has been made in the art of projecting pictures upon screens that the time has come for re-writing that old article, or, rather writing another dealing with the later phases and developments of the methods by which Eye-gate can be opened still more widely for the admission of information and of ideas In education the first thing is to interest The one great obstacle that lies in the way of all those who wish to teach is the difficulty of awakening the mind In all our teaching we rely too much upon the ear, whereas you can wake up the mind much more rapidly by the eye Far be it from me to say one word against oral teaching It is invaluable and indispensable, but picture teaching beats it hollow, especially in its initial stages We all recognise this in infancy, and the first book by which we attract a child is a picture-book In the Books for the Bairns, which are perhaps the most successful of all the publications I have ever issued, the essential feature is that there should be a picture on every page. But we are all children of a larger growth, and the picture is only one degree less necessary for adults than it is for children We are slow in the uptake, and dull to grasp a fresh idea. In order to understand things we have got to see them, and the great advantage of pictures is that a picture will at a glance explain much more clearly and intelligently a multitude of facts which the most painstaking explanation by word of mouth or by the printed page would fail to make clear.

HOW PICTURES EDUCATE THE PUBLIC.

At the present moment everyone who has bestowed any thought upon the question is deeply impressed with the necessity of stimulating the mind of our people, and compelling the ordinary man and the ordinary woman to take an interest in things that ought to interest them, but do not, and we are all more or less in despair as to how it is to be done In some things the public is interested And how is the public interested? Take, for instance, the war What interested the man in the street in the war? Very largely the pictures of the war The illustrated weeklies laid themselves out to interpret the telegrams and the war correspondence by bringing before the man in the street a living vivid image of the scenes which are actually being witnessed by human eyes in the far-off veldt In like manner the yacht race owes no small part of its popularity to the pictures of the yachts It may be argued that the pictures followed the interest rather than preceded it, but they acted and re-acted upon each other, and undoubtedly while many were interested in the war before they had seen the pictures, a great number of people first began to take interest in the war because of the pictures of its progress

Not only do pictures attract attention, but they produce a deeper impression Let any one look backwards in his own history, and he will find the things that have lodged most indelibly in his memory have been things he has seen rather than things that he has heard I can see before my mind's eye to-day as vividly as if it were yesterday a picture which I saw forty-five years ago of one of the battles in the Crimea It probably was wholly imaginary, especially the white horse that figured conspicuously in the centre , but after the lapse of all these years that white horse is still vividly impressed upon my mental retina Almost as far back do I remember my first panorama Out of one of the painted pictures I still see the head of a bear looking out of a hollow trunk Nearly everything else I was then taught has more or less faded away or blended in the indeterminate vague expanse , but the picture stands out Hence, if we are really to set ourselves earnestly to the task of quickening the mind of our people, we must resort to pictures." More pictures, and ever more !

ESPECIALLY THE LIVING PICTURE.

Now, just when our need is the greatest, science has come to our aid and provided us with an admirable instrument for presenting pictures to the eye of the multitude much more vividly and with more life-like realism than has ever heretofore been possible The living picture, which has long been one of the most popular turns in the music-hall entertainment, must now take its place as one of the potent weapons with which the well-equipped educationist goes forth to combat the hosts of ignorance At present the potentialities of the living picture have only been realised by the showman. It has still to be utilised by the School, by the College, by the University The magic lantern is very good in that it enables you to show excellent pictures on a large scale before a great crowd , but with very few exceptions the picture thrown by the stereopticon upon a sheet was as motionless as an oil-painting Dissolving views and mechanical arrangements only to a very small extent introduce an element of motion But if a picture is good, a moving picture is infinitely better, for there you have not only form and colour but the motion which is life , you have the dramatic element vividly present before your eyes It renders possible the presentation of a living drama without the expense of having to maintain a whole dramatic troupe, and to provide a stage and its accessories

THE WARWICK TRADING COMPANY

Anyone who has paid a visit to an exhibition, nay, anyone who has even walked down a crowded street, must have been impressed by the fact that nothing in the world attracts the attention of the ordinary man, woman, or child so much as something that moves. The most marvellous mechanism that ever was invented by human ingenuity, if it stands motionless in a glass case, will attract fewer observers than the simplest apple-paring machine if the latter is only at work. It is, however, unnecessary to argue the question of interest, because the music-halls have settled that for us long ago. The most magnificent pictures in the world would fail to command the attention of music-hall audiences, who will sit in rapt attention before the animated photographs which are thrown upon the screen in an interval between the performances of a juggler and those of a contortionist.

The Bioscope Projector.

What now has to be done is to yoke this modern invention, which has half a dozen different names, to the service of propaganism and of education. Whether we call it a kinetoscope, a biograph, or a bioscope is immaterial. All that is indispensable is the thing itself.

In order to form some idea as to what this thing itself is, how it has worked, and to what extent it has made its way amongst us, I spent an afternoon this last month at the headquarters of the Bioscope Company. The animated picture business was introduced into Europe in 1894 by Messrs.

Maguire and Baucus. They afterwards formed the Warwick Trading Company, Limited, with the following directors: J. D. Baucus, chairman, A. J. Ellis, F. Z. Maguire, J. O. Nicholson, H. W. Mack, directors, and Chas. Urban, managing director. The Warwick Trading Company, Limited, is one of the most enterprising of the firms which have taken hold of an American invention and naturalised it on British soil. It has its head offices at Warwick Court, in Holborn. It has a theatre and photographic film plant at Brighton for photographing its pictures and manufacturing its finished film subject-rolls for the market, and a large and growing factory for manufacturing the machines and sensitized film stock in an outlying district of London.

"QUICK WORK."

The company have just taken over two four-story buildings in the vicinity of Warwick Court for a further extension of their laboratories, repair shops, film manufacturing plant and shipping rooms. Extension of film plant was necessitated by the great demand from exhibitors and theatrical managers for quick deliveries of films, to all points of England, of any event of topical interest, such as the Derby, Grand National, Henley Regatta, processions, etc. This means organisation and systematic execution of the work in hand, requiring two forces of dark-room operators, one working force during the day and the other all night. Any negatives which reach Warwick Court by four o'clock in the afternoon can be manipulated so that twenty-five to fifty prints (according to length) can be supplied to the exhibitor for showing at the halls the same evening.

The demand for some subjects reaches 300 to 750 copies for immediate delivery. This number of complete films are usually finished within forty-eight hours after the receipt of the negative.

Lightning delivery of films to the provincial exhibitor by passenger and express trains also means hustling. In short, the present phase of the animated picture business can be likened to the preparing and distributing of a special edition of an illustrated journal.

As millions of people have seen the animated pictures who have never seen or, if they have seen, have never had explained to them the way in which the pictures are produced, it may not be without interest to enter into some detail to explain exactly how the results with which we are familiar are produced.

The first thing indispensable is the lantern; the second is the light; the third the bioscope mechanism; and fourth the pictures. Of the lantern itself there is not much need to speak. It differs in no respect from the ordinary magic lantern. Indeed, an ordinary magic lantern can be fitted with the apparatus necessary for producing animated pictures. It is different, however, when we come to the light. The better the light, the better the pictures. Magic lanterns are operated either with oil lamps, with gas, with electricity, with the oxy-hydrogen light, or with the lime light. It is possible to exhibit animated pictures with the oil light, but the result is naturally not so good as when the oxyhydrogen is used, or the lime light. Concerning oil lamps, it is unnecessary to speak. Oxy-hydrogen light is very good when gas is procurable; but it entails the carrying about of cylinders charged under great pressure. Electric light is the best for projecting animated pictures, and very many and elaborate are the apparati used to press it into the service of the lantern.

THE MAKING OF THE PICTURES.

We now come to the projecting mechanism and the pictures, without which the best of lanterns, the most brilliant of lights, would be of no avail. This brings us to the camera, which is specially made for the taking of animated pictures. It is a very ingenious piece of mechanism, and marvellous for the perfection of its parts and the facility with which the whole thing works. Every amateur photographer is well aware of the difficulty of posing a subject and of taking a picture even when he is not hurried for time; but the essence of an animated picture is that the pictures must be taken with immense rapidity and in rapid succession. The bioscope camera differs from an ordinary camera in the fact that it has what resembles the handle of a barrel-organ on one side. The handle is indispensable for operating the mechanism and winding the long ribbon of sensitised film upon which the photographs are taken. Instead of exposing a plate, the camera used for the production of animated pictures exposes a film in the shape of a long ribbon not more than 1½ inches in breadth, which is wound round a spool by the aid of cog-wheels working in the holes punched on both sides of the film. The film is fed into the dark chamber of the camera in coils 150 feet or longer, from whence it passes through the mechanism opposite the lens, and is coiled upon another spool in a chamber immediately below. When the camera is in working, it would appear that the operator was winding off the film steadily at the rate of about 50 feet a minute. Nor can the eye detect any halt in the steady roll of the film off the reel across the ray that passes through the lens. But if the film were constantly moving, the resultant image would be badly blurred. The nicety of the mechanism consists in the fact that, although the turning of the handle is continuous, the cog-wheels are so arranged that when the film passes through the mechanism it halts for the fortieth of a second, during which the ray of light reflected from the object photographed strikes the film through the lens and registers itself indelibly. By this means 150 feet of film can be exposed in three minutes, and during these three minutes no fewer than 2,400 distinct photographic pictures will have been impressed upon the sensitive surface of the film. It is marvellous, almost miraculous, and a short time ago would have been regarded as absolutely beyond the bounds of possibility. But all difficulties have been triumphantly surmounted. The bioscope camera is no sooner in position and properly fixed than the operator literally grinds off small pictures about the size of a postage stamp, but each complete in itself, at the rate of 800 a minute, or 16 a second.

AN AMAZING CALCULATION.

As the film registers the impressions at the rate of 16 a second, it is obvious that between one picture and another the difference is almost imperceptible; but if you compare the first with the twentieth, or still more with the sixtieth, each successive movement can easily be seen without the least difficulty. It is a somewhat appalling thought that one's casual motions, the almost accidental actions, may be registered by this photographic coffee-mill, and reproduced indefinitely for evermore. When watching the machine in action, it occurred to me to calculate how many miles of film would be required to preserve the exact living picture of all one's waking life. Supposing that a man lives to fulfil the three-score years and ten of the Psalmist, and supposing that one-third of his life is spent in sleep, how many miles of film do you think it would require to register all his acts and deeds, his goings and comings from the time of his birth until his death? It is no use going into the very minute figures, but broadly speaking it would require 200,000 miles of film in order to

The Bioscope Camera.

make a complete register of the acts of a single life. On these 200,000 miles of film there would be impressed no fewer than 12,000,000,000 separate pictures.

But if the camera were kept trained upon a single individual through the whole of his waking hours, whether he was at rest or whether he was in motion, it would undoubtedly enable those who come after us to reconstruct the actual living life of a man of the twentieth century better than any amount of description. Of the 12,000,000,000 pictures, 10,000,000,000 would probably consist of endless repetitions, which would be endlessly boring to the beholder. But without going to such extremes it is possible for anyone with the aid of this instrument to preserve a realistic picture of human life under conditions of the present day. It is astonishing how vivid a picture, complete in all its details, can be reeled off in three minutes. It is not too much to say that a dozen 150-foot reels would enable anyone to form a more vivid, comprehensive and complete picture of human life from the cradle to the grave in half an hour than he could possibly realise from the reading of half a lifetime.

There is hardly any kind of effect which cannot be reproduced by this ingenious instrument. Nothing is more difficult to reproduce than the flight of birds, but one of the first pictures shown me at Warwick Court was the feeding of the pigeons of St. Mark's in Venice. Nothing could be more life-like than the fluttering and hovering of the great cloud of pigeons which find their daily bread in the huge square. A much less pleasing, but for the purposes of demonstration perhaps even more effective illustration of the capacity of the bioscope, is afforded by the picture of a cock-fight in Manila. There upon the sheet you see the poor wretched birds, fortunately without other weapons than those afforded them by Nature, fighting main after main with all the savage vigour and combative spirit which they displayed in the Philippines twelve months ago.

INTERESTING OPERATIONS.

I was initiated in the whole art and mystery of the making of the pictures, and spent some time in the dark cells in which much of the operation goes on. There is, to begin with, the unperforated film to be passed through a perforator, which punches a row of holes in either side with such exactitude that every hole fits every cog in any one of the 900 bioscopes which are now in active use. After the perforation, the film is carefully packed in light-proof cases, ready for use. After it

The Bioscope in Italy : The Pigeons of St. Mark's.

has all been exposed in the camera, and every inch of the 150 feet has halted for one-fortieth of a second behind the eye of the lens, it is then taken off the reel and wound round the horizontal metal cross, from the four arms of which a number of pins project vertically. The film is wound round these pins, beginning at the centre, which is mounted on a vulcanite roller inserted in an iron standard. When the film is wound in the frame, so as to form a kind of square spiral, it is lifted from the iron base, and the vulcanite roller used as a handle, so as to enable the operator to immerse the film in the developer without soiling his hands. After being developed and further treated, it is then wound off the developing frame upon a large wooden ribbed drum, heated with gas-jets in the centre and revolving rapidly by electric motor, the drying process assisted by utilising a battery of electric

fans. Here it remains for half an hour or forty minutes, until it is dried, and the negative is then ready for printing. The developed ribbon of film, having been wound off the drying drum, examined and cleaned, is attached to another ribbon of film upon which the picture is to be printed. The two films are then passed together through a machine which is in many respects the counterpart of the camera and of the projecting machine ; that is to say, the film is passed through a machine very much like the projector, but the light which is thrown upon the aperture across which the double film travels is only used for the purpose of printing the picture from the negative, not to project it. The rate at which the film passes varies according to the density of the negative or the brilliancy of the light. At Warwick Court they used electric lights, and wound off 150 feet of film in about five minutes. After having been printed, the ribbon is again wound upon a frame and immersed in a developing and fixing solution, after which it is again wound off upon the drying drum, where after another twenty minutes' drying it is examined and cleaned, wound off upon a reel, enclosed in a tin box, and is ready for use.

GREAT EVENTS RECORDED.

The rapidity with which the whole process can be accomplished is amazing. On the Oxford and Cambridge boat-race day 150 feet of film, containing 2,400 pictures, was ready for exhibition in three hours after the arrival of the camera at the works. As a rule 150 feet is regarded as a good working length for an animated picture. It is not well to weary the audience by too long a film. One of the longest films was that representing the funeral of Queen Victoria. Every stage in the long procession from Osborne to St. George's Chapel was photographed by the Warwick Trading Company, eleven cameras and operators recording every stage of the ceremonies and procession. Their works were kept going night and day after the funeral, nor were they able for some time to overtake the orders which poured in from all parts. Everyone wanted them at once. To-day there is but little demand for these pictures, the interest in the Royal funeral having long ago spent itself. It is with films as it is with newspapers. A million people will buy to-day's paper for ten who purchase the paper of the day before yesterday. The complete set of these films of the funeral ran from 4,000 to 5,000 feet.

N

A very excellent picture, more recent than that of Queen Victoria's funeral, is that which exhibits the funeral procession of the Empress Frederick.

The cinematograph is, however, by no means exclusively or even primarily employed for funeral processions. It is more at home in pageants and festal processions. Some pictures taken of the procession on the occasion of the opening of the first Australian Parliament in Melbourne give a very vivid idea of the ceremonies and processions in all Australian cities visited by the Royal couple.

One of the simplest but nevertheless one of the most effective pictures exhibited is that showing the procession of the torpedo-boat destroyers on the occasion of the opening of the Manchester Ship Canal. As you sit watching the screen, the canal-gates open, and the long black hull of the destroyer forges its way through the foaming water. It is difficult to realise that you are not actually seeing a veritable ship. The effect, when again and again renewed, is a marvel of realistic accuracy. The camera on that occasion was located on a tug which went about a quarter the speed of the torpedo-boats whose movements were photographed.

WAR PICTURES.

One of the greatest successes of the cinematograph has been in the presentation of scenes from the seat of war, and yet it may be safely said that here we have witnessed one of its greatest failures. The success lay in the machine; the failure was due to the revolution which has taken place in modern warfare. The war was hardly well begun before the Warwick Trading Company had despatched three operators to accompany the British troops operating in various sections of South Africa and in their march to Pretoria. Each operator was equipped by the Warwick Trading Company with two mules, a Cape cart and camping and bioscope outfits. Upon long marches of the troops the "Warwick" carts took their places side by side with the regular war correspondents. When reconnoitring or scouting the cameras were slung over the back of one mule,

The Bioscope Cart on the March—Transvaal.

the other being mounted by the operator who accompanied the troops, while the assistant watched the balance of the outfit in camp and re-loaded a relay instrument ready in case of accident. Mr. Rosenthal, the chief bioscope correspondent, with his camera, rode all the way in the front of the British army through Bloemfontein, Kroonstad, and Pretoria. He used 15,000 ft. of film in photographing scenes on march, and he would have used 5,000 more if the ubiquitous De Wet had not seized the fourth 5,000 ft. of film at his lucky haul at Roodevaal. But although these operators were able to secure some marvellously living pictures of every phase of army life and historic incidents in the Transvaal, they were never able to secure a single battle picture although being in battle many times. On one occasion Mr. Rosenthal had a horse killed under him. On others shells burst in his immediate neighbourhood; but although he was constantly at the front, taking living pictures wherever he could find them, he utterly failed to secure any photograph which could be described by any stretch of the imagination as a battle picture. The reason for this is that there are no battle pictures nowadays. The nearest approach to such a picture is a photograph of a battery in action, but an equally good picture could be obtained by photographing a battery firing at

Portability essential for Skirmish and Scouting Work.

Woolwich or at Aldershot. Mr. Rosenthal's bitter disappointment in this respect brought into clear relief the fundamental difference between ancient and modern war. Although he was seven months in the forefront of the British army, and present at all the battles that took place during that period, he never saw a single Boer at range near enough to be photographed. In all the battles in which he took part the enemy was not visible. The bullets hissed and skipped around our men, but there was nothing on the horizon, east, west, north or south, to show where lay the marksmen with the Mausers. In war in the antiquated style, which still seems to be believed in in Germany and France, there was ample opportunity for the camera to obtain the most thrilling pictures. But war in the days of Maskelyne powder and long-range guns won't lend itself to pictorial display.

Bioscope Correspondent's Camp Equipment.

Mr. Rosenthal, after leaving South Africa, followed the allied armies to Pekin, and although he found plenty of traces of ruin and devastation wrought by the avenging troops of the so-called Powers, he came too late to see any actual fighting. Mr. Rosenthal may be regarded in some respects as the latest evolution of the special war correspondent. He was the first to be recognised in the official capacity of accredited war correspondent, and although he represented no paper, his position was never questioned. The Warwick Trading Company, as the purveyor of films to the showmen of the world, necessarily adopts the methods and organisation of a great newspaper. It has its correspondents and camera operators all over the world. Wherever anything is likely to happen of importance or of scenic interest, there its "special" waits, camera in hand, to preserve for the benefit of British music-halls and provincial lecture-rooms the living image of things as they are.

An American cinematograph company was fortunate enough to have had its instrument in position to have photographed Mr. McKinley at Buffalo immediately before his assassination, and to have photographed the distracted crowd as it rushed tumultuously hither and thither on receiving the terrible news of the President's murder.

PRIVATE ORDERS INCREASING.

With the cinematograph company, as it is with the newspaper, everything depends upon serving up their films hot from the press ; and they also resemble a newspaper in the fact that it is becoming more and more necessary to localise the institution. The demand for living pictures of events in the various localities increases daily. Soon every local flower show will consider that it is behind the times unless it has preserved a cinematograph record of the opening ceremony or the distribution of prizes. The cinematograph is becoming not merely an indispensable adjunct to the chroniclers of local history, but it is being adapted more and more as a family record. If, for instance, there is a wedding in your family, and you wish to preserve a permanent record of the ceremony, all that you have to do is to write to Warwick Court, and when the bridal procession leaves the church and comes out into sunshine, the bioscope camera will photograph the whole party, bridegroom, bride, bridesmaids, best man and parson, and all the merry mob of rice-sprinkling, slipper-throwing friends. The bridal procession is not a long affair, and the whole *cortège* could be photographed on fifty feet of film, which will be developed, printed and supplied ready for exhibition for a reasonable sum.

It is difficult to photograph interiors owing to the lack of good light, but as things are going now it will soon be as impossible for a fashionable wedding to take place without the bride receiving as a wedding gift a film, which will enable her to reproduce for her children and grandchildren after them a picture of how the bridal party looked on the day she was wed, as it would be for a bride to appear without a veil or a bridesmaid without flowers. Families that are *comme-il-faut*, which assumes that they can afford to be *comme-il-faut*, will have a family record consisting of a kind of record-chamber of films, beginning with a living picture of the bridal party, followed by the christening of each of the children. Thus we shall have each important family event, such as a coming of age, or a silver wedding, commemorated in like manner,

Lord Stanley passing Bioscope Film Negatives at the Front.

while the funeral films would supply a more sombre element to the collection. It will then be possible for every member of the family to call back as it were from the dim shadows of the misty past a living image of those who lived and loved and laughed in the days long gone by. If in addition to those photographic films of living pictures there should be stored permanent cylinders with phonographic records of the actual voices that have long since been stilled, it is evident that modern science is at least providing for those who can pay for it an immense improvement upon the simple written record of the old family Bible.

The bioscope can hardly be said to have reached the stage of development when it can be regarded as one of the domestic necessaries of a well-appointed household. But notwithstanding its costliness, it has established its reputation as a money-maker in the hands of showmen who know how to use it. A very short time ago, if anyone had asked what chance there was of popularising an invention which would entail an expenditure of £50 before the start, and necessitate a purchase of at least £50 worth of films in order to supply an hour's entertainment, he would have been told that the risk was too great, and the prospects of a yield too small. But so far from this being the case, there are now at this moment 700 cinematograph operators busily engaged in showing living pictures up and down the country, and six times as many in other countries, and the demand for films and machines grows steadily.

THE REAL MISSION OF THE CINEMATOGRAPH.

But the cinematograph, although launched with brilliant success as a showman's attraction, has yet to begin its real work of usefulness. At present it is little more than a thing to make people stare, which is very good in itself; but while it ministers to the curiosity and adds one more to the endless dissipations of modern life, it has never been systematically yoked to the cause of popular instruction. The school boards, for instance, have not yet begun to purchase bioscopes. Not even the Recreative Evenings Association has ventured to embark upon the small expenditure that would be entailed in purchasing and working a cinematograph, although the Salvation Army in England and Australia, the Ragged School Union, and Royal Mission to Deep Sea Fishermen have realised the value of the bioscope in their benevolent and educational work. Yet it is obvious that no adjunct of the schoolroom could be conceived more certain to stimulate the inattentive mind of the scholar and rouse him to a living interest in the lessons over which he pores with too often listless mind. Whether it be in geography or history, it is easy to see the immense variety of uses that could be made of the living picture. With the

The Bioscope in China ; Chinese mounting a Big Gun at Taku.

aid of the cinematograph the teacher could in very truth carry his scholars with him round the world from China to Peru. Instead of learning dry, more or less unmeaning facts, every lesson in geography could be linked on to a living representation of the country and the people to which the lesson applied. In the history class also, when we have impressions of bioscope films as cheap and as varied as a library of books, pupils will not read about the historical scenes ; they will actually see them in progress before them. All the advantage of seeing a well-mounted historical play at the Lyceum or Drury Lane could be placed at the disposition of every child in our public schools.

It may be said that this would leave too little to the imagination. But this is a mistake. Even if the scheme were carried out to its very ultimate, and every important historical event were cinematographed as part of the history-lesson of the day, there would still be ample room left for the exercise of the imagination. Suppose, for instance, that the battle of Hastings or the battle of Waterloo were represented in a series of living pictures. There would still be both before and after an endless vista in which the imagination of the scholar could revel. The fact is the chief difficulty of the instructor is not to find fields in which the imagination can work, but to get the imagination to work at all, especially the visualising eye of the imagination. None of us adequately conjure up with a sufficient degree of vividness the details of the historical scenes upon which we dwell. If, however, we could actually see, for instance, the execution of Charles I. or the burning of Cranmer there would be projected into our consciousness a real bit of actuality, and our imaginations would build to the right and left of it, making an endeavour at least to construct the edifice of as solid and palpable visible material as that which has been thrown upon the screen.

The Bioscope Company have already made a beginning in this direction, for besides the pictures which they photographed from a living page of contemporary history, they have endeavoured to reconstruct the past. They have selected, with a sound instinct, the romantic, miraculous, and pathetic story of Jeanne D'Arc. This is an importation from France, for as yet no one has attempted to stage, for photographic reproduction, anything approaching to the elaborate drama of which Jeanne D'Arc was the heroine. In the cinematograph spectacle of Jeanne D'Arc there are twelve scenes, covering 800 feet of film, the exhibition of which lasts for about fifteen minutes without a stop. This, however, is to make the worst possible use of it. Each of the twelve scenes should be opened and closed by the telling of the story of the events to which it belongs. In securing the Jeanne D'Arc scenes 500 persons were employed who were clothed in costumes and armour of the period. This is very French, and would shock many English people, although when I was down in Glasgow there were everywhere bills on the hoardings announcing that the story of Jeanne D'Arc was to be presented every day by the cinematograph to the citizens of Glasgow.

THE PASSION PLAY BIOSCOPED

This brings us directly to another great field for the use of the cinematograph, upon which it has only begun to enter, and that is the field of religious instruction. Lantern services have long been recognised as one of the most effective adjuncts of religious propaganda. But the best magic lantern is nothing to the bioscope. It is a mistake, however, to treat them as if they were in antagonism to each other, for every bioscope is primarily a magic lantern, and can be used to project ordinary pictures by simply turning the bioscope mechanism, and allowing the lights of the lantern to play directly upon the screen, without passing through the apparatus necessary for projecting living pictures. In the printed catalogue of the Warwick Company, with descriptions which cover more than 300 pages, there is only one set of films relating to religious subjects. It is one of the longest, and it is divided into thirty sections, with a total length of 2,500 feet of film. It is entitled "The Life and Passion of Christ," and is known as the Horitz Passion Play series. The excellent village fathers of Oberammergau were approached by the cinematograph companies with urgent requests and lavish offers of money to be allowed to photograph the Passion Play for the purpose of reproducing it as a living picture, but without meeting with their consent. Nothing daunted, the Bioscope Company representatives approached the Horitz Passion Play authorities, and finally induced them to give special performances of the entire production. A special outdoor stage of huge dimensions was constructed, special ' photographic " scenery (in black and white) was designed and painted, and over three weeks' time of a special staff of operators was consumed before satisfactory results were obtained, owing to occasional unfavourable weather conditions arising which were detrimental to photographic success, etc. Although this series was photographed over two years ago, the Warwick Trading Company has, for obvious reasons, withheld them from the market until just recently. This series will be in considerable demand, and according to those who have exhibited other similar series, even of a crude representation, and have witnessed its exhibition, the effect of its production, even as a middle turn in a music-hall, has been excellent. It is as if from the stage of the music-hall the revellers were addressed upon the most solemn of all themes by the most eloquent of all preachers. The incongruity of the surroundings will probably not deter a fervid evangelist from seizing the opportunity of presenting the Story of the Cross, and the Warwick Company maintain that, instead of being denounced by the pious for the pictures of the Passion, it ought to be imputed to them for righteousness. It is, however, a mistake to think that the films of the Passion are chiefly used at music-halls. They are, on the contrary, used at special services. Those who lecture on the Passion Play with a magic lantern can well imagine how much greater must be the effect produced when the whole of the events of the sacred tragedy move before the spectator on the screen. The seating capacity of our churches would be fully taxed if some enterprising minister would thus represent this interesting production and cut short a dry sermon.

IN RELIGIOUS AND SOCIAL WORK.

With this exception, little or nothing has been done to utilise the bioscope for purposes of religious teaching. It is noteworthy, however, that the Salvation Army, that most modern of all churches, is the only religious body that has acquitted itself with the bioscope, and has laid in a complete stock of the apparatus necessary for producing its own films. Its example will probably be followed by the Church Army and other religious organisations, who will use it in the first instance for the exhibition of what may be called the philanthropic department of their activities. But in time all those who are engaged in the attempt to convert their fellow-men will utilise this admirable instrument for compelling the members of their congregations to realise the need there is for consecrated service in the salvation of the world.

Mission work is another vast field which has hardly been attacked. The bioscope is useful at both ends. In the field at home, where funds are collected for missions, it would give a much more vivid, living interest to the details of mission work than has hitherto been possible. The missionary meeting would be transformed, and become one of the most popular of all the week-night services if it were illustrated by living pictures introducing the audience to lifelike presentations of the far-off scenes and peoples amongst whom the proceeds of their collection boxes maintain the emissaries of the Cross. At the other end, a complete library of the films of the parables and living pictures of the Bible stories would be an endless and inexhaustible source of attraction to the simple children of Nature amidst whom missionaries labour. The picture itself would be little short of miraculous, and would probably do more to carry conviction as to the truth of the Christian religion to their untutored minds than the most eloquent discourses.

IN MISSIONARY WORK—

But in its adaptation to these fields of missionary enterprise there is the initial expense to be overcome. If, however, showmen find the bioscope pays its expenses and leaves something over, churches may make the same discovery. It is possible that no particular church or chapel may consider itself justified in going to the expense of a hundred pounds for providing the complete set of apparatus, but there is no reason why a diocese or a Free Church Federation in any particular county should not provide a bioscope as part of the regular stock-in-trade of its church militant, and maintain a cinematograph missionary who would make his rounds from church to church or from schoolroom to schoolroom. The churches have at least an organisation which could be utilised at once. There is no reason why the bioscope might not even be made a source of revenue. People pay to go and see living pictures in the music-hall, and there is no reason why they should not pay to see them in church. At the same time those who have money and are desirous of doing good by endowing some institution for popular evangelism might do very much worse than set aside a few thousands for the purpose of endowing a section of the Church to which they belong with a set of bioscopes to begin with, and a small annual income for the purpose of buying fresh films. Diocese could exchange films with diocese, or county with county. The Sunday School Union, the Religious Tract Society, the British and Foreign Bible Society, the London City Mission, could all follow the example of the Deep Sea Mission, which has already an admirable set of films, which they have found to be of great service in bringing home to their members the needs of their interesting and adventurous congregation. It would not require very much organising genius on the part of the Free Churches to form a Free Church Bioscope Society, which would aim at securing for every Free Church Federation in every county in England a first-class bioscope and a good collection of films, and providing a competent lecturer and operator who could be dedicated to the work. I throw out this suggestion for what it is worth, and should be very glad to receive communications from those in any part of the kingdom who wish to make the experiment. It requires organisation, for the expense is more than most individuals or even separate churches could be expected to incur. With a little organisation, however, a good business man ought to be able to set the bioscope perambulating on its mission of evangelisation in all the counties of the land.

AND SURGERY.

There is one other sphere of usefulness to which allusion must be made, and that is the

service which the bioscope can render to medical science. One of the most important parts of the training of doctors is the witnessing of operations. The bioscope renders it possible to reproduce endlessly, under circumstances which permit of the most close and leisurely study, scenes which at present can only be witnessed in the operating theatres of our hospitals. A great surgeon performs some difficult operation with perfect success, and all those who witness it cherish the memory of that exhibition of skill as long as they live; but what of the enormous multitude of medicos who have never witnessed it and have no opportunity of seeing it? But even of the few who were privileged to be present in the operating theatre, how many would wish to see it over again, if only to imprint more indelibly on their minds the way in which the work was done! The bioscope offers to all an opportunity of witnessing reproductions of the most difficult and delicate operations of modern surgery. The time is coming when every operation of exceptional importance will be photographed with the most scrupulous care by scientifically trained operators, and films of every supremely successful operation will form part of the necessary plant of all medical colleges. Victims for the operator's table cannot always be laid on for the sake of improving the education of our budding medicos, but a very little extension of the scope of the cinematograph would render it possible for every medical student in the land to see every important operation performed by masters of the surgical art with the same certainty that he would be able to buy his *Lancet* or his medical dictionary. Surgical science is of no country, and pictures speak a universal language. But at present, with very few exceptions, no arrangements are made for securing the permanent preservation of the sight of important operations. The suggestion is well worth while bringing before the attention of leaders of the profession and heads of colleges and of the institutions where doctors are being trained for the next generation. A lecturer in surgery would find his task enormously facilitated if a first-class bioscope, with a carefully-selected collection of films, formed part of the permanent apparatus of his class-room.

The Bioscope in Manilla; American Troops firing on party of Philippine Rebels.

CPSIA information can be obtained
at www.ICGtesting.com
Printed in the USA
BVHW011747190622
640142BV00003B/19

9 781296 824013